The

Mexican
Americans

The

Mexican
Americans

Alma M. Garcia

THE NEW AMERICANS
Ronald H. Bayor, Series Editor

GREENWOOD PRESS
Westport, Connecticut • London

Library of Congress Cataloging-in-Publication Data

García, Alma M.
    The Mexican Americans / Alma M. Garcia.
        p. cm.—(New Americans, ISSN 1092–6364)
    Includes bibliographical references and index.
    ISBN 0–313–31499–3 (alk. paper)
      1. Mexican Americans—History. 2. Mexican Americans—Social conditions. 3. Mexican
Americans—Social life and customs. 4. Immigrants—United States—History. 5.
Mexico—Emigration and immigration—History. 6. United States—Emigration and
immigration—History. I. Title. II. New Americans (Westport, Conn.)
    E184.M5 G34   2002
    973'.046872—dc21   2001054549

British Library Cataloguing in Publication Data is available.

Library of Congress Catalog Card Number: 2001054549
ISBN: 0–313–31499–3
ISSN: 1092–6364

First published in 2002

Greenwood Press, 88 Post Road West, Westport, CT 06881
An imprint of Greenwood Publishing Group, Inc.
www.greenwood.com

Printed in the United States of America

The paper used in this book complies with the
Permanent Paper Standard issued by the National
Information Standards Organization (Z39.48–1984).

10 9 8 7 6 5 4

Copyright Acknowledgments

The author and publisher are grateful to the following for granting permission to reprint from their
materials:

"Legal Alien" by Pat Mora is reprinted with permission from the publishers of *Chants* (Houston: Arte
Público Press—University of Houston, 1984).

To the strong and independent women in my family: my grandmother, María B. Araíza; my great aunt, Esther Araíza Holmes; and foremost and always, my mother Alma Araíza García.

Contents

Series Foreword

Oscar Handlin, a prominent historian, once wrote, "I thought to write a history of the immigrants in America. Then I discovered that the immigrants were American history." The United States has always been a nation of nations where people from every region of the world have come to begin a new life. Other countries such as Canada, Argentina, and Australia also have had substantial immigration, but the United States is still unique in the diversity of nationalities and the great numbers of migrating people who have come to its shores.

Who are these immigrants? Why did they decide to come? How well have they adjusted to this new land? What has been the reaction to them? These are some of the questions the books in this "New Americans" series seek to answer. There have been many studies about earlier waves of immigrants—for example, the English, Irish, Germans, Jews, Italians, and Poles—but relatively little has been written about the newer groups—those arriving in the last thirty years, since the passage of a new immigration law in 1965. This series is designed to correct that situation and to introduce these groups to the rest of America.

Each book in the series discusses one of these groups, and each is written by an expert on those immigrants. The volumes cover the new migration from primarily Asia, Latin America, and the Caribbean, including the Koreans, Cambodians, Filipinos, Vietnamese, South Asians such as Indians and Pakistanis, Chinese from both China and Taiwan, Haitians, Jamaicans, Cubans, Dominicans, Mexicans, Puerto Ricans (even though they are already

U.S. citizens), and Jews from the former Soviet Union. Although some of these people, such as Jews, have been in America since colonial times, this series concentrates on their recent migrations, and thereby offers its unique contribution.

These volumes are designed for high school and general readers who want to learn more about their new neighbors. Each author has provided information about the land of origin, its history and culture, the reasons for migrating, and the ethnic culture as it began to adjust to American life. Readers will find fascinating details on religion, politics, foods, festivals, gender roles, employment trends, and general community life. They will learn how Vietnamese immigrants differ from Cuban immigrants and, yet, how they are also alike in many ways. Each book is arranged to offer an in-depth look at the particular immigrant group but also to enable readers to compare one group with the other. The volumes also contain brief biographical profiles of notable individuals, tables noting each group's immigration, and a short bibliography of readily available books and articles for further reading. Most contain a glossary of foreign words and phrases.

Students and others who read these volumes will secure a better understanding of the age-old questions of "who is an American" and "how does the assimilation process work?" Similar to their nineteenth- and early twentieth-century forebears, many Americans today doubt the value of immigration and fear the influx of individuals who look and sound different from those who had come earlier. If comparable books had been written one hundred years ago they would have done much to help dispel readers' unwarranted fears of the newcomers. Nobody today would question, for example, the role of those of Irish or Italian ancestry as Americans, yet this was a serious issue in our history and a source of great conflict. It is time to look at our recent arrivals, to understand their history and culture, their skills, their place in the United States, and their hopes and dreams as Americans.

The United States is a vastly different country than it was at the beginning of the twentieth century. The economy has shifted away from industrial jobs; the civil rights movement has changed minority–majority relations and, along with the women's movement, brought more people into the economic mainstream. Yet one aspect of American life remains strikingly similar—we are still the world's main immigrant receiving nation, and as in every period of American history, we are still a nation of immigrants. It is essential that we attempt to learn about and understand this long-term process of migration and assimilation.

Ronald H. Bayor
Georgia Institute of Technology

Acknowledgments

I am grateful to many individuals who provided me with invaluable support and encouragement at various stages in the preparation of this volume: Wendi Schnaufer, Acquisitions Editor, School and Public Library References, Greenwood Press, for her constant support and encouragement, and Frank Saunders, Production Editor, Greenwood Press, for his production assistance in the book's final preparations. Various students assisted me in preparing statistical and demographic illustrations: Diann Naidu, Randy Reyes, and Kamal Samuels. I would like to offer my special thanks to my friend Lou Dombro for taking several of the photographs that appear in this book. The Mexican Heritage Corporation of San Jose graciously permitted me to use several pictures from its archives documenting the Mexican cultural heritage in the greater San Jose area.

My most special thanks and appreciation go to Professor Matt Meier, Santa Clara University, pioneer in the discipline of Mexican American Studies and my longtime mentor and friend; Professor Richard A. García, California State University at Hayward, and Professor Mario T. García, University of California at Santa Barbara, my intellectual mentors, colleagues, and, above all, brothers who have always been my role models; and Professor Francisco Jiménez, Santa Clara University, cherished friend and colleague whose autobiographies *The Circuit* and *Breaking Through* have brought to life the struggles of Mexican immigrants who have survived against all odds in their efforts to make a better life for their children. Their stories stand as dramatic testimonies to the persistent need for all Americans to struggle for social justice. As César Chávez said: "The truest act of courage, the strongest act of humanity, is to sacrifice ourselves for others in a totally non-violent struggle for justice . . . to be human is to suffer for others . . . God help us to be human."

1

Background

At the beginning of the twenty-first century, Americans continue to deal with the impact and consequences of immigration from various countries to the United States. As with other immigrant groups, Mexican immigration to the United States created generations of "New Americans." Mexican immigration differs from other immigrations in one major way: Mexico shares a 2,000 mile-long border with the United States. Mexican immigrants never had to cross an ocean to reach American shores. In fact, unlike all other immigrant groups, the American Southwest belonged to Mexico until the country's defeat by the United States in 1848. The history and culture of contemporary Mexican society have always influenced the lives of Mexican immigrants living in the United States. A brief overview of the land and key historic periods in the history and culture of Mexico provides a background to contemporary patterns of Mexican immigration and settlement in the United States.

GEOGRAPHY

Located in North America between the United States and Guatemala, bordering the Caribbean Sea and the Gulf of Mexico on the east and the Pacific Ocean to the west, Mexico is a land of stark contrasts. In the north, vast arid deserts stretch out across the states of Chihuahua and Sonora. High, rugged mountains extend from Mexico's border with the United States to its southern borders. In the country's southeastern tip, the Yucatán peninsula reveals lush tropical plains once home to the ancient Mayas. The Central Valley of Mexico is the country's geographic and symbolic heart: the site of Mexico's capital since Aztec times. The coastal state of Veracruz, on the Gulf of Mexico, is Mexico's principal seaport and the site of vast oil fields. On Mexico's Pacific side, large coffee plantations in the state of Chiapas thrive on the fertile soils on the steep hillsides. Mexico is a country of diverse regions, cultures, and peoples. Mexican historians have long claimed that the study of the history and culture of Mexico begins with the basic understanding that many regional "Mexicos" have always made up the nation.

EARLY CIVILIZATIONS

An overview of Mexican history begins with Mexico's early civilizations and continues through the Mexican Revolution of 1910. The earliest groups to arrive in Mexico migrated from the north, near the Bering Strait, around 8000 B.C.E. These nomadic tribes roamed the countryside hunting buffalos, mammoths, and mastodons. When these herds died out, around 7000 B.C.E., some tribes living in what is now the state of Puebla discovered how to cultivate crops such as corn and beans. Agriculture transformed the nomadic tribes into village-dwellers, and by 2000 B.C.E., large villages existed in the Valley of Mexico, in what is now Mexico City, and in the southern highland region with its fertile soil, which was ideal for farming. An evolving and complex society emerged around 1000 B.C.E. The Olmec Indians led the first major developments in pre-Columbian Mexico. The Olmecs settled in the Southern Gulf of Mexico Coast and their empire thrived between 1200 B.C.E and 400 B.C.E. Major contributions included the development of a counting system and a sophisticated and accurate calendar. The Olmec civilization is most well known for its colossal human sculptures made of forty-ton blocks of basalt.

Archaeologists identify the Classic Period (300–900 C.E.) in ancient Mexico as the one during which the most significant cultural and artistic achievements developed. The rise of cities, particularly in the Valley of Mexico, led to the development of complex societies characterized by social classes, commerce, transportation systems, and religious centers. Cultural centers in the Classic Period included those of the Maya in Yucatán and Guatemala, the Mexican Highlands of Teotihuacán, the Zapotec cities of Monte Albán and Mitla in Oaxaca, and the Totonac cities of Tajín on the Gulf Coast. One of the most famous archaeological sites in this period is the Toltec's monumental pyramids to the sun and the moon in Teotihuacán and the Zapotéc capital of Monte Albán.

These civilizations declined as a result of the frequent warfare that existed throughout the Classic Period, dramatic declines in favorable climatic conditions for agriculture, and threats from new tribes, such as the Chichimecas, who invaded the central valley. From 900 to 1520, a variety of tribes continued to engage in warfare. Later pre-Columbian cultures thrived but never reached the cultural heights of the Classic Period's civilizations.

Beginning in 1300, the Aztecs, a highly warlike people, entered the Valley of Mexico and settled on Lake Texcoco, which is now Mexico City. They established their capital of Tenochtitlán on an island in Lake Texcoco. The Aztecs selected this site because one of their legends said that they should build their capital on the site where they found a cactus with an eagle sitting on it, holding a serpent in its mouth. This symbol became the national symbol of Mexico. The population of this Aztec city reached the amazing number of 300,000. The Aztecs ruled over a loose confederation of surrounding states and spread their social, cultural, and, most important, their religious influence throughout the Valley of Mexico. In 1519 when the Spanish arrived in what is now the state of Veracruz, Hernán Cortés encountered an Aztec empire ruled by the emperor Moctezuma. The arrival of the Spanish signaled the defeat of the Aztecs and the creation of a Spanish colony that would eventually rebel against the Spanish Crown and establish its independence in the nineteenth century.

SPANISH CONQUEST

Cortés and his expedition entered the Aztec Empire in 1519. When Moctezuma first heard of the arrival of these strangers from the East, he believed that Cortés was the Aztec god Quetzalcoatle—the Feathered Serpent—who, according to legend, flew away from the world but promised to return from the East. Moctezuma also realized that the Spaniards represented a military threat to his Aztec Empire, and he tried to appease Cortés with gifts of gold and other precious metals. After a preliminary setback, the Spanish subdued the Aztecs in 1521 with the surrender of Cuauhtémoc, who was to become the last Aztec emperor. The Spanish Conquest incorporated a vast territory into the Spanish Empire. In the two centuries that followed, the Spanish maintained governmental control over its colony, building large, landed feudal estates owned by Spaniards and worked by indigenous peoples. The Spanish accumulated great wealth from the silver mines and other raw materials discovered throughout Mexico, facilitating its economic and political superiority over other European powers by means of the wealth accumulated in the "New World."

During the sixteenth century, Spanish America experienced the continued expansion of the Spanish monarchy. During these early years of "discovery," Spain brought to the New World its culture and language. Once in New Spain, the Spanish continued their exploration of the entire region while engaging in persistent warfare with native tribes. The Spanish built settlements, established their form of local and regional government, and supported the Christianization efforts of the Catholic Church. Tragically, the Spaniards brought European diseases with them that led to the near decimation of native populations. Much has been written about the conflicts and contradictions of the "Age of Discovery" and its legacy for the inhabitants of the Americas. Nevertheless, historians mark the sixteenth century as a watershed in Spanish history. "It is almost impossible to believe that a country of ten million people, distributed among several kingdoms and crowns, could produce such a number of notable personages, some absolutely extraordinary—navigators, explorers, conquerors, missionaries, jurists, theologians, men of science and of letters, architects, painters, sculptors" (Jiménez, 1994: 212).

By the seventeenth century, Spain had institutionalized one of the major hallmarks of its society in the colonies with the introduction of the "hacienda" system of landholding. The hacienda system replaced the "encomienda" system of land ownership that had been designed primarily to maintain New Spain's indigenous population in a condition of slavelike servitude. Under the economienda system, native populations gave tribute to the Spanish monarch who in turn entrusted them ("encomendar") to a Spaniard. This system assisted the Catholic clergy in their evangelization efforts. With the passing of time and the continued need of the Spanish monarchy to excise more wealth from its colony, the hacienda system was subsequently introduced. It involved the granting of land rights to individual Spaniards. Large landed estates reverted to the ownership of Spaniards, who soon formed a landed oligarchy that would dominate New Spain's economic, political, social, and cultural life. Such land ownership patterns and political arrangements became one of the sources of conflict that would erupt in New Spain's War of Independence in 1812. Control of the large haciendas eventually transferred to the hands of a new social class: the "Creoles" who were Spaniards born in New Spain. The Creoles and the European Spanish split over dominance in the Americas. Political turmoil between Spain and other European countries further exacerbated the social class conflicts in the New World. France and England challenged and usually emerged victorious over the rapidly declining Spanish Empire. The persistent efforts to encroach on

Spanish landholdings by the United States, England, and France added to Spain's troubles.

SPANISH CULTURE IN THE NEW WORLD

Spain's contributions to the development of the cultural life in New Spain go hand in hand with its military conquest. Although pre-Columbian cultures such as the Aztec and the Mayan left a rich heritage of arts and sciences, Spain contributed its own cultural legacy. Many times Spanish culture, particularly language, integrated indigenous elements, creating a uniquely New World culture. The ultimate result of the introduction of Spanish to the Americas, like the introduction of English to North America, was the expansion of the Spanish language to the twenty countries in the "New World."

The earliest contributions to Spanish literature consist of the records of explorers and clergy to the Americas. During the entire sixteenth century, these explorers produced important literary and travel narratives that represent a rich source of historical investigation and contributions to the cultural legacy of Spain. Historical accounts of these early days of the Spanish Empire in the New World provide contemporary readers with a firsthand account of life in the colonies. Spanish clergyman who traveled throughout the colonies recorded detailed accounts of the land, its customs, and the native peoples. Although their evangelizing efforts are today criticized by many, their writings remain a source of literary heritage. Many clergy, both European Spanish and Creole, wrote detailed histories of their religious orders and their experiences in the New World. The most well-known literary works of this time include Hernán Cortés's letters to the Spanish monarch and the *True History of the Conquest of New Spain,* written by Bernal Díaz del Castillo, who was one of the soldiers that accompanied Cortés, and Alvar Núñez Cabeza de Vaca's *Shipwreck.* By the seventeenth century, even more famous literary works emerged throughout the Americas. Sor Juana Inés de la Cruz remains one of the most famous writers; as a woman she is of special note in a literary world dominated by men. Sor Juana was born in Mexico in 1648 and studied at a convent in Mexico City where she became a nun at a very early age. Her writings focus exclusively on Mexican society and culture. Her work stands as a hallmark of Spanish Baroque literature. Sor Juana's writings cover an impressive variety of genres, including plays, poetry, an autobiography, and spiritual essays.

The development of certain architectural styles complements the literary contributions of this period in the history of the Americas, including Mexico.

The introduction of Spanish architecture remains as a visible representation of the Spanish influence, even now in the twenty-first century. Government buildings, homes of the landed aristocracy, and, perhaps most famous, convents, churches, and cathedrals stands as a legacy to Mexico's colonial past. Those found in Cholula, Mexico, stand as classic examples of this architectural period. In the early sixteenth century, Spain transplanted its preference for gothic-style buildings. Religious orders such as the Jesuit, Dominican, and Augustinian supervised the construction of magnificent Gothic cathedrals. These structures, massive in size, accommodated the large numbers of newly converted indigenous populations, even though a large number were forced conversions. The Spanish Conquest left a legacy of forced Christianization of many of the inhabitants of its "New Spain." In addition, as in Spain, these enormous structures served as military sites for refugees during frequent uprisings. The cathedrals in Mexico City, Puebla, and Guadalajara represent outstanding examples of colonial buildings. The cathedral in Mexico City was the largest church built by Spaniards in the New World and continues to be the heart and soul of Mexico's Catholicism. The eighteenth century brought the baroque style of architecture to Mexico; its ornate styles were made possible by the immense deposits of silver and gold throughout Mexico.

Architectural styles differed in most northern regions of Mexico due to its limited amount of building materials. In the towns established along Mexico's frontier, adobe became the primary building material. The near absence of stone and timber prevented the building of baroque-style churches, convents, and other buildings. Interestingly, certain regions of Spain faced the same limitations and also used adobe. A person who has traveled through Castile and Extremadura in Spain will recognize the influence of these regions when traveling through what is now the American Southwest.

MEXICAN INDEPENDENCE

The Spanish Conquest of Mexico created a highly stratified society. At the top, Spaniards (born in Spain) and Peninsulares (Spaniards born in Mexico) dominated almost every aspect of life in the colony. They controlled the government, owned all the land, and maintained a strong coalition with the Catholic Church. Through intermarriage, many other racial/ethnic groups developed within New Spain. Intermarriages between Spaniards and indigenous people created a completely new group called "Mestizos" who eventually formed the majority of present-day Mexican people. Indigenous groups and enslaved Africans remained at the bottom of the social class ladder.

At the beginning of the nineteenth century, Europe found itself in a state of political uprising. In Spain, King Charles IV's reign was built on corruption and repression. Eventually an opposition movement succeeded in forcing Charles IV to abdicate, and his son became King Ferdinand VII. Almost immediately Napoleon gave refuge to Charles who began a campaign to regain the Spanish throne. Napoleon's attempt to place his brother Joseph Bonaparte on the throne in Spain led to the Peninsular War of Spain in 1808.

These political upheavals were felt in New Spain where a growing resentment against colonial rule continued to increase. Although there were many groups in Mexico, such as the Spaniards ("Peninsulares"—Spanish peninsula), various opposition groups joined together in a common cause to overthrow the Spanish. The Spaniards represented a small group of ruling elite whom the rest of Mexican society resented for their oligarchic rule. The Mexican War for Independence pitted the existing social classes against the ruling class of Spaniards. Miguel Hidalgo y Costilla, a local priest, began organizing a combination of Mestizos and indigenous groups. His revolt is best remembered for his proclamation of independence: the "Grito de Dolores" (the Cry of the city of Dolores), a call to revolt issued on the night of September 15, 1810. Hidalgo issued the call for independence from his church pulpit when he shouted to the large crowd: "Mejícanos, Viva Mejíco" (Mexicans, Long Live Mexico). These are the famous words that are repeated every year by the Mexican president on Mexican Independence Day.

Soon after his "Grito de Dolores," Hidalgo led a band of his followers to the town of San Miguel where he again issued a cry that has become a central part of Mexico's historical and cultural past. Hidalgo proclaimed, "Long Live Our Lady of Guadalupe [The Mexican image of the Virgin Mary] and death to the Spaniards." Hidalgo's troops won important victories in the towns of Celaya and Guanajuato. Eventually Hidalgo and his followers fought their way to Mexico City, but, tragically, Hidalgo, with his limited military skills, made a poor strategic move when he turned his troops away from Mexico City to regroup. The Spanish troops began to win several critical battles that increased the disorganization of the opposition's forces. Eventually Hidalgo and his military coleader Ignacio de Allende were captured, court-martialed, and shot. Other leaders continued the struggle for independence. The Spanish government retaliated with a series of repressive measures against the insurgents, but their strategy backfired as more and more groups joined the independence movement. As a result of a coalition of anti-Spanish leaders, such as Agustín de Iturbide and Vicente Guerrero, Mexico gained its independence from Spain in 1821. New Spain became the young nation of Mexico, and Hidalgo had succeeded in turning the course of Mexican history. He remains Mexico's greatest patriot.

The decades after 1821 proved to be some of the most turbulent in Mexican history. The political coalitions that had been formed to gain independence from Spain soon disintegrated, producing intense civil strife. Some groups favored establishing a monarchy to rule Mexico whereas others dreamed of creating a form of government patterned after the United States. The former leader of the independence movement, Iturbide, gained control of the country and declared himself emperor of Mexico until he was overthrown by the military. Finally, in 1824, the various factions agreed upon a republic headed by an elected president and a Congress. Guadalupe Victoria became Mexico's first president.

The new republic soon faced one of the most turbulent episodes in Mexican history to have a long-range impact on contemporary Mexican society: Mexican immigration to the United States and relations between Mexico and the United States.

THE U.S.–MEXICO WAR OF 1845

Mexico experienced dramatic upheavals during the first half of the nineteenth century. Although a democratic republic existed on paper, political chaos prevailed throughout the country. Some groups opposed the constitution; others favored military intervention. Shifting political coalitions produced one of the most confusing periods in the country's history. For example, one military leader, General Antonio López de Santa Anna, gained the presidency eleven times between 1833 and 1855. For many, Santa Anna represented a dictator; others, however, continued to support him. Santa Anna's disastrous political decisions led to one of the most critical turning points in Mexican history: the war between Mexico and the United States.

Prior to 1848, the most northern region of Mexico—the American Southwest and particularly Texas—was sparsely populated. After Mexican independence in 1821, the Mexican government encouraged greater numbers of Mexicans to move into this border region. The government recognized the potential threat of American settlers crossing the U.S.–Mexico border who had started to take up residence in Mexico's northern territory. Under the leadership of such well-known historical figures as Sam Houston, adventuresome Americans settled in Texas. By 1835, an estimated 65,000 Mexicans lived in Texas; about 50,000 were Americans—most of whom opposed the

Mexican government that enforced restrictions on them. Santa Anna set siege on San Antonio, where serious uprisings had developed. The famous Battle of the Alamo witnessed the efforts of Americans and some Mexicans who joined in opposition to the Mexican government. Santa Anna's victory put a temporary halt to the Texas uprising.

In his pioneering book *North from Mexico* (1948), the noted historian Carey McWilliams analyzed the clash of cultures that developed inevitably as more and more Anglo-Americans established permanent residence in Mexican territory:

> In Texas, the Spanish-Mexican settlements were directly in the path of Anglo-American expansion. Unlike the rest of the borderlands, Texas was not separated from the centers of Anglo-American population by mountain ranges and desert wastes; geographically it invited invasion. In a series of belts or strips, its rich, alluvial plains stretched from the plateaus to the gulf. The rivers that marked these belts could be crossed, at all seasons, at almost any point, without much trouble. (McWilliams, 1948: 98)

An overwhelming distance, characterized by expansive semiarid land, existed between Mexico City and the closest Mexican settlements in Texas. The Mexican government had little chance of protecting its northern borders from Anglo-American influx because too many physical barriers stood between the center of Mexican power and the Texas region. Mexican culture differed vastly from Anglo-American culture. Language represented the greatest cultural barrier between the groups. Most Anglos and Mexicans were not bilingual and, in addition, lived in different areas. Mexicans were concentrated in small towns along the border, and Anglo-American settlers lived on ranches and farms farther removed from settlements. The escalating tension between the U.S. and Mexican government exacerbated cultural tensions between the two groups. President Jackson's plan for Texas intended to "trigger these United States into an explosion across the continent" (Hernandez, 1994: 19). By 1836 this explosion led to the declaration of Texas's independence from Mexico, an action that would culminate in war between Mexico and the United States. Developments in Mexico also contributed to the declaration of war between the two countries.

Between 1836 and 1848, a complicated series of political developments shaped the course of Mexican history. With the declaration of independence, border raids and skirmishes became an everyday occurrence. Texans raided Mexican settlements, and Mexicans sent forces into Texas, whose independence it never recognized. Interestingly, a significant number of Mexicans living in Texas sided with the Anglo Americans against the Mexican government. In fact, two Mexicans joined the other forty-eight signers of the declaration of Texas independence and a third signer became vice president of the Texas republic.

Mexico refused to recognize these actions and attacked U.S. soldiers in Texas. These military skirmishes culminated in a declaration of war against Mexico in 1845. American General Zachary Taylor claimed victory over the Mexican general Santa Anna's forces in the north. General Winfield Scott landed in Veracruz and led an invasion force that captured Mexico City in 1847. One of Mexico's most revered national monuments is the statue outside of Chapultepec Castle commemorating the heroic actions of six young military cadets who gave their lives fighting against Scott's invading army. Mexico surrendered in 1848 and signed the Treaty of Guadalupe Hidalgo that ceded Mexico's northwest territory to the United States. The states of California, Wyoming, Utah, Nevada, and certain areas of Arizona, New Mexico, and Colorado became part of the United States. In 1853, the United States gained the remaining parts of Arizona and New Mexico through the Gadsden Purchase. Mexico also recognized the annexation of Texas by the United States. The Treaty of Guadalupe Hidalgo also provided that the United States would recognize the rights of Mexicans holding land titles. The increased numbers of Anglo Americans into the Southwest, however, eventually resulted in the takeover of these Mexican land grants. The California Gold Rush resulted in an even greater influx of Anglo Americans, and within a matter of years, few Mexicans retained title to southwestern lands. Hostilities between the two groups persisted long after the war ended.

MEXICO UNDER BENITO JUÁREZ

The annexation of this vast territory by the United States produced a complex social order in this land seceded by Mexico. Those Mexicans residing in this land became U.S. citizens as a result of the Treaty of Guadalupe Hidalgo. Although the treaty stipulated that their property, wealth, and civil rights would be respected, former Mexican citizens soon confronted the harsh realities of military defeat, and by the latter part of the twentieth century, those Mexicans living in the Southwest lost almost all their rights and privileges. The War of 1845 created a generation of new "Americans" who did not fit the classic pattern of immigrants; they did not cross oceans or other borders to enter a new country. On the contrary, their country of origin—

Mexico—became part of the United States, the country to which subsequent generations of Mexicans would cross the newly established international border as immigrants.

As a result of its defeat, Mexico experienced a wide range of economic, political, and social catastrophes that produced new conflicts. Santa Anna returned to power as an even stronger dictator, but his authoritarian rule sparked an opposition movement led by Benito Juárez. Juárez, a Zapotec Indian, seized control of Mexico in 1855 by establishing a liberal democratic republic with a new constitution. The United States played a key role in championing Juárez and his followers. The U.S. government pledged its support for Juárez, recognizing him as the legitimate national head of state of Mexico. By 1858 a very strong group of upper-class Conservatives joined with the majority of the Catholic hierarchy and forced Juárez from the presidency. Juárez left Mexico City but established himself and his followers in Veracruz, where he continued the struggle against the Conservative group. Mexico found itself in what would prove to be a tragic civil war. Juárez's army eventually recaptured Mexico City in 1861, but his victory proved to be short-lived.

This historic period witnessed one of the most unusual European interventions into Mexican politics. The Juárez government found itself almost bankrupt as England, France, and Spain demanded repayment of their loans. Mexico's default on these loans resulted in a joint invasion of Mexico in 1862. Led by Napoleon III, France set out to conquer Mexico. In May 1862, Juárez's army resisted the French Invasion and won a famous victory against the French, whose army was the best in the world. This event is still celebrated both in Mexico and in the United States by Mexican immigrants and Mexican Americans. Despite this defeat, the French captured Mexico City, sending Juárez and his followers into exile. Through a combination of political intrigues, this conservative opposition group, with the support of Napoleon III, appointed Archduke Maximillian of Habsburg as emperor of Mexico in 1864. Juárez continued to maintain his opposition forces with the support of the United States. This combination of pressure on France resulted in the removal of its troops from Mexico in 1867. Maximillian was taken prisoner and executed by a firing squad in the city of Querétaro, Mexico, in 1867.

Juárez returned to power, serving as president from 1867 to 1872, the year of his death. The political developments that followed the presidency of Juárez unleashed an unprecedented upheaval in Mexican history: the dictatorship of Porfirio Díaz from 1876 to 1911, and the Mexican Revolution that succeeded in overthrowing him. The Revolution, the first modern world revolution of the twentieth century, led to one of the largest mass immigrations to the United States. This generation of Mexican immigrants fled their country and sparked the creation of a group of "New Americans."

2

The Mexican Revolution and Immigration

When Porfirio Díaz took over the reins of the Mexican government in 1876, neither his supporters nor his opponents could have understood the impact that his dictatorship would have on the development of twentieth-century Mexico and the short- and long-term impact of the consequent mass immigration of Mexicans to the United States. The social fabric of both Mexico and the United States would never be the same. Dictatorship led to revolution, and revolution to the international migration of Mexicans to the United States.

MEXICO UNDER DÍAZ (1876–1911)

When Díaz became president in 1876, Mexicans still admired him for his military victory against the French in 1862. His popularity soon deteriorated as he initiated political, economic, and social policies that produced extreme inequalities throughout Mexico. Díaz believed that Mexico needed to establish a stable government after having experienced seventy-five changes in the presidency between 1821 to 1876. His presidency soon took on all the characteristics of a dictatorship. Díaz gained the support of various powerful sectors of Mexican society, such as the large landowners and the upper-level clerics of the Catholic Church who agreed with his plan to create a modern Mexico. Unfortunately, their vision of a "modern Mexico" was one in which civil rights were suspended, the role of the state and local government diminished, and the powers of the central government expanded.

Díaz initiated economic policies that he believed would transform Mexico into an international power. His program for economic modernization increased the dissatisfaction among the peasants, working class, and emergent middle class. The Díaz regime encouraged foreign interests, especially British, French, and American, to invest in the country's economy in an attempt to modernize Mexico by stimulating economic growth driven by external investments. Within a few years, foreign companies controlled Mexico's agriculture, mining, oil, and railroads. Although these foreign ventures did bring some level of economic development to the country, the majority of Mexicans soon found themselves in dire economic circumstances. Many indigenous groups suffered harsh treatment under the Díaz regime. His government confiscated communal lands, revoked political rights, and, tragically, relocated many tribes, such as the Yaquis, from their communal lands in Mexico's northwest to the jungles of the Yucatán Peninsula. Unlike other indigenous groups, the Yaqui Indians had a long history of conflict with first the Spanish government and then, after independence, with the Mexican government. The Yaquis lived in small villages in Mexico's most northern regions, in what is now Arizona. The Yaquis prided themselves in their independence, and their history is a record of long and sustained conflict with the national government. Under the Díaz regime this conflict intensified, leading to their expulsion. Many Yaquis died or were killed as they were forced to leave their lands and resettle in Yucatán.

THE MEXICAN REVOLUTION OF 1910

By 1900, opponents of the Díaz regime began to mobilize themselves against the federal government, even though such opposition groups experienced swift and harsh repression at the hands of federal troops. In some cases, the United States, in an attempt to maintain stability in Mexico, assisted Díaz in suppressing these uprisings. The presidential election of 1910 served as a major catalyst for the Mexican Revolution. A group of middle-class liberals who favored the establishment of a republic in Mexico was headed by Francisco I. Madero, who launched his presidential campaign against Díaz in December 1909. The presidential elections of 1910 proved to be the ultimate downfall of the Díaz dictatorship. Díaz won the elections through a series of fraudulent practices and in so doing added to the intensity of Madero's opposition. As Díaz celebrated his seventh presidential victory, Madero and other revolutionary leaders such as Pancho Villa and Emiliano Zapata joined forces in city after city on their way to Mexico City for the final showdown with Díaz. Madero had traveled to the United States where he formally denounced the Díaz presidency and published his political plan, "Plan de San Luis Potosí," in which he called for a national revolt on November 20—the date on which Mexicans and Mexican Americans continue to celebrate the start of the Mexican Revolution. At this early stage, the opposition against Díaz met with many defeats, but the various factions continued in their efforts. In May 1911, they emerged victorious. Outside the National Palace in Mexico City, Díaz encountered masses of his opposition calling for his resignation. Díaz realized that the end was at hand, and with his departure from the capital on May 26 and his exile in France, Mexican revolutionaries claimed victory for overthrowing the dictatorship. However, they soon found themselves embroiled in one of the bloodiest social revolutions of the twentieth century.

Madero became president on November 6, 1911. Tragically, opposition to Madero soon led to violent upheavals as one group tried to emerge victorious over others. Madero was assassinated only three months after he won the presidential election. From the time of his assassination, Mexico was torn apart as revolutionary factions fought against each other in attempts to consolidate presidential power. Violence permeated every aspect of Mexican society. Leaders of revolutionary factions assassinated their rivals until they themselves were killed by competing groups. It is estimated that between 1.5 and 2 million Mexicans lost their lives during the Revolution. The Mexican writer Mariano Azuela captured this turbulent period in Mexican history in his novel *The Underdogs* (1915).

In 1913, General Victoriano Huerta gained control of the presidency, but he was soon challenged by another military figure—Venustiano Carranza. Under the leadership of President Woodrow Wilson, the U.S. government supported Carranza, providing him with both military and diplomatic assistance believing that he would restore a climate of peace and economic stability in Mexico that would favor American business ventures. President Wilson ordered American troops onto Mexican soil at the Pacific port of Veracruz as a response to the arrival of munitions supplied by Germany to Huerta's forces. Carranza denounced this American action and, as a result, refused American support for his troops.

Carranza eventually occupied Mexico City in 1914. Carranza and his forces battled against such opponents as Francisco "Pancho" Villa in the northern region of Mexico and Emiliano Zapata in the southern region. Carranza emerged victorious in 1916. Under his leadership delegates to a constitutional convention succeeded in drafting and adopting a new document, the Mexican Constitution of 1917, which continues to serve as the blueprint of Mexican politics and society. This constitution established a liberal republican form of government with the central government in control of education, land reforms, and subsoil rights such as those for oil and for the Catholic Church. It also restricted the presidency to a single six-year term. By 1924 Mexico's chaotic revolutionary period ended, and the Mexican Revolution became consolidated into what is now modern Mexico. The Institutional Revolutionary Party of Mexico, known as the PRI, emerged as an all-powerful political party and dominated both national and state elections. The PRI was the longest-lasting political party maintaining its control of Mexican national politics until the presidential elections of 2000, when Vicente Fox Quesada, the candidate of the Partido Acción Nacional (PAN—National Action Party), the major opposition political opposition party, emerged victorious.

IMMIGRATION TO THE UNITED STATES

From the beginning of the Mexican Revolution, Mexicans sought refuge in the United States. They left their small villages and set out to "El Norte"—the North—as they called the United States. The railroad system built under the Díaz regime transported the mass migration of Mexicans to the American Southwest. Hundreds of thousands of Mexicans made this trip across the Rio Grande. The United States did not keep complete immigration records for Mexicans entering the country. Many crossed and then recrossed "la frontera," as Mexicans called the U.S.–Mexican frontier. In addition, many entered without checking at border entry points. Existing figures show a constant increase in Mexican immigration from as early as 1894 to 1920 (see Table 2.1).

The U.S. Census started keeping records for Mexican immigration in 1930, although record keeping for immigration figures continues to be difficult even to the present day due to such factors as large numbers of undocumented immigrants and patterns of reentry to the United States by deported immigrants. Data gathered in the 1930 Census show that the total population of Mexican immigrants actually grew from 367,510 in 1910 to 700,541 in 1920. By the beginning of the Great Depression, approximately 1 million Mexicans resided in the United States. The majority of Mexican immigrants who came during these years settled along the U.S.–Mexican border in such states as Texas, Arizona, and California, with about half of these residing in Texas. Communities of Mexican immigrants were established in places such as El Paso and San Antonio, Texas, and San Diego and Los Angeles, California. By 1920, El Paso, Texas had the largest Mexican

Table 2.1
Mexicans Admitted to the United States, 1894–1920

1894	109
1895	116
1896	150
1897	91
1898	107
1899	161
1900	237
1901	347
1902	709
1903	528
1904	1,009
1905	3,637
1906	1,997
1907	1,406
1908	6,067
1909	16,251
1910	18,691
1911	19,889
1912	23,238
1913	11,926
1914	14,614
1915	12,340
1916	18,425
1917	17,869
1918	18,524
1919	29,818
1920	52,361

Source: U.S. Immigration reports as quoted in Charles H. Hufford, *The Social and Economic Effects of the Mexican Migration into Texas* (San Francisco, CA: R & E Research Associates, 1971), p. 23.

population of any city in the United States and had more Mexicans than Anglos. San Antonio had the second-largest population of Mexicans.

The majority of immigrants were displaced peasants, unemployed and dissatisfied working-class persons who fled the impoverished conditions and violence prevalent throughout Mexico. Some immigrants, however, came from the middle and upper classes of Mexican society who left for political and economic reasons. Many prominent elite families, such as the Terrazas family from the state of Chihuahua, represented exiled supporters of the Díaz regime who had fled Mexico and settled in El Paso, Texas. These families brought their wealth to the United States and formed an early leadership group among the Mexican immigrant community. Regardless of the socio-economic and political background, this wave of Mexican immigrants left their homeland—a country engaged in one of the most violent social revolutions.

During this period, Mexicans crossed the border into the United States with relative ease. Marked social and geographic continuities created a borderland on the American side that differed very little from the Mexican immigrants' own country. Ernesto Galarza, a prominent Mexican immigrant who spent his adult life in the United States and became the most influential educator, political activist, and scholar in the Mexican-American community, wrote his autobiography, *Barrio Boy* (1971), in which he recounts his family's immigrant journey to the United States. Galarza recalls his first impression of the United States as he left Mexico. He says that everything looked the same; one side of the border looked like the other side. The American flag flying over the border inspection post was the only marker indicating that he and thousands of other Mexican immigrants were now in the United States. Mexicans wanting to enter the United States reported to the immigration office on the American side and provided the officer with a few pieces of relevant information such as name, date and place of birth, and destination in the United States.

The need for unskilled and semiskilled workers for the rapidly industrializing American Southwest represented one of the major reasons for the ease with which Mexican immigrants entered the United States during the late nineteenth and early twentieth centuries. Throughout the Southwest, a booming economy in mining, ranching, and agriculture followed a national and international industrialization period which was characterized by industrial expansion and production. New factories turned out textiles, chemicals, steel, iron, and electricity. Rapid industrialization developed along regionally specialized production centers. In the Northeast and parts of the Midwest, a large supply of Western European immigrants entered light manufacturing

Araíza family portrait prior to immigration to the United States in the early 1900s. Courtesy of Araíza Family Archives.

factories such as textiles. The Pacific Northwest shipped lumber to the East Coast. The Great Plains region supplied unlimited amounts of beef. The Lake Superior region developed the extraction of iron and copper. Cotton became "King" in the South, supplying the textile mills in the Northeast with raw materials.

The South and Southwest served as suppliers of the raw materials and agricultural products needed to supply the industrial centers and the growing working class they employed. This region developed only a limited number of short-lived industries. All along the U.S.–Mexico border and other cities in the Southwest, centers of mining and agriculture emerged as regional parts of a national industrialization process. Mexican immigrants formed the backbone of the Southwestern economy by providing an abundant, constant, and cheap source of mostly unskilled labor. These jobs provided employment but also created strong barriers to the upward social mobility for the masses of immigrants. Unskilled Mexican workers contributed to the economic boom, but they failed to reap its rewards. They were concentrated in such industries as the railroads, construction, mining, and agriculture. Although Mexican men dominated the working class in Mexican immigrant communities, large numbers of Mexican women also became part of the paid labor force. Widowed and young, single women worked as domestics, laundresses, seamstresses, and garment workers. In whatever industries they found themselves, Mexican immigrant workers resided in largely segregated occupations with little chance of improvement. Economic discrimination created a dual labor force with Anglo-American workers concentrated in higher-paying occupations than Mexicans. Unskilled workers found it practically impossible to improve their occupational status because most unions restricted membership to Anglos. These patterns of discrimination affected the development of Mexican immigrant communities during this period and subsequent generations of Mexican Americans who, for the most part, continue to face patterns of inequality.

The Immigration Act of 1917 represented an early attempt to restrict the flow of immigrants to the United States. The years leading up to the passage of this legislation were marked with increased concern with the large numbers of immigrants from all parts of the world, including Mexico. Exaggerated and often inaccurate reports of Mexicans posing health problems and representing a bad moral influence on American citizens contributed to this early episode of anti-Mexican immigrant sentiments. The Immigration Act of 1917 called for a head tax of $8 and a literacy test. Mexican immigration hardly increased from 1917 to 1918. Although they were not eligible to be drafted, many Mexicans feared conscription to the American armed forces fighting in World War I and returned to Mexico, discouraging others from immigrating to the United States. American employers experienced economic difficulties caused by a shortage of labor due to decreases in Mexican immigration and the numbers of American citizens drafted into the armed services. Sufficient pressure was exerted by employers and eventually the Department of Labor suspended the immigration law to allow Mexican immigrants to enter the country as agricultural workers. By the middle of 1918, Mexican immigration resumed and continued to increase rapidly. Many companies, especially the railroads and mining, actually entered Mexico to recruit laborers. These immigrants became known as "Los Enganchados" (The Hooked Ones). A popular Mexican ballad captured the feelings of those who came as farm workers to the fields in the United States. The ballad tells of the journey to "El Norte"—the unfair treatment, low wages, and unsanitary conditions experienced by immigrants. More than anything, the ballad tells of the homesickness of the immigrants as they worked in the fields, longing to return to their homeland but always keeping the American dream: making a better life for themselves and, most important, the lives of their children, who would eventually form a generation of U.S.–born citizens—Mexican Americans.

IMMIGRANT CULTURE

Like all immigrant groups, the Mexicans who entered the United States brought with them their cultural traditions and ways of life. Their Mexican culture provided them with a strong sense of community—an important survival strategy as they lived, worked, and raised their children in their new country. In Mexican immigrant communities throughout the United States, particularly in the Southwest, Mexican culture thrived within the immigrants' families, religion, and community activities.

The proximity of Mexico to the United States represented a major factor in the development of cultural practices among immigrant communities. For the immigrant, "La Frontera"—the border between Mexico and the United States—did not serve as a barrier from one side to the other. They crossed La Frontera, but they did not turn away from Mexico. They lived and raised their families in Texas, California, Arizona, New Mexico, and even in states far removed from the border such as Kansas and Illinois, but they continued to keep Mexico alive as its culture flourished in their immigrant communities. Many Mexican immigrants even believed that they would return to Mexico when the revolution ended. In reality, most of them remained in the United States. The immigrants' longing for their homeland resulted in their conscious efforts to create "little Mexicos" in the United States. Anthropologist Manuel Gamio (1932) interviewed Mexican immigrants who arrived in the United States from Mexico in the 1910s and 1920s. One immigrant told of how she wanted her family to eat the Mexican food she prepared exactly as she did in her hometown. She said that her family could live their everyday lives as if they were still in Mexico. She and her husband spoke only Spanish in their home. Her family lived in a neighborhood of Mexicans, and she said that she could walk all around her community and hear only Spanish and see only Mexicans. Many immigrants would tell their children that when they left their home they were in the United States, but when they came back into their home, they were in Mexico. All along the border, Mexican immigrants attempted to re-create their lives as they had been before they left Mexico. Although they could not be completely isolated from the Anglo-American world, Mexican immigrant culture survived in the United States.

The family became the most important cultural institution that Mexicans carried with them to their new immigrant communities. Mexican immigrant families were diverse, but common patterns existed. During this immigration period, Mexicans came to the United States as a family unit. In other immigrant groups, single men formed the majority of immigrants. Mexicans traveled as families, sometimes extended families. Some industries, such as the railroads, recruited entire Mexican families in an effort to keep a stable workforce. In his autobiography *Barrio Boy*, Ernesto Galarza tells the story of how his mother, his uncles, and he made the long trip to Sacramento from his home village in the rural state of Nayarit, Mexico. When they arrived in California, his extended family continued to live together. Other extended family members eventually made a similar journey, settling in Galarza's thriving Mexican community. The process through which immigrant communities serve as magnets for other immigrants is called chain migration. As Mexican immigrant communities experienced large-scale chain migration, the Mexican immigrant family, with its native customs, values, and kinship systems, allowed Mexicans to maintain strong Mexican identities.

Mexican families retained many traditional cultural practices. One immigrant, interviewed by Manuel Gamio for his classic book, *Mexican Immigration* (1930), recalled how his family would get together for family celebrations such as baptisms and weddings. They would listen and dance to Mexican music. The family table would be full of the traditional dishes from their home state of Puebla. Such religious and family celebrations also forged new traditional family networks. Baptisms and weddings created the kinship bond of coparenthood called "compadrazco." Parents would select a couple to sponsor the baptism of their son or daughter, becoming the "madrino" and "madrina" (godfather and godmother, respectively). This religious and cultural practice provided a safety net for the child; godparents were expected to step in to raise their godchild if either or both parents died. This practice also exists among other immigrant groups such as Italians. Among all groups, immigrants believed that these family kinship networks were key to their cultural and economic survival in their new country.

Mexican folk customs and practices existed both inside and outside of immigrant families. Traditional folk songs and music from their homeland served as popular forms of entertainment. Family celebrations usually included some form of musical entertainment. Some families could afford to hire a small group of musicians who played a variety of musical styles. Mexican folk ballads—corridos—represented human interest stories set to music. These corridos expressed the emotions and life histories of Mexicans. Although they continued to listen to the best-known corridos from Mexico, songwriters composed new corridos that expressed the specific attitudes and feelings of the immigrants. Such new songs told of the immigrant journey and the adjustment to problems in the United States. One very popular corrido told the story of Aurelio Pompa, who was executed in California for killing an Anglo. Mexican immigrants throughout the Southwest believed in his innocence, stressing that he acted in self-defense. The "Corrido of Aurelio Pompa" could be heard in Mexican immigrant communities from California to Texas.

Music formed an important part of the immigrant's life. Most communities organized Sunday concerts in neighborhood parks. Summer concerts were particularly popular and were usually accompanied by dancing. Dance forms included waltzes, polkas, and a version of the American foxtrot. German immigrants to Texas introduced the polka to Mexican immigrants. These public concerts also served as a site for courtship among young Mexicans. Girls waited on one side of the dance floor in the park or plaza to be asked to dance, always under the watchful eyes of parents or chaperones.

Family gatherings in a backyard, neighborhood park, or at some other location for a celebration usually included storytelling. As in other immigrant communities, the oral tradition provided immigrants with a connection to their homelands. Oral literature included Mexican tales called "cuentos," legends, and children's stories. Ghost stories were very popular and usually included a moral lesson. A story with many variations is that of "La Llorona"—the weeping woman who supposedly killed her children by drowning them, then repented for her horrible deed and wandered the earth crying for her murdered children. Many Mexican immigrant children came home to bed immediately when their mothers called them in from play out of their fear that La Llorona would steal them.

Religion played a key role in the daily life of Mexican immigrants. The majority of Mexican immigrants practiced Catholicism but blended specific Mexican cultural practices with the traditional Catholic beliefs and rituals. Historically, the Catholic Church in Mexico maintained a stronghold on political power through its accumulated wealth, landholdings, and dramatic influence on social life. Although some clerics championed liberal causes, Mexico's clergy is best known for its alliance with conservative groups.

At the level of the everyday citizen, the church exerted a tremendous force by shaping every aspect of society from birth to death. As immigrants, Mexicans continued to practice Catholicism, but the church took on an additional role in their communities: as an important source of comfort and cultural continuity. In most Mexican communities, the majority of priests were mostly Irish Americans and Italian Americans due to the shortage of Mexican priests. Parish priests, such as those at Sacred Heart Church in El Paso, Texas, made serious attempts to deal with the specific cultural needs of their Mexican parishioners. Within Mexican immigrant parishes, it was common practice for priests to learn Spanish and try their best to understand Mexican religious practices that were often very different from the formal practices of the Catholic Church. Many of the wealthy immigrants sent their children to Catholic schools. In places such as Los Angeles, San Antonio, and El Paso, Mexican immigrants continued to follow the religious rituals that they had brought with them. For example, many Mexicans retained their devotion to the Virgin of Guadalupe. According to Mexican Catholics, the Virgin Mary appeared to a Mexican peasant in 1531 and directed him to convince the Spanish bishops that she wanted a shrine built on the hilltop outside of Mexico City. Her indigenous features led her to become a national symbol for social justice for the masses of peasants. This is the present-day site for the National Basilica, the most revered shrine in Latin America.

Devotional societies to the Virgin of Guadalupe existed in both rural and urban communities in Mexico, and immigrants transferred their local societies to their American settlements. These societies attracted more women than men. Throughout the Southwest, the Society of Our Lady of Guadalupe organized religious celebrations such as the annual Christmas Shepherds' Play called "Los Pastores." Religious parades in honor of the Virgin of Guadalupe attracted hundreds of Mexican immigrants. The Catholic Church and its activities helped Mexicans to adjust to their lives in the United States and to maintain a strong sense of pride in their Mexican culture. Many Mexican

Home Altar of Tina Fuentes, Lubbock, Texas. Courtesy of Sam Braudt.

homes displayed home altars, usually cared for by women. Home altars were small shrines located on top of a dresser or table, which consisted of one or more religious statues of Christ, the Virgin Mary, and other popular saints. Candles, either natural or, in later years, electric, were kept as illumination. Fresh or plastic flowers adorned the home altars that could be located either in one room or in many. Among the most religious, these home altars became the focal point for daily prayers.

Mexican immigrants will always have a special relationship with the United States due to its proximity to Mexico. Although specific periods of immigration can be identified, such as the mass migrations in the aftermath of the Mexican Revolution, a continuous influx of immigrants helps to maintain many aspects of Mexican culture.

3

Continued Immigration, World Wars, and Aftermath

Beginning with the first wave of Mexican immigration to the United States during the Mexican Revolution, the relationship between Mexican immigrants and the United States has been characterized by periods of alternating cycles of hospitality and antagonism. The changing nature of the economy and the political climate affected which of these cycles confronted the newly arrived Mexican immigrants. An understanding of the sociopolitical climate that led to the Immigration Act of 1965 requires an overview of developments within Mexican immigrant communities prior to 1965. Two major factors are discussed in this chapter: (1) continued immigration and labor unrest (1920–1940), and (2) World War II and its aftermath (1940–1965).

CONTINUED IMMIGRATION AND LABOR UNREST (1920–1940)

The country's experiences during World War I shaped American immigration policies in the 1920s. As a result of a serious labor shortage of workers during the war, American immigration policies represented legislative efforts to attract greater numbers of Mexican immigrants to work in war industries. As early as 1917, the U.S. government relaxed all laws limiting Mexican immigration. Interestingly, the U.S.–born children of Mexican immigrants were not allowed to enter the army, which enforced segregation of all groups considered "nonwhite." Records show that many Mexican Americans changed their last names in order to avoid serving in segregated battalions.

One young man living with his immigrant parents in Texas took on an Anglo-sounding last name and served in Europe. Many such men who managed to break the army's restrictions were killed in action, and several were decorated for their bravery in service to the United States (McWilliams, 1948).

The liberalization of U.S. immigration restrictions led to a significant increase in Mexican immigrants living in the border states. In the twenty years between 1920 and 1940, the Mexican population living in the United States increased by 22 percent. The population grew from 8.8 million in 1920 to 14.4 million in 1940, with migration from central and southern states in Mexico to border states increasing dramatically. Large numbers of Mexicans who moved to the border states eventually entered the United States and settled in existing Mexican communities throughout the Southwest. Immigrants concentrated in such cities as San Diego and Los Angeles. In El Paso, the Mexican immigrant and U.S.–born Mexican-American population became the majority group over all other groups. Within these communities, Mexican cultural traditions were reinforced as a result of this new influx of immigrants. Just as in the mid-1900s, immigrants retained many of their cultural practices long after they settled in this country. The demand for Mexican food products, the popularity of Mexican music, and the preference for Spanish as the main language all contributed to Mexican cultural continuity. One immigrant who came to the United States recalls that many of his adult nieces and nephews lived in his apartment until they were able to find a place of their own. While they were living with him, they tried to re-create their everyday life in Mexico and in so doing exposed his children to traditional Mexican practices (Gamio, 1930).

With the end of World War I, the United States attempted to return to prewar normalcy, but national and international economic instabilities produced widespread and collective anxiety among Americans. The 1920s witnessed the rise of extreme prejudices and discriminatory practices among those groups of Americans that embraced racial "purity" ideologies. The Ku Klux Klan reached a membership of about 5 million. Politicians and ordinary citizens across the country began to express anti-Mexican immigrant feelings. The so-called "Mexican Problem" referred to the widespread but largely unsubstantiated belief that Mexican immigration created the country's economic disaster in the 1930s. Racial prejudices contributed further to the resentment against Mexican immigrants and immigrants from other countries. All these factors led to a renewal of antagonism against Mexican immigrants as witnessed by the passage of restrictive immigration laws. For example, earlier in 1921 and 1924, U.S. immigration quota regulations exempted immigrants from Mexico in order to maintain a constant flow of workers for expanding American industries. Nevertheless, anti-immigrant groups and most American labor unions continued their efforts to curb Mexican immigration. With the stock market's final collapse in the early 1930s, a demand for the development of more restrictive immigration policies decreased as the country began its long road to economic recovery.

Unfortunately this recovery process led to serious violations of the civil rights of Mexican immigrants. Feelings of intense hostility against Mexican immigrants culminated in a government policy of "repatriation" that developed to placate those sectors in American society that continued to exert pressure on the government to send Mexicans back to Mexico. Many Mexican immigrants had already left the depression-stricken United States even though Mexico did not escape the impact of the Great Depression. It is estimated that about 500,000 Mexican immigrants left the United States. Not all these immigrants made the return journey to Mexico voluntarily. Tragically, many Mexican immigrants were forcefully "repatriated" by the government and sent back to Mexico. Between 1929 and 1935, large numbers of immigrants were forced to leave their Mexican communities in the United States. The highest rates of deportations (called "repatriation" by the Hoover administration) took place in California, where the majority of Mexicans resided. Government officials and law enforcement agencies combined their efforts to appease the business and labor union sectors by conducting these mass deportations. All too frequently, the American-born children of Mexican immigrant parents were deported along with their families. This chapter in Mexican immigrant history continues to be a source of resentment in Mexican communities throughout the United States.

Beginning in the mid-1920s, deteriorating sociopolitical and economic conditions in the United States gave rise to a significant development: labor unrest within many Mexican immigrant communities. At the same time that many immigrants were being deported, other groups of Mexicans and Mexican-American laborers started collective efforts to improve their working conditions. Mexican immigrants had entered a variety of industries during the 1920s and 1930s. Mexicans workers, primarily male immigrants, represented the dominant labor population in such industries as mining, agriculture, and the railroads. Eventually, many Mexican immigrants established themselves in such states as Washington, Colorado, Michigan, and Kansas (Gamio, 1930).

The anti-immigrant climate and the deteriorating working conditions soon developed into labor activism. Mexican workers established unions that initiated several large-scale strikes. California's agricultural workers experienced

the majority of these strikes. One Mexican immigrant recalled his participation in the Cantaloupe Strike of 1928. He remembered attending the early
meetings of the newly established union and later casting his vote for the
strike. Working conditions in the fields were harsh, and the wages were low.
He had come to the United States with his family, hoping to make a better
life for his children. He lived in a nearby community of Mexican immigrants
who also found themselves working long hours with little to show for their
efforts. During the early months of the strike, the Mexican consulate provided important support, demonstrating to Mexican immigrants that the
Mexican government continued to maintain an interest in those Mexicans
who had left the country to live in the United States. The Cantaloupe Strike
of 1928 proved an early victory for Mexican immigrants, and other strikes
soon took place throughout the Southwest (Gamio, 1930).

Mexican immigrant women entered the labor force along with their fa-
thers, husbands, and brothers. Women, however, worked in service sector
jobs such as domestic workers. Some women did work in agriculture. Emma
Tenayuca remains an important figure in Mexican-American history for her
union activity among the pecan-shellers in south Texas. Tenayuca was born
in San Antonio in 1916. She became a labor leader during her high school
years, organizing a workers' march to Austin in 1931. Over the next years,
Tenayuca fought for the rights of Mexican immigrant workers in the agricultural fields of Texas. She is most remembered for her leadership among
the pecan-shellers who went on strike in 1938. According to an oral history
interview, an immigrant woman who had worked as a pecan-sheller for almost a year recalled hearing Tenayuca speak at a rally. The woman knew
that going on strike would be difficult, particularly since she was raising her
four children by herself, but Tenayuca inspired her, giving her the courage
to vote in favor of the strike. Tenayuca developed into a nationally known
labor activist throughout the 1930s and early 1940s (Gonzales, 1999).

The labor strikes by Mexican immigrants prior to World War II reflect
the ongoing problems between Mexican immigrants and the United States.
Many strikes succeeded in improving working conditions for the immigrants,
but many proved unsuccessful. As the economy improved, resentment against
immigrants subsided gradually. Increased numbers of Mexicans began to
enter the United States. Their numbers would grow even more when the
United States found itself engaged in World War II.

WORLD WAR II AND THE BRACERO PROGRAM

The Spanish word for hired hand is "bracero," from the word "brazo" or
arm. Bracero became the word used to refer to contract laborers recruited

from Mexico under specific legislation. With the entrance of the United States into World War II, the country's need for a large supply of workers increased dramatically. War industries needed workers to fill in for the Americans fighting in Europe and Japan, even though large numbers of American women, including Mexican-American women, had entered the paid labor force, many in jobs usually reserved for men. The U.S. government joined with the Mexican government and designed the Bracero Program to guarantee a steady supply of Mexican immigrant workers. During the years of the Bracero Program, it is estimated that approximately 350,000 changed their status from temporary workers to immigrants living on a permanent basis in the United States. As a result, the Bracero Program produced another significant wave of Mexican immigration.

The Bracero Program began in 1942 following Pearl Harbor and the American entrance into the war. The U.S. Congress ratified Public Law 45, and Mexican President Ávilo Camacho agreed to its provisions for the recruitment of braceros. About a quarter of a million Mexican men made the trip to the agricultural fields and war industries and in so doing supported the American war effort. These workers harvested food supplies and worked in a variety of industries such as the railroads and mining. The first group of braceros numbered about 1,500. The U.S. government allocated $120,000.00 for this program from 1943 to 1947. The numbers of braceros brought to the United States increased steadily from 1942 through 1947. Mexican immigrant workers harvested such crops as lettuce, carrots, strawberries, peaches, apricots, melons, and other vegetables. In addition to California, workers traveled to other areas such as the Rocky Mountain states and the Midwest. Some braceros became railroad workers and were particularly important for the war effort.

Braceros worked under specific guidelines outlined in Public Law 45. The workers were guaranteed minimum wages, adequate living conditions, and the right to end their participation in the program and return to Mexico. Many growers in the agricultural industry, particularly in California, maintained that these provisions were unnecessarily protective, but they were practically forced to accept the guidelines due to the extreme shortage of farm laborers. Close to 200,000 Mexican contract workers migrated to the United States and could be found in twenty-one states. California became the temporary home for about half of all braceros workers who were recruited to come to the United States to work in agriculture. Braceros served as a steady source of cheap labor. Interestingly, Texas did not favor the Bracero Program, preferring undocumented Mexican immigrants whose wages were far below the minimum wage guaranteed to braceros.

The program stipulated that the immigrants were to return to Mexico at the conclusion of the war. In 1945, when World War II ended, most growers wanted the U.S. government to extend the program. Pressure was exerted on various congressmen, and in January 1947 a bill was passed to extend the Bracero Program until 1948. The bill stipulated the program would end in 1948. Nevertheless, the agricultural business sector continued to experience labor shortages. Their efforts to extend the program and make it renewable every two years led to the passage of another congressional bill. American involvement in the Korean conflict, beginning in 1950, produced a marked increase for contract laborers from Mexico. The Mexican government, however, in response to widespread abuses of braceros, said that it would only participate in the program if the U.S. government improved its monitoring of the treatment of the workers. With such a guarantee assured, the Mexican government agreed to an extension of the Bracero Program, which continued in operation until 1964 when various factors led to its end.

The new Bracero Program retained its original guidelines. The Mexican government recruited the workers who would enter the country as contract laborers. As a result of the large numbers of Mexicans who wanted to become braceros, the Mexican government designed a lottery system to be used in the selection. Immigration records show that about 4.8 million Mexican workers participated in the program over its twenty-two years. Once the workers entered the United States, employers hired those they needed. In the case of agricultural workers, the growers agreed to provide housing, transportation, and a guaranteed term of employment. In addition, employers also agreed to protect the civil rights of the contract laborers.

Although large numbers of growers benefited from the use of braceros, a rise in anti-immigrant groups developed, particularly in California. Many American workers and their unions complained that these immigrant workers kept wages down and took jobs away from them. Even those workers outside of the agricultural sector agreed with this argument; they feared that eventually Mexican braceros would leave the fields and seek work in the urban industrial centers. Nevertheless, the influx of braceros not only continued but also increased every year. The largest number of braceros entered the United States in 1975. Approximately 25 percent of all braceros resided in the states of Texas, California, New Mexico, and Arizona.

Inevitably, the development of sustained abuses led to the mobilization of social groups intent on ending the Bracero Program. Interviews and newspaper articles document a long list of serious complaints made by the braceros: poor housing, inadequate food, interruptions in employment without pay, and episodes of anti-immigrant violence. Critics of the abuses of the Bracero Program included such groups as the California Migrant Ministry and the National Catholic Welfare Council. During these years, César Chávez and Ernesto Galarza emerged as key leaders in support of ending the widespread abuse of braceros under the Bracero Program.

Ernesto Galarza stands out as a major figure in calling attention to the blatant abuses of the Bracero Program. As both a sociologist and political activist, Galarza pioneered the idea of organizing Mexican and Mexican-American farm workers. He directed his mobilization efforts against such California agricultural growers as DiGiorgio and the table grape industry. Galarza focused his efforts on the development of a consumer boycott, involving the organizing of picket lines outside supermarkets carrying the DiGiorgio label. Galarza became the director of research and education for the American Federation of Labor's farm workers union—the National Farm Labor Union (NFLU)—founded soon after World War II. Galarza worked tirelessly on behalf of the farm workers, producing a documentary film, *Poverty in the Valley of Plenty*, intended to gain the support of clergy, students, and local and national political figures and organizations. Ultimately, these early efforts at mobilizing Mexican and Mexican-American agricultural workers came to an end with the application of the antiunion provisions of the Taft-Hartley Act.

After a study by the Department of Labor under the Eisenhower administration, Congress debated legislation to end the program but sustained pressure by an alliance of growers, primarily from California, blocked the bill to terminate the Bracero Program. Nevertheless, more opponents of the program mobilized to terminate what they consider a seriously flawed binational agreement. By 1960, the National Council of Churches of Christ in America and the National Consumers League joined together to oppose the continuation of the Bracero Program. The impact of the growing Civil Rights Movement provided the anti–Bracero Program with a renewed spirit. Opposition groups began to see some results in Congress. In 1963, Congress voted against the extension of the Bracero Program, and it came officially to an end in 1964. It is estimated that about 8 percent of the total number of braceros eventually settled in the United States. All through the 1950s and early 1960s, increased numbers of Mexican immigrants, usually undocumented, would make the long journey to the United States, becoming a growing generation of "New Americans" who, like the generation before them, brought their dreams and hopes with them to what would become their new homeland. This generation of New Americans and the one immediately following it, the generation of the 1970s and 1980s, would experience the effects of a new series of immigration laws beginning with the Immigration Act of 1965.

THE IMPACT OF MEXICAN IMMIGRATION

The continued influx of immigration, both documented and undocumented, remains one of the major characteristics of Mexican immigration,
unlike the experiences of most other immigrant groups. Within Mexican
communities throughout the United States, various generations of immigrants have lived side by side with each other: the recently arrived and those
with immigrant experiences. In addition, the immigration reform laws passed
after 1965 led to the increased numbers of immigrants from other areas of
the world, particularly from Asia. This has produced Mexican immigrant
communities that have now been reconfigured by the presence of other immigrants living within the once exclusively Mexican areas. This diversity
within a given community promises to expand throughout the twenty-first
century, bringing with it a complex array of intergroup relations, including,
unfortunately, troubling ones such as those between young Mexicans and
Vietnamese immigrants in the east side of San Jose, California, and Los
Angeles, California.

The impact of Mexican immigration is greatest on labor market conditions
in the United States. One of the important consequences involves the different characteristics of recently arrived Mexicans with the native American
population, including American-born individuals of Mexican descent. Employers are able to place very low wage ceilings on Mexican immigrants in
comparison to those of American citizens. The large numbers of undocumented Mexicans represent a constant source of cheap labor, particularly in
California and Texas. Arriving in this country with limited skills and receiving very low wages, the standard of living of the majority of Mexican immigrants continues at the brink of poverty.

The continued influx of Mexican immigrants from 1965 to the present
has resulted in fluctuating periods of anti-immigration sentiments within
certain sectors of American society. Anti-immigrant movements appear, fade
away, and then reappear, creating ongoing tensions between immigrants and
the rest of society. The anti-immigrant movement, specifically the English
Only movement, gained strength in the late 1980s and early 1990s when
various local and state politicians integrated these issues into their campaigns.

Interestingly, studies show that even the most recently arrived immigrants
express strong feelings that their children, both immigrant and U.S. born,
gain excellent English-speaking skills. At the same time, however, Mexican
immigrant parents also maintain high expectations that their children be
bilingual, retaining some degree of fluency in the Spanish language. With
the steady flow of Mexican immigration, immigrant communities will con-

tinue to include significant numbers of Mexicans with limited English language ability, which reduces chances of occupational and economic advancement. This issue represents a major and ongoing social problem for both types of Mexican immigrants. Low wages, limited English skills, and recurring periods of anti-immigrant feelings all combine to place severe constraints on the general upward mobility of Mexican immigrants.

4

The Immigration Act of 1965 and Other Acts

The Immigration Act of 1965 proved to be a piece of legislation that would have a major impact on American society. This act removed the provision of "national origin" from immigration laws, opening the doors to increased numbers of immigrants—"New Americans"—who would shape the American landscape from 1965 to the present. In the decades leading up to the Immigration Act of 1965, the United States experienced increasing numbers of Mexican immigrants, both documented and undocumented. The post–1965 period in American immigration history will remain a turning point in U.S.–Mexico relations and in American history.

OPERATION WETBACK

With the end of World War II, the United States took center stage in global politics. Immigration policies emerged as a cornerstone of U.S. relations with such countries as Mexico. The final years of the Bracero Program witnessed a rising tide of undocumented Mexican immigrants whose presence in the United States produced an ongoing national debate. At the same time that the numbers of Mexican immigrants participating in the Bracero Program were declining, American employers, particularly growers, continued to demand a steady source of cheap labor and turned to the ever-growing numbers of Mexicans willing to leave Mexico's economic problems and make the trip north as undocumented workers. These workers were called "mojados," meaning "wetbacks," referring to their crossing the Rio Grande River into the United States. Those who entered the United States by crossing under the long stretches of barbed wire were called "alambristas" from the Spanish word for wire, "alambre." Interestingly, current research on Mexican immigration points out that the number of undocumented Mexican workers had been on a steady increase even in the early years of the Bracero Program because many employers disregarded the program's guidelines restricting Mexicans to agricultural work. Employers actively recruited undocumented workers to work in canneries, construction, and service industries. Since these workers were not protected by the Bracero Program, employers could pay lower wages than those established by the program. Undocumented workers who were trying to escape the conditions of poverty in Mexico accepted such arrangements, although they lived in constant fear of deportation. The flow of Mexican immigrants increased as the Mexican economy worsened. Although Mexico experienced a certain degree of economic development after World War II, a large number of working-class Mexicans remained outside the reach of economic improvements. Wages could not match skyrocketing inflation rates; population rates increased geometrically. Large numbers of Mexicans migrated to urban centers in search of a better living. Few of these migrants found respite from their deteriorating economic circumstances, with urban poverty reaching new and tragic heights. These conditions pushed Mexicans toward the United States and ultimately fueled anti-immigrant sentiments.

Throughout the agricultural fields of Texas, California, and the Southwest in general, employers welcomed this new flow of undocumented workers. In his classic 1971 study, *Los Mojados: The Wetback Story*, sociologist Julian Samora records the lives of these undocumented Mexican workers. Samora describes their daily living and working conditions, stressing that employers favored undocumented workers whom they could pay the lowest wages, house them in worse than dilapidated housing, and, in general, maintain them under conditions that would have been in flagrant violation of the provisions of the Bracero Program.

Despite such terrible living and working conditions, the stream of undocumented workers continued to increase dramatically. Border crossings, as in the past, did not pose insurmountable difficulties because long stretches of the U.S.–Mexico border were difficult to patrol. Once in the United States, undocumented workers found it relatively easy to travel throughout the Southwest in search of work, blending in with documented Mexicans and American-born Mexicans and avoiding apprehension by the authorities. Employers themselves often assisted the workers in avoiding the Border Patrol and the Immigration and Naturalization Service (INS).

Growing hostilities continued against undocumented Mexican immigrants during the early 1950s. The Cold War period in American history harbored a climate of both anticommunism and anti-immigration. Among many sectors, a fear of communist conspiracy within the United States became associated with a deep-rooted suspicion of immigrants. Congress passed the Internal Security Act of 1950, barring the immigration of any member or former member of the Communist Party. It also included a provision that allowed for the deportation of members of the Communist Party already living in the United States if they were deemed threats to national security. Very few Mexicans, however, were affected by this act.

The INS developed "Operation Wetback" in an effort to reverse the tide of "illegal aliens" from Mexico. In June 1954, the INS began a program to deport undocumented Mexicans living in the United States, specifically in the Southwest. The Border Patrol employed questionable paramilitary tactics in rounding up Mexicans and deporting them back to Mexico. Julian Samora's work provides extensive documentation for many of the violent excesses carried out by the Border Patrol under Operation Wetback. Although the program lasted less than a year, it is estimated that over 1 million Mexicans were deported. Many of these ultimately returned to the United States as Operation Wetback was scaled down and eventually ended. Within a few months after the Border Patrol ended these deportation raids, the flow of undocumented Mexicans resumed. Nevertheless, the escalation of the Cold War and the perceived threat of unrestricted immigration to the United States led to major revisions in the existing immigration laws.

THE MCCARRAN-WALTER ACT OF 1952

In 1952 Congress passed the McCarran-Walter Act in an attempt to integrate the major provisions of past immigration laws. The deep-rooted restrictionist sentiments by numerous legislators formed the spirit and letter of the act. A stipulation renewed the existing quotas from Northern and Western European countries who would be awarded an annual admission quota that represented 85 percent of the total quotas. President Truman supported the views of other political figures in opposing the continuation of quotas that discriminated against immigrants by their country of origin. Truman also cited the labor forces shortages in various American industries, particularly agricultural workers. Nevertheless, Truman's veto was overridden by Congress.

The McCarran-Walter Act consisted of a series of provisions aimed at the types of immigrants favored for entrance into the United States. First, the act stipulated that immigrants with professional or technical skills would receive preferences. Relatives of these immigrants were also to be given preferential treatment. The passage of the McCarran-Walter Act represented the strengthening of a historical legacy of hostility and suspicion of immigrants, particularly those from countries outside Western Europe. The prevailing Cold War ideology intensified such restrictionist policies. Interestingly, the 1952 act provided for the end of racial quotas, but, ironically, the stipulations limiting immigration from Asian and African countries worked in practice as virtual race quotas. In addition, a general selective admissions provision provided for a system of preferential treatment of immigrants. Of specific importance to Mexican immigrants, the McCarran-Walter Act stipulated that countries in the Western hemisphere were exempt from quota ceilings.

President Truman and his advisors continued to support less restrictionist immigration policies, going so far as to support the repeal of the McCarran-Walter Act. Truman appointed a special commission in 1953 to examine the provisions of the immigration act. Its report, *Whom Shall We Overcome*, recommended the end of the national origins system of immigration preferences called for in the McCarran-Walter Act. Later, in 1960, Republican President Dwight D. Eisenhower, not a Democrat like Truman, joined in the opposition by urging Congress to reconsider its restrictionist policies. Eisenhower's recommendations were reaffirmed by his successor, President John F. Kennedy, who declared his support in 1963 for legislative revision of the current immigration quotas. Kennedy's lobbying for such action was cut short with his assassination, but President Lyndon B. Johnson furthered the cause for immigration reform. Johnson, like Kennedy and Truman before him, recognized the growing need for an end to restrictionist immigration laws. He gained bipartisan support in the Congress as legislators felt the increased pressures of the growing civil rights movement for racial and ethnic equality within the United States. The resultant legislation, however, would develop out of a complex set of factors that ironically combined elements of liberalization and renewed restrictionism regarding immigration. The Hart-Cellar Act of 1965 ushered in a new period in immigration history in the United States; its effects continue to shape American society.

MEXICO'S ECONOMIC CRISIS AND INCREASED MEXICAN IMMIGRATION

Like other developing countries in the 1970s, Mexico designed its national economic policies in an effort to meet the demands of a changing global economy. Economic problems, both national and international, led to a severe crisis, particularly for Mexico's working class. Over time, one of the major consequences of these economic difficulties involved an increase in immigration to the United States as Mexicans attempted to escape from the "Crisis," as Mexico's economic difficulties were called.

After World War II and on through the 1970s, the Mexican government adopted a specific model of economic growth and social development based on a reliance on rapidly expanding global financial markets. As a result of a combination of dramatic growth in international capital and profits, Mexico, like other countries in Latin America and some in Asia, initiated key economic policies designed to take advantage of an expanding global economy. Between 1958 and 1970, the Mexican government believed that the country was on the road to stable economic growth. Mexican economists thought that the country needed to obtain foreign loans to underwrite an expanding industrial sector. Their belief was that with a vibrant economy, a country such as Mexico could use profits from industrial investments to repay a growing national debt to foreign countries.

An unprecedented expansion of the international financial order led to dramatic increases in capital flows to Mexico, particularly from the United States. Throughout the 1970s, Mexico witnessed the growth of foreign investments used to bolster its industrial sectors. The government created the "maquiladora" (assembly plant) program in 1965 in an effort to develop its border region by attracting foreign investors to set up their plants in Mexico under specified conditions. Establishing maquiladoras required that Mexico reconfigure its borders in a way to maximize the profits of foreign investors and thus, ultimately, improve its own economic conditions.

Maquiladora plants developed within an export-processing zone in Mexico's border with the United States. Mexico invited American manufacturers to set up their factories in Mexico. Foreign companies employed Mexican workers at much lower wages than American workers in similar industries. In the maquiladoras, workers assembled such items as circuit boards and televisions. These assembled products were then shipped back to the United States without the additional charge of paying import taxes to the United States. The Mexican government provided large subsidies to encourage the expansion of the maquiladora program; it allowed American manufacturers and other foreign investors to import duty-free machinery parts and raw materials to their Mexican plants. In only a few years the program witnessed dramatic growth, with increasing numbers of plants built all along the U.S.–Mexico border.

Several factors contributed to the development of such export-processing zones in Mexico. During the late 1960s and 1970s, American electronics industries were at a disadvantage with Asian industries, whose production systems provided them with a competitive advantage that allowed them to provide cheaper goods to be exported to the United States. In addition, the rising wage demands of labor unions in the United States increased dramatically during this period. American companies looked for regions, such as Mexico, where they could employ a cheaper labor force in order to maximize their profit margins and become competitive with Asian countries, particularly Japan. Such a plan was only possible through the development of a binational agreement between the United States and Mexico in which Mexico established an export zone and facilitated the passage of legislation to regulate the flow of this new source of foreign capital. Similarly, the U.S. government enacted legislation that would exempt U.S. industries operating in Mexico's export zones from certain import taxes.

From its beginnings, American manufacturers viewed the maquiladora program as a means to a steady supply of cheap labor. As in other export processing zones, the cheapest labor force consisted of young females—most with relatively little experience in the paid labor force. Work on the assembly lines required long hours of tedious work as various products were completed for shipment to the United States. Women in the maquiladoras encountered a variety of occupational hazards, some more serious than others. Eye strain, back stress, breathing problems due to the harsh chemicals required in many plants, and other health problems combined together, creating working conditions that compromised the well-being of the women on the assembly line. In addition, the large numbers of women willing to take jobs in the assembly plants worked against the development of unionization and other forms of collective action through which the workers could exert pressure on their employers to improve the harsh working conditions. The film *The Global Assembly Line* documents the everyday lives of women working in the assembly plants in Mexico, Taiwan, and the Philippines. Through the use of extensive interviews with these women, the film presents a dramatic portrayal of worker exploitation on a global scale. One young woman working in a Mexican maquiladora stated that she and her coworkers had no choice: they either starved, or they accepted their lives as workers in the assembly plants.

As a result, Mexico's northern region and its proliferating export processing zones came to represent the hallmark of Mexico's new economic development plan of the 1970s. The manufacturing assembly plants, established by the influx of American foreign investors, were allowed to flourish as the Mexican government aimed to increase its economic standing in the international world economy. With Mexico experiencing widespread and unforeseen economic difficulties, it was forced to reassess its hopes for achieving an "economic miracle." First, the Mexican economy occupied an extremely vulnerable position within the global economy. Its assumption of an astronomical foreign debt used to subsidize its export sector was almost impossible to be repaid; the government found it difficult to make payments on the interest. As a result the International Monetary Fund and foreign creditors, including the United States, succeeded in exerting pressure on Mexico to adopt severe economic policies to curb national spending. Cuts in wages and in a wide variety of social services led to rising levels of social discontent among Mexico's working and middle class. The devaluation of the Mexican currency—the peso—led to further discontent among the middle class. Other international factors deepened Mexico's economic crisis. The U.S. economic recession in 1971 and the 1973 oil crisis curbed imports from Mexico, accelerating the collapse of the Mexican economy.

Mexico had hoped to alleviate some of its key social problems, specifically unemployment and poverty, by implementing economic policies that favored the role of foreign investment in stimulating its economy. Mexico believed that its border industrialization program would serve as a safety valve that would ease the conflict among sectors of its society experiencing the most economic hardship. Rising unemployment rates, particularly among young males working in large urban centers, represented one of Mexico's most pressing problems, one that in the past had led to serious social unrest. Although the Mexican government designed the maquiladora program to reduce unemployment, American manufacturers never changed their preference for a labor force consisting of young females, which they considered to be the cheapest form of labor in Mexico. As a result, Mexico witnessed very little change in male unemployment rates. In addition, working conditions in the maquiladoras led to a rapid turnover rate among its female labor force. Both factors ultimately led to a sharp increase in Mexican immigration, both documented and undocumented. In their book *Immigrant America* (1996), Alejandro Portes and Ruben G. Rumbaut describe the general socioeconomic background of Mexican immigrants settling in the United States beginning in the mid-1970s. In comparison to other immigrant groups, particularly Korean and Southeast Asian, Mexicans had the lowest educational levels and occupational status. Most had only a few years of grade school, entering the labor force overwhelmingly as unskilled laborers. Immigration increased as Mexico's economic crisis increased, pushing more and more Mexicans to search for a better life in the United States for themselves and their families. As the numbers of Mexicans coming to the United States sharply increased, legislation and public opinions regarding this large immigrant flow into the United States, at both a national and local level, underwent important changes.

THE HART-CELLAR IMMIGRATION ACT OF 1965

The Hart-Cellar Immigration Act of 1965 marked a significant development in U.S. immigration policy, serving as an amendment to the McCarran-Walter Act. Several factors led to the passage of the Immigration Act of 1965. After World War II, the Cold War witnessed the United States become the major power in the Western bloc, emerging as the leading defender against communism. The fight against nazism and fascism made it necessary, according to many U.S. foreign policy experts, for the United States to present itself to the international community as a champion of the "free world." As such, Congress called for a reform of existing immigration policies that maintained national origin quotas which could be interpreted as racially discriminatory. President John F. Kennedy urged Congress to reform the country's immigration policy. After Kennedy's assassination in 1963, President Lyndon B. Johnson furthered the call for immigration reform. Johnson's campaign for civil rights culminated with the Civil Rights Act of 1964, which served as a further impetus for immigration reform. Johnson and the Democrats in Congress viewed immigration reforms in terms of basic civil rights. Labor unions changed their historically anti-immigrant attitudes and became another source of support for the Immigration Act of 1965. Labor unions opposed any immigration reform that would not limit immigrants to occupations with an insufficient number of American workers. This would have the greatest impact on Mexican immigration and their relations with the larger American society.

Congress passed the new immigration act called the Hart-Cellar Act. This legislation eliminated the "national origin" quota system for immigrants from specific regions in Asia and Africa. Congress drew up this act, also referred to as the Immigration Act of 1965, as an amendment to the McCarran Act of 1952. For example, under the McCarran Act the total quota for Asia was 2,990 in comparison to 149,667 for Europe. The McCarran Act set the quota for Africa at 1,400, an even smaller number than Europe and Asia. The Immigration Act of 1965 abolished this national origins quota system, replacing it with several provisions that would shape immigration in the post–1965 period.

The law designed a preferential system to replace the quota system with its specified ceilings for particular countries. It set quotas for immigrant visas for geographic groupings with the Eastern Hemisphere receiving 170,000 visas with a maximum of 20,000 per country. The Western Hemisphere was originally allotted 120,000, but this was later changed to a 20,000 per country ceiling. Mexico would become the country with the largest number of documented immigrants to enter the United States. Moreover, the Immigration Act of 1965 allowed for unlimited numbers of spouses, unmarried children, and parents of U.S. immigrants to enter as immigrants.

These changes in the preferential allocation system led Congress to anticipate greater immigration from Asian countries, but in fact Mexico represented the country sending the most immigrants. Under these provisions, Mexican immigration contributed to the increased diversity of American society. Declining economic conditions in Mexico served to "push" Mexicans from Mexico to the United States just at the time when immigration reforms were "pulling" Mexicans to the United States. Second, American industries, particularly in California and the Southwest, had become dependent on the Bracero Program and its supply of cheap immigrant labor, contributing to the further "pulling" of Mexican workers to the United States.

Although many legislatures and sectors of the general public in the United States continued to oppose increased immigration, they anticipated that increasing the numbers of documented immigrants would at least curb what they still called "illegal immigration." This term, however accurate in referring to persons entering the United States without the necessary documents, is viewed as a politically charged one usually used pejoratively. The more accepted term, particularly used by Mexicans, is "undocumented workers." Entering the United States without documents is a dangerous undertaking, but, throughout the 1960s and 1970s, large numbers of Mexicans left their country to begin a new, and hopefully better, life in the United States. In their collection of immigrant oral histories, *American Mosaic: The Immigrant Experience in the Words of Those Who Lived It* (1980), Joan Morrison and Charlotte Fox Zabusky provide a segment from an interview with one Mexican immigrant who came to the United States in 1977. A small excerpt from this interview captures the usual immigrant experiences of undocumented persons.

> I was born in a small town in the state of Michoacán in Mexico. . . . I wanted to come to the United States to work to earn more money. My uncle was here, and I thought if I could come to him, I could live with him and work and he would help me. It's not possible to get papers to come over now. So when I decided to come, I went to Tijuana in Mexico. (p. 347)

This immigrant's story is representative of the stories of many of the Mexican immigrants who risked their lives to try and make a new start in the United States.

Historian Reed Ueda, in his book *Postwar Immigrant America* (1994), states that the Immigration Act of 1965 actually produced conditions that worsened the problem of undocumented Mexican immigrants in the post–1965 period. Given the economic urgency to come to the United States, Mexicans considered the procedure set up under the Immigration Act of 1965 as too burdensome and time-consuming. In addition, as discussed earlier, the ending of the Bracero Program coincided with the Immigration Act of 1965, and, as result, many of these temporary workers preferred to stay in the United States, risking apprehension by the INS. In fact, from 1965 to 1975 the INS arrested and deported 500,000 workers, mostly Mexican, but including some from Central America and the Caribbean. Most were low-skilled workers who were employed in seasonal occupations.

An increase in undocumented immigration from Mexico represented one of the most important consequences of the Immigration Act of 1965. The 1995 film *Mi Familia/My Family* captures the long and arduous journey undertaken by Mexican immigrants and their settlement in cities such as Los Angeles and San Diego. Undocumented Mexican immigrants entered the United States with little or no skills. Men entered the labor market at the lowest rungs of the occupational ladder. Women took jobs as domestic workers or low-skilled factory workers. After 1965, continued economic difficulties in Mexico and the dislocation of those employed in the maquiladoras created conditions for an increase of Mexican women turning to immigration to the United States as a means to survive. In her book *First Generation: In the Words of Twentieth-Century American Immigrants*, June Namias (1978) includes an oral life history of a Mexican woman who left Mexico and experienced the hardship of coming by herself to the United States.

> If you come here [United States] alone first, it's more complicated. When I know the place and everything, I bring my brothers and my mother and my sister. She marry a good man, they got a big house. . . . But if you are here first you don't know nothing. It's more good to come like that than alone. (p. 179)

Once in the United States, both men and women worked side by side as farm workers, primarily in the agricultural fields of California and Texas. In his award-winning autobiography *The Circuit: Stories of a Migrant Child* (1997), Francisco Jiménez recalls poignantly the difficulties of a young boy living with his farm-worker parents who migrated from harvest to harvest, never knowing if they would find work. They lived in tents with little of the basic necessities. They also lived with the constant fear of being deported to Mexico. Jiménez gives a vivid and sad account of how the immigration officer came to his elementary school, took him into custody, and deported his entire family.

The increasing flow of undocumented Mexican immigrants in the years after the implementation of the Immigration Act of 1965 can be explained by an understanding of the process of formal, legal immigration in the post–1965 period. More visas became available, but the bureaucratic procedure of filing out forms and obtaining other necessary documents proved too time-consuming for the majority of those wanting to enter the country legally. The steady flow of undocumented Mexican immigration fueled anti-immigrant sentiments within American society. Resentment against Mexican immigrants, both documented and undocumented, increased within the general U.S. public. More importantly, the anti-immigrant climate led to the passage of new immigration laws.

IMMIGRATION REFORM AND CONTROL ACT OF 1986

The Immigration Reform and Control Act (IRCA) of 1986 was designed to curb undocumented immigration but resulted in an increased influx of illegal immigrants. Three major provisions attempted to accomplish the objective of the act: (1) employer sanctions, (2) amnesty provisions for undocumented immigrants residing in the United States, and (3) increased funding for law enforcement programs, particularly along the U.S.–Mexico border. Employer sanctions penalized those employers who hired undocumented workers. More important, IRCA also contained a provision that granted amnesty to undocumented workers who had resided in the United States continuously since January 1, 1982. IRCA set a May 4, 1988, deadline for amnesty applications to be filed with the INS. After November 1986, employers were required to verify the eligibility of their employees to work in the United States by completing an INS form and verifying those documents used by employees to establish their eligibility.

Although IRCA was designed to curb the flow of immigration, in reality it merely kept the flow constant. Many undocumented immigrants made trips back and forth to Mexico and therefore were not eligible for amnesty. Many undocumented parents had children who had not entered the United States with them and had not been reunited with them until after 1982. Given the nature of the Mexican immigration, a significant number of im-

migrant families experienced these circumstances, and, therefore, they hoped
for an amendment that would allow for greater flexibility for family reuni-
fications in cases where a family's children were not eligible for amnesty under
IRCA. By 1990, undocumented Mexican immigration had decreased only
somewhat since 1980. Ongoing economic difficulties in Mexico and the
demand for cheap, unskilled labor contributed to gradual increases in undocumented immigration until the present.

IRCA affected all undocumented persons living in the United States at
the time of its implementation. Agricultural employers, particularly those in
California, experienced specific effects under this immigration legislation.
IRCA contained a Special Agricultural Worker (SAW) Program that gave
producers of perishable crops an exemption from the employers sanctions
until December 1, 1988. SAW allowed agricultural growers harvesting perishable crops to continue their long-established practice of recruiting and
hiring undocumented workers, almost exclusively Mexican workers. The provision covered most crops but not livestock. Still another IRCA provision
allowed for the importation of nonimmigrant workers to the United States,
on a temporary basis, if employers anticipated a shortage of workers.

The IRCA sparked renewal of a national debate on immigration to the
United States and the issue of undocumented workers then residing in the
United States. Opponents cited their belief that immigrant workers depressed
wages for American workers. Other opponents, usually smaller in number
but often more vocal, argued that legislation that facilitated the inflow of
immigrants, even legal immigrants, would serve to undermine the national
character of the United States. Such opposition reverted to xenophobic pleas
for an end to limit, if not end, immigration. On the other hand, Mexican-
American organizations opposed IRCA because of their views that its eligibility provisions would work against the reunification of those families whose
members did not immigrate to the United States at the same time, a common
practice among Mexican immigrants. In addition, many Mexican Americans
believed that IRCA would contribute to increased discrimination against
U.S.–born Mexican Americans as a result of employers' unwillingness to
comply with the IRCA employer provision for checking employee eligibility.

Supporters of IRCA, including many Mexican Americans, viewed the act
as a sign of a new era in immigration. They pointed out that the sponsors of
IRCA advocated a pro-immigration political ideology that rested on the proposition that immigrants contributed to the overall betterment of the United
States. The passage of IRCA and its implementation marked a new period
of immigration. In 1990, 1.5 million immigrants, a record number, entered

legally to the United States; in 1991, the number rose to 1.8 million. The 1990 number included about 880,000 formerly undocumented workers. For 1991, 1.1 million of the total number gained legal status in the United States.

The pro-immigration climate of the IRCA period persisted in the following years of its passage. In 1990, Congress passed additional legislation that set revised numerical ceilings and revised the system of preferences. It established a flexible cap of 700,000 for all admission categories. This would revert to 675,000 in 1995. A three-tiered preference system was adopted favoring (1) unification of family members, (2) admission of immigrants with designated skills and professions, and (3) increased applications from countries underrepresented in immigration admissions. Congress projected a yearly admission number of 700,000 plus another 100,000 with refugee status. Congress also set up a Commission on Immigration Reform in 1990 in order to design new procedures for curbing undocumented immigration to the United States.

In 1990, Congress passed an additional bill that demonstrated the continuation of legislative attempts to control undocumented immigration. The Immigration Act of 1990 became effective in November 1991. The bill was designed to assist the growing number of American businesses that were experiencing a shortage of highly skilled and educated professionals, particularly in the high-tech industries. The Immigration Act of 1990 provided for a stipulated number of visas for those immigrants with the ability to (1) find employment in these industries or (2) set up a business in key target areas in the United States characterized by high unemployment.

This act did not result in any significant increase in Mexican immigration as a result of its provisions calling for such high socioeconomic backgrounds of immigrants to be targeted by the Immigration Act of 1990. Mexican immigrants continued to flow into the United States in unprecedented numbers. Many took advantage of the less restrictive immigration legislation, primarily as a result of the Immigrant Act of 1965 and through the various legislations of the 1990s. Still, the number of undocumented Mexican workers continued to increase with the continued economic chaos in Mexico, the prospects for an improved life in the United States, and the ineligibility of the majority of Mexican immigrants to qualify for those immigrant acts that benefited highly skilled, professional workers. Nevertheless, the presence of both documented and undocumented Mexican immigrants setting up permanent residences in the United States from the 1960s to the present contributed significantly to the increased diversity of peoples and their cultures in the United States. Even though immigration remains a complex issue,

Mexican immigrants as new Americans continue to transform the American social fabric by establishing thriving immigrant communities, particularly in the Southwest.

CONSEQUENCES FOR MEXICAN IMMIGRANT COMMUNITIES

Throughout the 1980s and the early 1990s, the U.S. Congress passed other immigration laws and amendments that contributed to increased Mexican immigration and the constant renewal of Mexican immigrant communities within the United States. According to Portes and Rumbaut (1996), leading experts on immigration issues, these Mexican immigration patterns that developed in the post–1965 period reinforced historical patterns of entry, destination, and socioeconomic status.

The majority of Mexican immigrants came to the United States with family members. Immigrant families, nevertheless, frequently left some children with relatives in Mexico and arranged for their immigration once they set up a stable home situation in the United States. Most Mexican immigrants who took advantage of the conditions stipulated in the Immigration Act of 1965 and the IRCA of 1986 settled in the states of Texas and California. As a result of chain migration patterns, this wave of immigrants favored setting up residences in areas having well-established Mexican immigrant communities. A strong support network among Mexican immigrants facilitated the adjustment for more recently arrived immigrants.

Another historic trend evident in immigrant patterns in the post–1965 period involved the socioeconomic circumstances of these immigrants. Between 1970 and 1980, Mexican immigrants were concentrated in the lowest occupational categories with only 6 percent of all Mexican immigrants in the professional category. Mexican immigrants ranked the lowest of all immigrants in this category. Similarly, Mexican immigrants had the lowest percentage of business owners and entrepreneurs among all immigrant groups. In general, Mexican immigrants were more likely than all other immigrant groups to be semiskilled or nonskilled workers. Women Mexican immigrants were concentrated in the operator or service occupations, particularly as domestic workers, waitresses, and farm workers. Continued economic chaos in Mexico during this period contributed, along with immigration reforms, to both increased immigration and, specifically, the immigration of Mexicans with the lowest socioeconomic statuses.

Chain migration patterns further reinforced long-standing historic trends of Mexican immigration in the post–1965 period. Pushed out of Mexico as a result of a failing economy, Mexican immigrants arrived in desperate conditions, usually lacking sufficient economic resources to adjust independently to their new environment. As a result, Mexican immigrants relied on family networks for housing, start-up money, and other vital resources. Such patterns existed among other immigrants groups such as Koreans, Chinese, and Japanese. The majority of Mexican immigrants settled in the cities of San Diego, Los Angeles, El Paso, and Houston. Within these cities, preexisting Mexican immigrant communities provided a safety net for the newly arrived.

In general, the immigration reforms passed by Congress between 1965 and the mid-1990s increased the flow of both documented and undocumented Mexican immigrants. Their migration patterns continued long-established trends in Mexican immigration. Ultimately, this wave of Mexican immigrants contributed to the nature and character of the United States, a country moving toward the twenty-first century with a population consisting overwhelmingly of "New Americans."

5

A Demographic Profile of Mexican Immigrants in the United States

Mexican immigrants in the United States continue to contribute to the diversity of American society. Whether they made the journey to the United States at the turn of the twentieth century or arrived as recently as this year, Mexican immigrants and their American-born children have always searched for the "American Dream" as "New Americans." A demographic profile of this foreign-born population highlights the major statistical indicators of their experiences, revealing an additional dimension to the study of their history and culture. This examination of the Mexican immigrant population in the United States documents their socioeconomic status by examining such demographic characteristics as population growth, age, family structure, educational attainment, occupations, income, and poverty. A comparison with other immigrants to the United States will also contribute to an understanding of the experiences of Mexican immigrants.

POPULATION SIZE AND COMPOSITION

The statistics in the following demographic profile represent immigrants who are residing in the United States with legal documents; demographic data are difficult to obtain for undocumented immigrants. In 1999, population reports recorded 26.4 million foreign-born people living in the United States. Figure 5.1 gives an overview of immigration patterns from 1901 to 1998. A dramatic increase can be seen between 1985 and 1991, as more

Figure 5.1
Legal Immigration: Fiscal Years 1901–1998

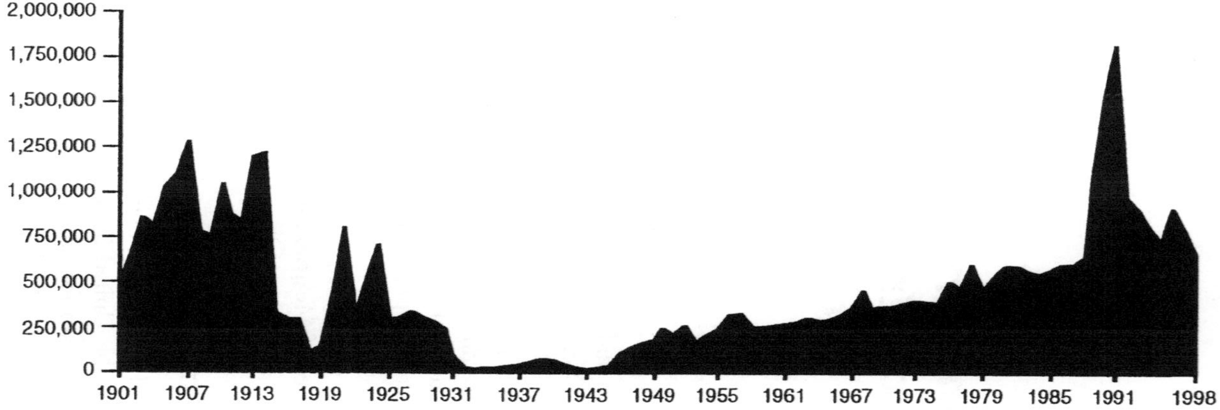

Source: U.S. Department of Justice, Immigration and Naturalization Service, *Office of Policy and Planning Annual Report*, no. 2 (May 1999).

immigrants took advantage of the immigration reforms, many, particularly Mexican immigrants, bringing large families to the United States.

The percentages of foreign-born people residing in the United States in 1999 are divided into the following categories: (1) Latin American, 50.7 percent; (2) Asian, 27.1 percent; (3) European, 16.1 percent; and (4) the remaining 6.1 percent from other parts of the world (see Figure 5.2). Foreign-born individuals from Central America, including Mexico, account for approximately two-thirds of the immigrants from Latin America in general and about one-third from the total foreign-born population. Persistent poverty in Mexico since the 1960s, the steady need for unskilled laborers in the United States, and the reforms in immigration laws, specifically the Immigration Act of 1965, led to a dramatic increase in Mexican immigration, both documented and undocumented, to the United States. In 1990, Mexican immigrants were the largest immigrant group to enter the United States, numbering about half of the total population from Latin America (see Figure 5.2). In 1997, the population from Mexico was approximately six times greater than Cuba, the Latin American country with the next highest rate of immigration to the United States.

Demographic records have reported that although Latin American immigrants take up residence throughout the United States, the majority concentrate in a few geographic areas. For example, 75 percent of all immigrants from the Caribbean reside in either New York or the general Miami area (see Figure 5.3). Mexicans reside largely in Los Angeles, Chicago, and San Francisco. The foreign-born population of Texas is almost entirely made up of Mexican immigrants.

AGE AND FAMILY STRUCTURE

Major trends can be identified regarding the age structure of foreign-born individuals by country and year of immigration. In general, the age structure of the foreign-born population in the United States has changed over the last forty years. The U.S. Census Bureau notes that between 1960 and 1990, the median age dropped from fifty-seven to thirty-seven years old and has not changed from 1990 to 1997. The median age (thirty-one years) of Mexican immigrants is lower than that of any other immigrant group. Another way to examine the age structure of any population is to determine the percentage of persons within a specific age group. The percentage of the total foreign-born population between the ages of twenty-five to forty-four increased from 1960 to 1997 (19 percent and 44 percent, respectively). The percentage of Mexican immigrants within this age group is 48 percent.

Figure 5.2
**Top Countries of Birth of the Foreign-Born Population from Latin America;
1990 and 1997 (in thousands)**

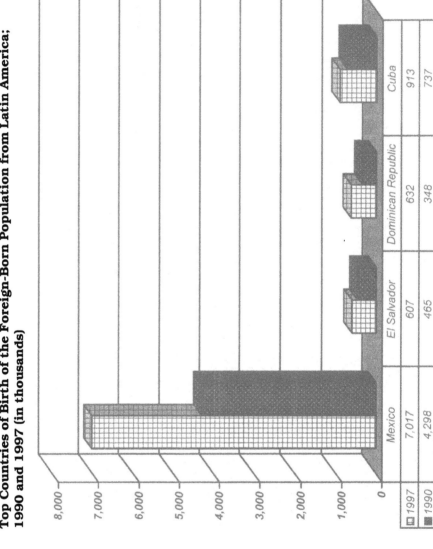

	Mexico	El Salvador	Dominican Republic	Cuba
1997	7,017	607	632	913
1990	4,298	465	348	737

Source: U.S. Census Bureau, 1999. P23–195.

Figure 5.3
Percent of the Foreign-Born Population from Regions of Latin America for Selected Metropolitan Areas: 1997

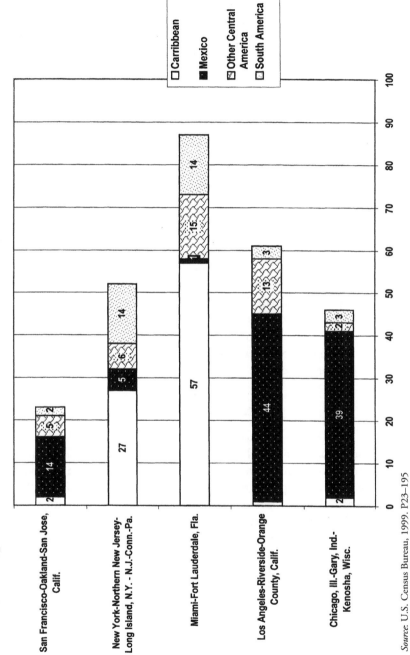

Source: U.S. Census Bureau, 1999. P23–195

Similarly, the population sixty-five years old and over decreased from 33 percent in 1960 to 11 percent in 1997 for all immigrant groups. The elderly population of Mexican immigrants (4 percent) remains among the lowest of all the foreign born. Demographers from the U.S. Census Bureau account for these changes in the foreign-born population in two major ways. First, the elderly population of foreign born, particularly the male population, is experiencing higher mortality rates than any other age group, primarily due to bad health and lack of adequate health care. Second, the number of younger immigrants to the United States, particularly from Mexico, continues to increase with women in this age bracket having very high fertility rates.

Foreign-born individuals are more likely to live in family households that are larger than the native population. In 1999, for example, 25 percent of foreign-born families consisted of more than five persons in comparison to 13 percent of the native-born population. For Mexican and Central American immigrants, 40 percent of all families consisted of five or more people in comparison to 11 percent for European immigrants. It should be noted that Mexican and Central American family households often include extended family members. Foreign-born individuals (60 percent) are more likely to be married than the native-born population (53 percent). In addition, the U.S. Census Bureau keeps records of the foreign-born population by type of household. Of all foreign-born groups (57 percent), Mexican immigrants (65 percent) have the highest percentage of households headed by a married couple.

EDUCATIONAL ATTAINMENT

With only a few exceptions, educational attainment levels for the foreign-born population in the United States lag behind those of the native-born population. Immigrants twenty-five years and older are less likely to have a high school diploma than native born (65.7 percent and 85.9 percent, respectively). Only about 36 percent of Latin American immigrants completed high school. Immigration records also report that almost 25 percent of the total foreign born received less than a ninth-grade education compared with 4.9 percent of the total population. Data for higher levels of educational attainment show that only about 16 percent of the foreign born have some college in comparison to about 26 percent of the native population. The foreign-born population and the native-born population have about the same percentage (25 percent) of individuals who have graduated from college.

The foreign born from Asia illustrate the differences among immigrants groups in terms of educational attainment, with 83.4 percent of Asians having a high school diploma. At the higher levels of education, more Asian immigrants (45.3 percent) completed college than those from Latin America (10.8 percent).

Educational attainment figures for Mexican immigrants reveal vast differences between them and the total foreign-born population. In 1997, about 69 percent of all Mexican immigrants twenty-five years and older had less than a high school education. They had the lowest high school completion rates (17 percent) of all immigrants (24 percent). Mexican immigrants had the lowest rates for four years of college or more (4.6 percent) in comparison to 24.5 percent for the total immigrant population in the United States (see Figure 5.4).

POVERTY

With a few exceptions, immigrants are more likely to live in poverty than the native-born population. For example, in 1998, 18 percent of immigrants lived below the poverty level in comparison to the U.S.-born population (12 percent). In addition, those immigrants who are not U.S. citizens are twice as likely (22 percent) to live in poverty than foreign-born naturalized citizens (11 percent). Latin American immigrants have higher poverty rates (28 percent) than Asians and Europeans (14.7 percent and 12.7 percent, respectively). Mexican immigrants (34 percent) in the United States have the highest poverty rates for any group of foreign born in comparison to 13 percent for the native population.

OCCUPATION AND INCOME

In general, Latin American immigrants, including Mexicans, are more likely to be unemployed than the native-born population but this difference, nevertheless, is small. In 1999, about 5 percent of immigrants in the labor force were unemployed (individuals looking for employment) in comparison to 4.5 percent of the native population. Men in both groups had almost identical unemployment rates, but differences between women were larger than those for men. The unemployment rate of foreign-born women was 4.3 percent and for native-born women, 6.2 percent.

Occupational distributions for specific foreign-born workers differ significantly by world region and by country. Differences also exist between foreign-born workers and the total population. Different levels of educational attainment represent one of the most important factors in determining the specific type of occupational distribution found for specific immigrant

Figure 5.4
High School Graduate or Higher Education by Nativity and Region of Birth of the Foreign-Born Population

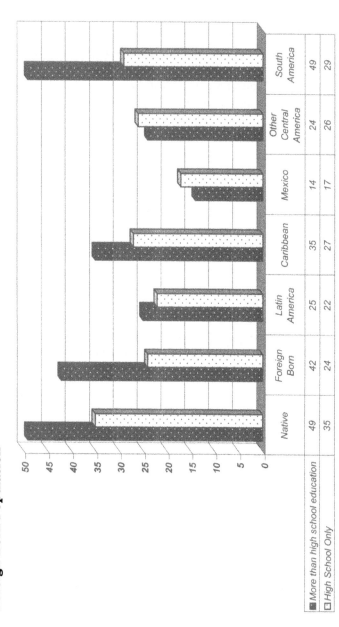

	Native	Foreign Born	Latin America	Caribbean	Mexico	Other Central America	South America
■ More than high school education	49	42	25	35	14	24	49
□ High School Only	35	24	22	27	17	26	29

Source: U.S. Department of Justice, Immigration and Naturalization Service, *Office of Policy and Planning Annual Report*, no. 2 (May 1999).

groups. As in all populations, the higher the educational attainment level of individuals, the more likely a person will be employed in a higher income occupation such as the professional classes.

Figure 5.5 provides an overview of occupational distributions in 1997 for different foreign-born groups in the United States. Data are organized by occupation as defined by the United States Census Bureau. Occupations are grouped into three major categories: (1) managers and professionals; (2) technicians, sales and administrative support; and (3) service and skilled workers and farm and manual laborers. The differences that exist among immigrants from various countries can be explained by various factors, including socio-economic conditions in the region of birth of immigrants, historical immigration patterns, length of immigration, English proficiency, and years of education. Of the total number of European immigrants, 38 percent held professional and managerial occupations. For Asian immigrants, 36 percent held similar occupations, but only 11 percent of all Latin American immigrants held professional or managerial occupations. Among Mexican immigrants the total percentage of managers and professionals is 6 percent, representing the lowest for all foreign-born workers in the United States. Among the foreign-born population, Mexican immigrants have the highest number of individuals in the service, skilled workers, and farm and manual laborers (83 percent).

Other demographic records show that at the opposite end of the occupational category—farming, forestry, and fishing—Mexican immigrants had the largest percentage (13 percent) in comparison to all immigrants (4.7 percent). Less differences are seen in the middle range of occupations: service workers and production, craft and repair workers. Statistics for all foreign-born workers in the United States indicate that approximately 45 percent of all workers within each country cluster in these two occupational categories. The 1996 median earnings of full-time, year-round workers born in Latin America were $18,600 for men and $16,700 for women. Median earnings for workers born in the Caribbean ($23,900 for men and $20,200 for women) and from South America ($25,200 for men and $21,100 for women) were not significantly different from each other. Among workers born in Mexico, the median earnings of both men ($16,800) and women ($13,700) were below the respective median for workers born in the Caribbean or South America. For native-born workers, the median income was $33,200 for men and $24,100 for women.

Figure 5.5
Occupation Distribution of Workers by Selected Regions of Birth of the Foreign Born: 1997 (percent distribution)

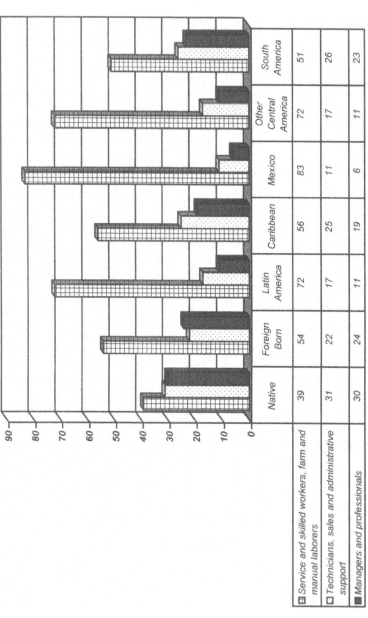

	Native	Foreign Born	Latin America	Caribbean	Mexico	Other-Central America	South America
⊞ Service and skilled workers, farm and manual laborers	39	54	72	56	83	72	51
☐ Technicians, sales and administrative support	31	22	17	25	11	17	26
■ Managers and professionals	30	24	11	19	6	11	23

Source: U.S. Census Bureau, 1999. Table 15–1D.

Edward B. Araíza became the owner of a gasoline station franchise in El Paso, Texas, in 1941.

MEXICAN IMMIGRANT BUSINESS OWNERS

Mexican immigrants represent a population that has lagged behind other foreign-born and native-born populations in terms of socioeconomic indicators. The last decade, however, witnessed the origins and development of a small but growing Mexican immigrant business sector. These businesses are often run by Mexican immigrant parents and their American-born children. Statistical data on Mexican-owned businesses usually provides information for both the immigrant generation and the second generation without differentiating between the two groups.

The research on ethnic businesses has concentrated primarily on the origins and development of enterprises within specific ethnic communities in the United States. Comparative studies between Japanese and Chinese immigrants trace the development of business owners within these immigrant communities as a response to segregated ethnic neighborhoods and limited occupational opportunities. In addition, some immigrant groups, like the Japanese, have brought greater levels of business experience with them to this country (Light, 1972; 1984; Light and Bonocich, 1988). Mexican immigrants have run their own businesses in Mexican communities since the first wave of Mexicans came to the United States. The majority of Mexican businesses relied on a Mexican clientele, although more recent businesses have expanded beyond the traditional Mexican and Mexican-American clientele.

According to records gathered by the U.S. Department of Commerce, Mexican immigrant businesses are found outside a given city's major business district. In some cities, such as Houston, more than 90 percent of Mexican immigrant and Mexican-American businesses are located far away from the

Amado García Rodarte immigrated to the United States in the early 1940s and started several businesses that catered to a Mexican clientele.

downtown business district, usually in the existing Mexican immigrant communities. Most businesses are run by a sole owner with only a few employees. In most cases, employees are also Mexicans. The two largest types of firms owned and run by Mexicans are service sector industries, such as restaurants and beauty shops, and in the retail trade sector, such as small "mom and pop" grocery stores and clothing stores. Many employers provide employment for family members and relatives who are recent immigrants, both documented and undocumented. This practice, found among other immigrant groups, represents one of the major factors accounting for chain migration patterns. California has always been home to the majority of Mexican businesses, and Texas is the state with the second largest percentage. In 1992, Hispanic-owned business (data exclusively on Mexicans not available) represented 39 percent of all minority-owned businesses, the largest percentage of all minority businesses. Hispanic men owned 27 percent of all Hispanic-owned business and Hispanic women, 13 percent (U.S. Census Bureau, Statistical Abstract, 2000, No. 874, p. 547).

Within the last decade, Mexican women have been entering the labor force in larger numbers than ever before. Mexican women, like other women, cluster in certain occupations. A growing number concentrate in the clerical and sales sectors, but large numbers reside at the lower rungs of the occupational ladder. Occupational data show, however, that a new trend is developing: Mexican women have now entered the world of business ownership even though it is estimated at a much smaller percentage than Mexican men.

The most common reason given by Mexican women for starting their own businesses involved a combination of their concern with the family's financial condition and interpersonal problems between themselves and their former employers (Garcia, 1995). The majority of business owners were married to husbands who were employed in skilled blue-collar jobs, most of which were unionized. Mexican women business owners believed that they could earn money by running their own small business and achieve the freedom and autonomy of business ownership. Most important, Mexican women expressed their hope that the extra income that they could earn by running their own business could be used to improve their children's lives, specifically through education. As one woman states:

I didn't start my beauty shop for the money. Before I started by own business, I worked in a beauty shop in a large department store, I worked hard and tried to save money. But I only found myself working harder and harder and never really having some kind of savings. I believe that a mother should help and work for the money if the money will be used to help her children find a better life. When my husband got a promotion and a good pay increase, we saved, borrowed some money from my father and then I bought this little shop. It was hard to make money at first, but I finally got it going. As my shop brought in more money, it went directly for the tuition at my daughter's private school. (Garcia, 1995: 75)

Business ownership is valued by both Mexican men and women, although access to the necessary start-up capital remains a serious obstacle to an increase in Mexican businesses among a large percentage of Mexican immigrants. As occupational and income levels continue to be low for Mexican immigrants, the future development of businesses will continue at a slow pace. Nevertheless, significant improvements are taking place as seen in the growth and expansion of Mexican and Hispanic business owners—usually second-generation individuals. The U.S. Hispanic Chamber of Commerce (USHCC), established in 1979, continues to expand its membership and services. The USHCC serves as a network to promote national business interests in Mexican and other Hispanic communities across the country. The USHCC includes a wide range of objectives: "strengthening national programs that assist the economic development of Hispanic firms; implementing national programs that assist the economic development of Hispanic firms;

increasing business relationships and partnerships between the corporate sector and Hispanic-owned business; celebrating Hispanic Business achievements at the USHCC's Annual National Convention, as well as Legislative and International events such as promoting international trade between Hispanic businesses in the United States and Latin America; monitoring legislation, policies and programs that affect the Hispanic business community" (www.ushcc.com/mission).

6

Family, Culture, and Life Cycle Rituals

After World War II, Mexican immigrants to the United States faced many of the same challenges experienced by other immigrant groups who, as a result of new immigration laws, entered the country in unprecedented numbers. They tried to balance their dreams of starting a life in a new country as "New Americans" with the hope of maintaining important aspects of their Mexican immigrant culture. Throughout their communities in the United States, but particularly in the Southwest, Mexican immigrants struggled to keep their Mexican identities alive. The result was a blending of the traditional with the new.

THE FAMILY

Mexican cultural values and traditions vary within Mexico, producing many distinct practices and behavior patterns. Many social scientists, particularly anthropologists, identify the importance of understanding these complex cultural differences that have existed since the beginning of Mexican history to the present. Every Mexican region, state, and even locality exhibit some cultural traits that may be found only within its borders. Regional groupings may, however, share certain similarities. Even so, it is possible to highlight certain key values that are usually held in common by a majority of Mexicans, including Mexican immigrants to the United States.

Mexicans place a very strong value on the importance of the family. Although Mexicans recognize the need for individuality, Mexican society places a high value on maintaining strong family ties. Siblings usually see their relationships with each other as unconditional, taking primacy over outside friendships. Parents see themselves as responsible for creating a family environment where blood ties are placed above all others. Family members inculcate within each other the value of working for the good of the family unit, often at the expense of individual gratification. Many behavior patterns reflect such sentiments. Family members also assist each other financially and emotionally, even when they have started families of their own. Historically, Mexican immigrants, particularly the working class, have not relied on banks or other lending institutions for loans. The first place they turn to for financial help is to other family members. Researchers, however, point out that many banks in the Southwest practiced discriminatory policies against Mexicans, denying them access to loans and other services. Children value the importance of providing financial assistance to their parents, even when they find themselves in difficult economic circumstances. Emotional support for each other has often resulted in low utilization rates for public assistance, particularly welfare, family social services, and counseling. This result has serious consequences in those instances when problems within a Mexican immigrant family require the intervention of outside professionals such as social workers and mental health care providers. Studies document significant rates of depression among some groups of Mexican immigrants, particularly those without an intact family network support system. Domestic violence is best handled by professionals rather than family members who lack expertise in coping with and ending cycles of domestic violence.

Strong family loyalties extend beyond the immediate nuclear family and include other relatives and kinship networks. It is common for families to consist of family members such as grandparents, aunts, uncles, and cousins. Many times a family will raise a niece or a nephew, usually until the rest of the family settles in the United States. In other cases, migration patterns result in the creation of immigrant neighborhoods where many relatives live in close proximity to each other. Child care is usually provided by relatives who may take turns baby-sitting others' children. Celebrations of birthdays, name days, anniversaries, and such religious events as baptisms, first communions, confirmations, and weddings become extended family events. Sponsors for many religious events are generally selected from among family members. Thus, family kinship networks are strengthened by religious practices. Mexican immigrants use these strong family ties for everyday living situations and emergencies. Taken together, Mexican immigrants are able to continue their tradition of placing a very high value on the family and in so doing retain an important aspect of Mexican culture long after new lives in the United States have begun.

RELIGIOUS LIFE CYCLE RITUALS

Every society maintains various practices and rituals linked to major changes in the life of its individual members. Key transformative events in a person's life involve traditional rituals and behavior that a given society creates to distinguish it from other societies. These rituals are often, but not exclusively, tied to religious beliefs. Societies practice life cycle rituals for many reasons. First, life cycle rituals contribute to strengthening the feelings of solidarity and integration among members. Second, individuals experiencing a specific life cycle ritual will gain a more in-depth knowledge and exposure to key values within their groups. Third, life cycle rituals reinforce kinship networks among its members. Thus, life cycle rituals deepen a group's sense of community and mutual bonding.

All immigrant groups continue to practice specific life cycle rituals and religious practices. Some immigrant groups share similar religious rituals, but even these are most likely to take on specific group practices. The majority of Mexican immigrants share a Catholic religious background, although other religious denominations such as evangelical Protestant groups have been gaining a following among Mexicans. An understanding of birth, marriage, and death religious rituals provides an additional dimension into the lives of Mexican immigrants.

BIRTH AND BAPTISM RITUALS

Baptism is one of the major religious ceremonies practiced by Christians. For Mexicans, including Mexican immigrants living in the United States, the religious ceremony of baptism signifies that the newborn is beginning its religious life as a member of a community of Catholics. Perhaps the most recognized tradition associated with this life cycle event is the ritual of "compadrazo," or coparenthood. This practice is not exclusive to Mexicans; Italians and Greeks also maintain the rituals and practices surrounding coparenthood.

With the birth of a child, the Mexican immigrant family selects a married couple, preferably one married within the Catholic Church, to be the sponsors at their child's baptism. Mexicans consider it an honor to be asked to serve as a child's godparents, refusing only under extreme circumstances.

Sacred Heart Church, San Jose, California. Many parishioners are recently arrived Mexican immigrants. The church provides them with many social services. Courtesy of Louis Dombro.

Given the tightly knit family structure among Mexican immigrants, it is not unusual for coparents to be related to the parents of the child to be baptized. The sponsoring couple enter into a religious and life cycle bond with the child's parents, becoming their "compadre" and "comadre" (cofather and comother). Their godchild usually refers to them as "padrino" (godfather) and "madrina" (godmother). These bonds can remain strong into adulthood.

Among some Mexican immigrants, the same couple may be asked to serve as the godparents of other children.

The married couple that agrees to become the godparents of a child has numerous responsibilities. Traditionally, the godparents assume, to varying degrees, the duty of assisting in the religious upbringing of the child. Each family usually follows its own traditions in delineating specific degrees of responsibilities. The godparents assume responsibility for many facets of the actual baptismal ceremony, usually by purchasing the christening outfit and all other clothing accessories. Announcements for the christening and celebration are most often personalized invitations. The godparents often give their godchild, particularly a goddaughter, a small piece of gold jewelry, which becomes a cherished memento of this event. Within many Mexican communities, items needed for such life cycle religious events can be found in the numerous stores that cater to these needs. Many shopping centers within Mexican immigrant communities even have specialty stores that carry only religious items.

The baptismal ceremony takes place traditionally on a Sunday afternoon at the local Catholic church. Parents can select another church and the officiating priest if they choose to do so. In many cases, parents prefer that the ceremony be conducted in Spanish, but this is not always possible given the low number of bilingual priests. During the ceremony, the godmother holds the baby as the priest says the prayers and anoints the child with holy water and oils. The family's economic circumstances are a determining factor in how elaborate a celebration is held. Sometimes the party held after the christening is held in the family's or godparents' home. Families with greater economic resources may rent a local hall or hotel function room for the party. In either case, the baptism and its celebration cement a bond between parents and coparents, between child and godparents, and among the Mexican immigrant community in general. Similar to the baptism ritual, Catholics celebrate a child's First Communion, the day on which a child partakes in the sacrament of the Holy Eucharist and takes the Communion wafer during the celebration of the mass.

LA QUINCEAÑERA: THE MEXICAN DEBUTANTE

The "quinceañera" (from the Spanish word for fifteen—quince) refers to the cultural practice of celebrating a young girl's fifteenth birthday and is similar but not identical to a cotillion or a "sweet sixteen" party. The quinceañera functions, like other cultural practices brought by Mexican immigrants to the United States, as a link between the immigrants to their

Alma M. Garcia (author), a third-generation Mexican American on her First Holy Communion day.

homeland. Although a quinceañera can be quite expensive, it remains a common celebration even among those Mexicans with limited resources who cannot afford to be extravagant. The young girl being honored on her quinceañera and her escort (her "chamberlain"—probably from the English "chamberlain") are accompanied by fourteen couples. Quinceañeras begin with a Catholic mass, with the entrance and behavior of the entourage resembling a sort of wedding. The young girl wears a long white gown, carries a bouquet, and walks down the center aisle of the church. A traditional quinceañera is described in the following manner:

> an elaborate event, equal to a wedding, in both time and expense. . . . The first part of the quinceañera involves a mass in church where the girl gives thanks for guidance and makes a promise before the altar of the Virgin of Guadalupe. There is a procession up the aisle, with the girl on her father's arm, preceded by her attendants. During the mass, the religious medal is presented to the girl by her padrinos [sponsors similar to godparents], and blessed by the priest. (Stern, 1976: 42–44)

Many Mexican immigrants believe that a quinceañera is another step beyond a girl's baptism. The ceremony and its deeply rooted Catholic religious connotation serves to bring the quinceañera to a higher level of religious responsibility. She is, in effect, renewing her baptismal vows, pledging herself once again to the service of God. Her public display of commitment to her Catholicism brings honor to herself and to her entire family, particularly her parents whom the community recognizes for raising a traditional Mexican daughter. Many quinceañeras may, on the other hand, represent more of a "sweet sixteen" party and less of a traditional Mexican cultural and religious practice. But even if the quinceañera is predominantly a secular celebration, the quinceañera, her family, and all those joining in the day's activities are reminded of their Mexican cultural roots. With the increased diversity of immigrant experiences, those American-born Mexicans who have never lived in Mexico find themselves reminded of their Mexican heritage.

A typical mariachi band may come to the quinceañera's house to serenade the birthday girl by playing the traditional birthday song:"Las Mañanitas." A typical party after the mass, if one is held, can be as elaborate as the finest wedding and as expensive and as time consuming to organize. A lunch or dinner is then followed by a dance that usually includes both traditional Mexican music and contemporary Mexican and American music. Arrangements for all aspects of a girl's quinceañera can begin as early as two or three years before the date. Reservations for both the church and the reception hall

Alma Araíza at her quinceañera, 1937.

or restaurant are also made well in advance. Many other aspects of the quinceañera are often shared by relatives and close friends of the parents of the quinceañera. To meet the demand of preparations for the quinceañera, many of the larger retail stores and some bridal stores carry a large selection of dresses and accessories. Among wealthier Mexican immigrants, a trip can be made to Mexico to purchase all the necessary items. Dresses can be store bought or special ordered just like wedding dresses. Gift registry services are also found at larger department stores, particularly those near large communities of Mexican immigrants and Mexican Americans. Recently, retail stores have designed web sites for quinceañeras in which they advertise the latest fashion and accessories, as well as provide links to photographers, florists, and other vendors. Many quinceañeras now have their own web sites, where all aspects of their celebration can be posted. Quinceañera chat rooms are gaining in popularity. These chat rooms provide soon-to-be quinceañeras with answers to a wide range of questions related to every aspect of the celebration. The continued and constant influx of new generations of Mexican immigrants will contribute to the practice of hosting a quinceañera. In addition, many American-born Mexicans are rediscovering the quinceañera as a means to teach their daughters, and all those who join in the celebration, the importance of cultural continuity and pride in one's heritage.

Trumpets are major instruments in mariachi bands. Courtesy of Mexican Heritage Corporation of San Jose, California.

MARRIAGE RITUALS

As with baptismal religious rituals, marriage rituals vary by region, arrival to the United States, and economic status. Nevertheless, generalizations can be made regarding the religious rituals associated with the marriage ceremony among Catholic Mexican immigrants. The marriage ceremony and its rituals continue to undergo many changes due to the impact of modern society. The following discussion is meant to provide an overview of traditional rituals that may now include the addition of other practices, particularly those derived from American society and the effect of cross-cultural influences of intermarriages.

Marriage rituals are rooted in Catholic dogma, which views marriage as a sacrament and the basis for a family lifestyle. The family is viewed as the only unit for procreation and for raising children as practicing Catholics. Such views led to the development of numerous rituals linked to this life cycle event. Among Mexican immigrants arriving in the United States in the early twentieth century, marriage rituals were preceded by highly structured dating rituals. Mexican tradition dictated the boundaries for interaction and socializing between single women and men. According to traditional practices, young girls were always under the watchful eyes of a family-appointed chaperone. Group activities represented the most common way for prospective couples to meet and begin a highly ritualized courtship pattern. Group functions, such as church-sponsored dances, family parties, or baptismal celebrations, represented an acceptable early stage of courtship. These interactions could then lead to family visits which were also strictly chaperoned. These meetings usually took the form of chaperoned visits on a Sunday afternoon after mass. Sometimes the prospective suitor brought his parents or a brother with him. After several such family visits, the parents of the girl would allow the couple to take a short walk together, but only if accompanied by a chaperone such as godmother or aunt. The final stage of courtship in this type of traditional Mexican immigrant setting involved the use of an intermediary, usually a family member, to go to the girl's father and ask for her hand in marriage. If the marriage proposal was accepted, then subsequent visits between families were arranged, and the girl's family was expected to serve as the host. After several visits, the family announced the engagement, and the couple could now interact with each other but under the continued scrutiny of her parents. These elaborate rituals were designed to safeguard the future bride's reputation by preventing any premarital sexual relations. Of all rituals associated with marriage, these traditional courtship patterns have been the first to undergo dramatic changes if not complete replacement with modern-day dating practices.

The marriage ceremony itself follows the traditionally accepted marriage rituals proscribed by the Catholic religion. Nevertheless, Mexican immigrant families retain certain specific traditions that provide a distinct character to their marriage ceremonies. Similar to the rituals associated with Mexican baptisms, married couples are invited to serve as sponsors for the wedding. These are usually selected by the bride and her family, but recently both sides of the family and the bride and groom assume an active role in this practice. Catholic marriages follow set liturgical rituals and take place within the ritual of a mass. Mexican cultural practices involve a series of ritual objects that play a prominent role in the marriage ceremony. As a symbol of financial support, the groom presents the bride with thirteen gold coins, called "arras." In cases of financial difficulties, decorative coins are substituted. Many brides attach these coins to a bracelet to be worn on special occasions throughout their lives. During the ceremony one of the bridesmaids or the maid of honor

Traditional Mexican immigrant wedding (1940).

places a long white rosary, resembling a rope, around the kneeling couple as a sign of their union. These "lazos" or ropes can be fashioned from such material as satin or a garland of white flowers. The couple keeps this lazo on for only a few minutes, and then it is removed by one of the wedding attendants. The patron saint of Mexico and Latin America in general is the Virgin of Guadalupe—the indigenous representation of the Virgin Mary. Many Catholic churches located in communities with a large number of Mexican immigrants usually display a statute of the Virgin of Guadalupe in a place of honor. If this is the case, another custom among Mexican immigrant brides is to place a special wedding bouquet at the feet of this statue during the wedding ceremony. One of the bridesmaids carries this bouquet and hands it to the bride who then walks to the shrine and lays the wreath as a symbol of her transition to a married status. All these special objects are often presented to the bride and groom by various couples whom they have designated as sponsors. Usually these couples are married and may be either friends of the wedding pair or their families. It is customary for these sponsors to form part of the wedding party, following the bridesmaids but before the maid of honor.

The marriage ceremony used to take place on Sunday mornings, but early Saturday afternoons have become more popular. As in baptisms, Mexican immigrant families prefer Spanish-language marriage ceremonies. Weddings often include mariachi music, the national musical form of Mexico. Mariachi music is played by four or more musicians dressed in the costume of Mexican "vaqueros" or cowboys. Instruments include guitars, violins, and trumpets. These musical groups can play during the marriage mass, as the newlyweds leave the church, at the reception and the dance, or a combination of all these moments in the wedding. Other types of music can also be heard at wedding celebrations depending on the preferences of the bride and groom.

FUNERAL RITUALS

Funeral rituals among Mexican immigrants, like those for baptism and marriage, vary by region of origin from Mexico, place of settlement in the United States, age of immigrants, economic status, and many other factors. Nevertheless, a general overview of some of the major rituals associated with traditional funerals will provide insight into the lives of Mexican immigrants living in the United States. Funerals combine many folk traditions and religious beliefs with contemporary rituals. It has been said that Mexicans have had a long-standing acceptance of death and dying. Such beliefs stem from two sources. First, Mexicans have been influenced by a contemporary and historical indigenous philosophy regarding an afterlife. Anthropological studies of Aztec and other pre-Colombian cultures reveal that these civilizations developed elaborate ceremonial funeral rites. Excavations at key archeological sites throughout Mexico uncovered a vast quantity of artifacts that provide a historical mirror into the fascinating world of beliefs about life and death. These civilizations viewed death as a natural part of life. Rather than deny the inevitability of death, they planned for the afterlife with elaborate rituals designed to assist the dead on their final journey. Similarly, Mexican attitudes toward death reflect their acceptance of the Catholic religion's teachings about death and salvation. Death leads to an afterlife in which redeemed souls enter what Catholics refer to as the "kingdom of God." As such, Mexicans, like other Catholics, accept death because it is the necessary path to heaven. Those individuals who are near death receive the last sacrament in the Catholic religion when their priests bless them with holy oils and pray for their souls' acceptance into heaven.

One of the most common funeral rituals found in Mexico has not been transferred to rituals practiced by Mexican immigrants living in the United States. In Mexico, the family of the deceased announced the death and funeral arrangements by placing an announcement in the local newspaper. The format for this announcement, different from an obituary, involved very little text. Instead, it resembled an advertisement with large, bold type that included the name of the deceased, the date of death, the names of the immediate family, the location of the wake, the time and place of the funeral mass, and the cemetery where the deceased would be buried. Many of these funeral announcements, or "esquelas" as they are called, could be quite large on the newspaper page, depending on the resources and preferences of the family. For the most part, Mexicans immigrants did not continue this practice in the United States because English-language newspapers did not usually publish this custom. In addition, with a few exceptions in cities such as Los Angeles and San Antonio, few Spanish-language newspapers were available. Interestingly, a growing number of Spanish-language dailies and weeklies can now be found in places with a large Mexican immigrant population such as San Jose, California, and El Paso, Texas. Nevertheless, this practice has all but disappeared.

With the accessibility of funeral homes, the older custom of preparing the body at the family's home, usually by women, is quite rare in Mexico. The deceased is taken to a funeral parlor where a wake is held. The coffin is usually open for viewing at this time. It is customary to have a priest lead those present at the wake in the recitation of the rosary. The wake takes place the evening before the funeral, which is held the next morning. It is also customary for family members and friends to take turns keeping an all-night vigil with the deceased. A funeral procession leaves from the funeral home and proceeds to the family's church of preference, usually a Catholic church. The coffin can be open for viewing during the entire mass according to the wishes of the family. As in baptisms and weddings, many families prefer that the mass be conducted in Spanish. At the conclusion of the mass, the coffin is closed and a procession to the cemetery follows, where the priest recites the prayers for the dead to conclude the burial ritual.

As in other cultures, particularly the Italian and Irish, family and friends gather at the home of the deceased for a meal during which time the mourning family is consoled. Traditionally, women friends and family have prepared Mexican food ahead of time and have it waiting to be served. This gathering provides for a collective grieving ritual and, in addition, brings family and friends close together, often from long distances.

Mexican life cycle rituals, despite the ongoing changes that are inevitable among immigrants now living in the United States, reinforced their cultural heritage, keeping their memories of Mexico alive for both themselves and for their children. With each passing year residing in the United States, Mexican immigrants begin to adopt new cultural forms taken from the larger society while trying to maintain some of their traditional ways of celebrating important life events.

7

Retaining Mexican Culture and Identity

Until recently, most social scientists have viewed the process of immigration as an uprooting of individuals from their cultural traditions and national identities once immigrants settled in the United States to become "New Americans." One general perspective focuses on how the immigration process transforms immigrants as they adapt to modern American society. Successful assimilation by immigrants, in this case Mexican immigrants, is seen as a process of transformation through which immigrants enter the cultural mainstream of American society. This chapter adds an additional perspective that suggests that cultural adjustment to a new society does not necessarily erase all the traces of an immigrant's traditional culture and identity. Immigrants find themselves in a new society in which their lives are characterized by tensions, conflicts, and cultural negotiations between themselves as immigrant parents and the larger American society. Current immigration studies find that immigrants often construct their sense of ethnic self in ways that may well be different from their country of origin, but still the formation of their new American identities retains aspects of the culture and traditions they left behind. There is a kind of new culture that emerges through the attempts of immigrants to adjust to the social reality of being both immigrants and New Americans. Mexican immigrants create immigrant worlds that differ from both the worlds they left in their country of origin and those that they encounter in their new country. New studies of immigrants' adjustment to American society suggest further that immigrants struggle to find the best of both possible worlds by blending their past cultural traditions and identity with those they encounter in American society. The lives of Mexican immigrants can be studied by examining their social experiences as Mexicans now living in the United States and the ways in which they try to find the best of both worlds: their Mexican past and their New American reality.

LIVING "MEXICAN" IN THE UNITED STATES

Historically, Mexican immigrants to the United States, like other immigrants, have attempted to re-create "little Mexicos" in their new communities. The continuous flow of Mexican immigrants strengthens their efforts to build new American lives within socially created worlds of Mexican culture, traditions, and identity. One key factor facilitating this process involves the development of immigrant enclaves, that is, Mexican communities whose boundaries contain elements of Mexican lifestyles and cultural traditions but within an American context.

Mexican immigrant enclaves can be found throughout the United States wherever large numbers of Mexicans set up residences. Within the immigrant enclave, Mexicans establish visible, concrete institutions that will help them maintain elements of their Mexican past. The residential patterns of Mexican immigrants tied them together as they lived side by side with their compatriots who also traveled to the United States in search of a better life for themselves and for their children. Extended family members and friends sought each other out in a conscious effort to survive in their new surroundings and build thriving immigrant communities. Neighborhoods such as East Los Angeles, East San Jose, and South El Paso have represented residential enclaves of Mexican immigrants since the turn of the century.

Residential enclaves are also known for the development of immigrant business whose clientele seek out specifically immigrant consumer items, particularly food items. Mexican immigrant entrepreneurs have been a mainstay of their surrounding Mexican immigrant communities. In the early years of the twentieth century, Mexican business enterprises were already prominent in Mexican communities in the United States. This continues to be evident in contemporary neighborhoods. Mexican businesses usually carry Spanish-language names to immediately identity themselves to their Mexican clientele. In his 1981 study of the formation of the Mexican immigrant community of El Paso (*Desert Immigrants: The Mexicans of El Paso, 1880–1920*), historian Mario Garcia lists the names of some of the business establishments whose "comerciantes" (business owners) serviced a primarily Mexican immigrant clientele: La Puerta del Sol, La Estrella, La Azteca, Gran Fotografía Mexicana, and Carnicería Mexicana. Walking through East San

Dance troupes perform traditional Mexican folk dances at fiestas and celebrations such as Mexican Independence Day. Courtesy of Mexican Heritage Corporation of San Jose, California.

Jose, Mexican immigrants continue to shop at La Tropicana, El Mercado, Las Palmas, and Guadalajara Restaurant. Interestingly, many of these stores have large, colorful Mexican murals on their inside and outside walls, painted in the style of the famous Mexican mural painters Diego Rivera and Clemente Orozco. Many immigrant homes display calendars depicting traditional scenes drawn from Mexican history, particularly Aztec motifs, which have been distributed free of charge by the business.

Mexican immigrants purchase Mexican food products sold at Mexican-owned grocery stores. These items include herbs and spices, pastries (pan de dulce), pinto beans, and special types of beef such as tripe and tongue. Mexican restaurants cater to a wide range of Mexican immigrants. These restaurants often specialize in regional Mexican cuisine. Many restaurants also carry "Americanized" Mexican food, particularly when they cater to American-born children of immigrants and Anglo customers. Perhaps more than any other business enterprise, Mexican restaurants are found both within the immigrant enclave and outside its boundaries. In some cities such as Los

Mexican Restaurant (Guadalajara Market #2, San Jose, California) in a Mexican immigrant community. Mural depicts various scenes from Mexican history. Courtesy of Louis Dombro.

Angeles and San Francisco, these restaurants have moved into more upscale and high-price establishments, but these are not usually marketed to immigrants for economic reasons.

Other stores carry tapes and CDs of the most current Mexican artists, particularly traditional music genres such as "mariachi" and "ranchero," but also current popular romantic music by artists such as Enrique Iglesias and Alejandro Fernandez. Pharmacies carry a large array of Mexican herbs, ointments, salves, teas, and other medicines that are usually imported directly from Mexico. Packages of such remedies usually carry instructions in Spanish. Often these medicines, usually in the form of teas, are labeled according to the ailment they are designed to cure such as headaches, kidney problems, and insomnia. Sometimes such medicines are designed for nonphysical ailments such as lovesickness, jealousy, or the "evil eye." Recently, modern pharmacies located in Mexican immigrant neighborhoods stock these traditional remedies alongside of regular medicines indicating the use of both types of medicines by their Mexican clientele.

Entertainment also provides a means for Mexican immigrants to live as Mexicans within the United States. Video stores carry Mexican-produced films, both current and classical, such as those featuring famous Mexican film stars María Félix, Flor Silvestre, and Vicente Fernandez. Many communities even have theaters that show only Mexican films, often organizing weekend film festivals featuring one particular artist. Attending Sunday afternoon films remains a major source of entertainment for many Mexican immigrants. Concerts by Mexican singing artists in venues in or close to immigrant enclaves draw large audiences.

Growing Spanish-language television industries such as Univision and Telemundo bring all types of programs, such as soap operas, talk shows, games shows, and musical variety shows, to Mexican immigrants and American-born Mexicans. Many programs are Spanish-dubbed versions of popular American programs. Perhaps the most popular type of television program is the Mexican soap opera. Unlike their American counterparts, Mexican soap operas run for a fixed time period, usually no more than a few months. These programs do not generally portray a diversity of social classes, but rather focus on the lives and times of the middle and upper classes with working-class Mexicans appearing usually in such roles as domestic workers. These shows continue to draw large audiences.

Individual Mexican immigrant families socialize with other immigrant families, often from the same area of Mexico, and share raising their American-born children to whom they hope to pass some Mexican cultural practices. Mexican families serve as repositories of Mexican cultural heritage.

Such traditions include a broad range of cultural practices involving Spanish-language retention, distinct Mexican music styles, food, and Mexican religious practices.

The use of piñatas to celebrate birthdays continues as a colorful cultural practice among Mexican immigrants. Piñatas are brightly colored paper-covered clay pots that can take almost any shape and form. Traditionally, piñatas came in all types of animal shapes, but recently the most popular ones are shaped as stars, spheres, or cartoon characters. These candy-filled piñatas contribute to the cultural practices of Mexican immigrants as they celebrate both birthday parties and Christmas. The piñata is hung on a rope between two trees or poles, and children take turns being blindfolded as they attempt to hit the piñata with a stick. The object is to be the first to break the piñata, spilling its candy to the ground for all the children to collect. Breaking the piñata is the high point of the birthday party. Recently, piñatas have been constructed entirely of papier-mâché, without the clay pot, in order to avoid accidents as the children compete to break it. Piñatas go back generations in Mexican culture, and Mexican immigrants transplanted this cultural practice to the United States. Most retail stores located in communities of Mexican immigrants stock a wide selection of piñatas. Many stores can provide custom-ordered piñatas for customers in shapes not usually carried in stock.

The custom of piñatas has crossed over to the general American public. Many retail stores, particularly grocery stores, now carry a large selection purchased by customers from all ethnic backgrounds. Stores such as Kmart, Wal-Mart, and Party America stock piñatas even in communities where few Mexicans reside. In keeping with the dot com retail trend, several entrepreneurs have started web sites featuring piñatas. The California-based Party America specialty store reports that its sales of piñatas tripled when it included them on its web site. Another company reports an astronomical increase in sales with their distribution reaching markets outside the United States, including Europe and Asia.

According to *San Jose Mercury News* (January 8, 2001: 1,16), reporter Anne Martinez in her article "Latino Ritual Becoming Party Staple in U.S.":

Piñatas have experienced such a strong crossover appeal, Hallmark couldn't resist launching its own line three years ago. Its updated selection now includes Blue's Clues, Scooby Doo and Winnie the Pooh. "It's become such a big part of birthday parties, we wanted to offer something to our consumers," said Kristie Ernstng, a Hallmark spokeswoman. "It's a way of taking different elements of cultures in America into a birthday celebration."

The Mexican tradition of piñatas demonstrates that Mexican immigrants retain important parts of their cultural practices and contribute to the diversity of American society as other groups incorporate the use of piñatas in their own celebrations.

THE MEXICAN GOVERNMENT AND MEXICAN IMMIGRANTS

Throughout the years, immigrants who left Mexico to set up residence in the United States continued to maintain a sense of Mexican nationalism— a patriotic loyalty to Mexico as their country of birth. The retention of such Mexican nationalism within Mexican immigrant communities is reflected in the yearly celebrations of Mexican holidays, particularly those that are of significance in the history of Mexico and Mexican nationalism. On September 16, Mexican immigrant and Mexican-origin Mexican Americans celebrate Mexico's independence from Spain in 1811 with parades, music festivals, and other forms of entertainment. On the Cinco de Mayo (May 5), Mexicans commemorate the 1862 victory of a small battalion of Mexican soldiers against the superior French army. These examples of Mexican nationalism and national solidarity are not the only representations of the strong ties maintained by Mexican immigrant communities. Historically, the Mexican government has played a key role in contributing to sentiments of sustained allegiance to Mexico by the immigrant population.

Historian George J. Sanchez's *Becoming Mexican American* (1993) provides an excellent overview of the process through which the Mexican government fostered a concerted effort to maintain relations with its citizens now residing in the United States. According to his study, Sanchez documents the direct intervention by the Mexican government and its Mexican consulates into the daily lives of immigrants in Los Angeles and other cities with a large population of Mexicans. From the early twentieth century, the Mexican government saw itself as an important force capable of protecting the rights of its Mexican citizens from abuses and exploitation within the United States. Although evidence shows that a significant sector within the immigrant community expressed skepticism over its role, the influence of the Mexican government extended directly in their new lives in the United States in various ways. For example, an active part in monitoring the relationship between Mexican immigrants and American society was taken. In addition, the Mexican government set up mechanisms to document abuses of Mexican immigrants, particularly farm workers. Mexican consulates set out to convince immigrants that the Mexican government took this role seriously. Consulate records and law records of American courts illustrate the active role taken by the Mexican government in protecting the rights of Mexican immigrants. In many instances, particularly in cases involving Mexicans living in Texas, the Mexican consulate registered formal complaints dealing with various types of abuses. Moreover, it also furnished legal advice and support in specific cases, for example, in the early 1920s in Lemon Grove, California, when the school board implemented a policy of segregation for Mexican and Mexican-American children.

During the early years of Mexican immigration to the United States, the Mexican government and its representatives in the United States organized various yearly events, such as the celebration of Mexican national holidays for its citizens living in the United States. In addition, it also took an active role in establishing Spanish-language schools and libraries in immigrant communities in order to maintain ties to their homeland. The themes of Mexican nationalism and patriotism represented the overall ideological themes of grade school textbooks, most of which were used in Mexican immigrant schools established by the Mexican government in the United States. The Mexican government used such educational tools for very specific reasons. It wanted to encourage Mexican immigrants to return to Mexico in an attempt to deal with persistent labor shortages, particularly in Mexico's northern states bordering the United States. As a result, the Mexican government wanted to make certain that returning expatriots would maintain a strong allegiance to Mexico. Conservative elements within the Mexican government and an influential business and political elite wanted to assure that returning immigrants had not developed a liberal political orientation through their exposure to the American political system of democracy, which contrasted sharply with Mexico's authoritarian political system. As a result, dramatic tensions existed within the Mexican immigrant community as it became aware of the political context within which the Mexican government set out to provide support networks for its citizens living in the United States, many of whom left Mexico for both economic and political reasons. Throughout the major periods of immigration, Mexicans came to the United States in search of a better economic life and, more importantly, for an understanding of the role of the Mexican government within their communities, as well as for political freedom from controlling elites.

A recent development in the relations between Mexican immigrants and the Mexican government involves the issues of dual citizenship and voting rights. The question of a country such as the United States allowing immigrants to maintain their citizenship rights from their country of origin has been an issue that has usually developed with an increase in immigrants. The question of whether Mexican immigrants can maintain dual citizenship is not a contemporary issue; political and legal debates date back to the early 1920s. In its arguments against dual citizenship, the U.S. government and other countries with large numbers of immigrants point to a potential international crisis between two countries, such as Mexico and the United States, when each country could claim a citizen with dual nationality. In addition, the political environment in the United States during the Cold War exacerbated the view that a person with dual citizenship, such as a Mexican immigrant, would be placed in a difficult predicament of divided loyalties. The fear was that in time of international crisis, particularly during a war, those individuals holding dual citizenship would not automatically pledge their allegiance to the United States.

The end of the Cold War did not end the suspicion of dual nationality by the U.S. government and other groups. Sectors in American society feared that Mexican immigrants would become a powerful voting block with liberal tendencies. In addition, the renewal of an anti-immigrant political climate in the mid-1980s and 1990s added support to the opposition of dual nationality. The Mexican government increased its support for the adoption by the U.S. Congress to pass legislation to legalize dual citizenship status for Mexican immigrants. The Mexican government had long favored the adoption of such a provision by its own legislative body. In 1996, Mexico passed a law allowing Mexicans living abroad to hold dual nationality but withheld voting rights. Eventually, dual nationality laws included the right for Mexican immigrants to vote in Mexican elections. In fact, many Mexicans living in the United States voted in the presidential election of 2000. The current president of Mexico, Vicente Fox, supported these laws and has gone further by calling for open borders between Mexico and the United States. Many issues continue to be debated regarding other specific aspects of dual citizenship, making this an issue that will continue into the early twenty-first century for Mexico, the United States, and, of course, Mexican immigrants themselves.

LANGUAGE

Surveys of Mexican immigrants have found that the majority of Mexican immigrants recognize the importance and value of learning to speak English. Responses to a national survey reveal that Mexican immigrants want their

American-born children to master the English language. Nevertheless, a widespread sentiment among Mexicans living in the United States is that they want their children to be bilingual, capable of fluency in both Spanish and English. Although bilingual education has lost support throughout the United States, Mexican immigrant parents attempt to provide their children with Spanish-language skills by speaking Spanish to them. Mexican immigrants find it necessary to learn basic-level English skills; many attend night school classes for non-English speakers. Many high schools, adult education facilities, and community centers located in areas with large Mexican immigrant communities offer such classes. Still, the combined use of Spanish and English can be found in legal notices, voting material, government agencies, and health care delivery systems.

SPANISH-LANGUAGE NEWSPAPERS

Studies of other immigrant groups such as Germans, Italians, and Jews from Eastern Europe have documented the importance of newspapers printed in the language of the particular immigrant group. For almost all immigrant groups in the United States, the establishment of newspapers in their native language (although English often appeared side by side with stories in the immigrant's vernacular) represented a major source of cultural continuity and solidarity. An immigrant press provided news from the immigrant's homeland and news from their new surroundings in the United States.

Mexican immigrants coming to the United States, as early as the turn of the twentieth century, established their own Spanish-language press. Between the years 1890 and 1920, for example, more than twenty Mexican dailies and weekly newspapers were started in El Paso, Texas, and surrounding border communities. Newspapers established during the Mexican Revolution of 1910 carried news articles discussing the victories and defeats of the various revolutionary factions. Mexican immigrant newspapers were usually established by wealthy Mexican expatriates, many of whom believed that they would return to Mexico when the revolution ended. Similarly, many of their subscribers shared these sentiments, intending to stay only a few years in the United States. The historical record shows that almost all of the Mexican immigrants who came to the United States fleeing the Mexican Revolution found themselves setting up permanent residence. Studies of Mexican immigrant newspapers illustrate how publishers change their focus by carrying more stories dealing with news and other events related to life in the United States. Nevertheless, the Mexican immigrant press continued to provide Mexicans with a sense of Mexican national identity. As the immigrant community began to include Mexicans from the upper, middle, and lower classes, the immigrant press reached a large circulation. One immigrant, Silvestre Terrazas, founded one of the most famous Mexican immigrant newspapers: *La Patria* (The Homeland). It was distributed along the border in the United States and in Northern Mexico.

Another newspaper, *La Opinión* (The Opinion), presents an important example of a Spanish-language press designed for a Mexican immigrant readership. Ignacio E. Lozano, a Mexican immigrant living in San Antonio, Texas, had started the Spanish-language newspaper *La Prensa* (The Press). Recognizing that Los Angeles represented a city with a much larger Spanish-speaking audience, Lozano founded *La Opinión* in 1926 to serve the needs of the rapidly growing numbers of Mexicans taking up residence in Los Angeles and its surroundings in southern California. Lozano believed that Mexican immigrants would benefit from news both from their homeland and their new country. Lozano never intended *La Opinión* to be a newspaper for Mexican expatriates "waiting" to return to Mexico. He set out to use print journalism in two major ways. First, he wanted to assist Mexican immigrants in retaining their native language. Second, Lozano wanted to encourage the successful adjustment of Mexican immigrants to the United States by preparing them to participate in American society and culture by providing them with local, state, and national news. Lozano and his family created a successful publishing dynasty and eventually formed Lozano Enterprises, a corporation designed to expand the Lozano publishing business. In 1990, Times Mirror Company bought 50 percent of the shares of Lozano Enterprises, adding this Spanish-language newspaper to its other holdings which included the *Los Angeles Times*, *Newsday*, and several other national newspapers. Using its increased access to financial resources, *La Opinión* dramatically increased its circulation, estimated at 110,00 weekly and 812,000 on Sunday.

Spanish-language newspapers continue to flourish in Mexican immigrant communities throughout the United States. These newspapers provide an important service to the wide audience of monolingual Spanish-speaking immigrants. In cities such as El Paso, San Antonio, Los Angeles, and San Jose, Mexican immigrants read about current events in both the United States and Mexico, and, in addition, they stay informed of local news particularly on topics such as immigration, elections, housing programs, and health care services, all of which represent important issues for Mexicans living in the United States. Interestingly, some English-language newspapers, such as the *San Jose Mercury News*, carry articles in Spanish on topics that are of immediate concern for Mexican immigrants. Major news articles covering the Mexican presidential election of 2000 appeared in Spanish in several of these newspapers. In addition, and perhaps more importantly, news stories on key issues in the United States appeared in Spanish. During the debates on immigration reform in the mid-1980s, Mexican immigrants could read both Spanish- and English-language newspapers to keep informed of all the latest developments related to the immigration debate at the local and national level.

As with other sources of cultural continuity discussed in this chapter, venues such as the Spanish-language press provided Mexican immigrants with an opportunity to retain a certain level of their native language, a key component in cultural retention.

TELEVISION AND MEXICAN IMMIGRANT COMMUNITIES

Spanish-language television broadcasting evolved slowly with the general expansion of the television industry in the United States beginning in the early 1950s. A San Antonio–based television station began broadcasting in 1955. One of the first programs was a weekly show called *Buscando Estrellas* (Star Search) and included a mix of entertainment and amateur talent contests. Every Sunday afternoon *Buscando Estrellas* reached large audiences of Mexican immigrant and Mexican-American communities. Many of the featured entertainers included Mexican stars who were particularly popular among Mexican immigrants. Throughout the 1950s and early 1960s, similar television variety programs expanded their productions, growing in revenue and audiences. Although many Mexican immigrant families found the cost of television sets prohibitive, it was common to gather at the home of a family member or friend who owned one. By the early 1960s, short news segments appeared alongside entertainment programs. Advertising revenues increased as business owners recognized the potential purchasing power of Mexican and Mexican-American immigrants (Subervi-Velez, 1994).

Three Spanish-language stations competed for the Mexican market: Spanish-International Network, Telemundo, and Galavisíon. Spanish-International Network eventually changed its name to Univision. These networks competed for control of Spanish-speaking audiences. The emergence of Spanish-language television stations put pressure on the more mainstream English-language stations to direct programming efforts for the Spanish-speaking audience already tuned into Telemundo, Univision, and Galavisíon.

The development of one of these broadcasting networks—SIN—sheds light on the changing character of its Latino and Mexican immigrant audiences. Both Mexican and American businessmen united to create SIN. Mexican investor and citizen Azcárraga Vidaurrta was limited to control only 20 percent of SIN under the stipulations of the Federal Communication Act. Americans became the primary SIN stockholders. Programming combined broadcasts originating in Mexico and Latin America. SIN eventually met with competition from another rising Spanish-language network: Univision. During the 1970s and early 1980s, these stations experienced alternating cycles of profit and loss, but by the late 1980s and 1990s, the growing Spanish-language audience contributed to their unprecedented stabilized growth.

Spanish-language stations aired a variety of programs. Many entertainment programs originated in Latin America, particularly Argentina, Venezuela, and Brazil. Over the last few years, Univision's programming has included an ever-increasing number of programs produced in the United States for Mexicans and Latinos. The introduction of national new programs in Spanish represented one of the most significant developments in the recent history of Spanish-language television broadcasting. "Noticieros" (news programs) reach Spanish-language audiences across the United States. Latinos and Mexicans, particularly in the Southwest, listened to nightly news programs featuring news from Latin America and, more significantly, from within the United States. Other stations soon had noticieros of their own which brought issues of specific interests to Latino communities on a regular basis. These news programs also ran stories that linked Latino communities with their Latin American neighbors on topics such as the elections in El Salvador, exposés of corruption in Mexican politics, and drug violence in Colombia. Univision now has its own news bureaus throughout Latin America and parts of Europe; nevertheless, about 44 percent of Univision's programs originate in the United States. The station is on the air twenty-four hours a day.

Over the last ten years, Univision has expanded the types of programs it airs on a regular basis. Many of these programs reflect the diversity of interest and ages of the entire Latino population in the United States: Mexican, Cuban, Puerto Rican, and Central and Latin American. For the ever-growing youth generation, Univision produces programs similar to *The Dating Game* and other programs popular in the United States. Other programs targeted to a teen audience include those developed from an "MTV" genre but featuring Latino pop stars and bands. Latin American soap operas—"telenovelas"—represent a mainstay of Spanish-language television. Musical variety shows, as in the early years, continue to draw large audiences. *Sabado Gigante* (Gigantic Saturday), hosted by the popular "Don Francisco"—Chilean-born Mario Kreutzberger—remains one of the most popular variety shows. During

Sabado Gigante's special program to celebrate the 2001 Cinco de Mayo holiday, Don Francisco broadcast his exclusive interview with President George W. Bush, who began the interview by stating, partially in Spanish, that he considered it his honor to be interviewed by Don Francisco.

All the Spanish-language television stations are reaching unprecedented numbers of Mexicans and all other Latinos living in the United States. Their programming reflects the changing demographics of diverse Latino groups. Univision, for example, met with great success when it introduced several musical specials, particularly its version of the Grammys: the *Premio Lo Nuestro a la Música Latina.* This musical award program, which was cosponsored with *Billboard Magazine,* draws one of the largest television viewing audiences in the Latino community. Another interesting programming feature involved a series of special programs commemorating the quincentennial of Columbus's voyage to the Americas.

Despite the ongoing competition among the major Spanish-language television stations and their respective internal organizational and financial changes and crises, the industry will expand as the Hispanic population of immigrants and American-born individuals continues to grow. As Subervi-Velez (1994: 350–51) concludes:

> As we move [through] the twenty-first century, Spanish-language and English-language media directed at Hispanics in the United States, and more recently directed towards Latinos in Mexico, Central America, the Caribbean, and South America, will continue to grow as such media are deemed profitable by national (U.S.) and international companies exploring and exploiting the global communications markets. . . . The richness and positive diversity of the Hispanic heritages should be a prime goal of all media in the United States.

THE CATHOLIC CHURCH AND MEXICAN IMMIGRANTS

The Catholic Church represents a major source of cultural continuity. Whether Mexican immigrants come from small rural Mexican villages or large urban centers, the Catholic Church plays a prominent role in their daily lives. Since the earliest period of large-scale Mexican immigration to the United States in the early 1900s, the Catholic Church has assisted Mexicans in a variety of ways.

The Catholic Church provides for the spiritual needs of its Mexican parishioners. Many Mexican immigrant communities, particularly those in California and Texas, were either established in close proximity to a Catholic

A statue of the Virgin of Guadalupe occupies a central location in most Catholic churches with large numbers of Mexican immigrant and Mexican-American parishioners. Courtesy of Louis Dombro.

church or in a neighborhood in which a Catholic church was eventually established. As in Mexico, Mexican immigrants consider the Catholic Church a vital part of their lives. Beginning with the far-reaching reforms of Vatican Council II (1962–1965), Catholic churches have worked closely with Mexican immigrants in using a combination of English and Spanish in religious ceremonies, including masses. Many parishes have masses that are entirely in Spanish, often incorporating traditional Mexican music such as mariachi music. Although the number of young men entering the priesthood has been declining significantly over the last years, many parishes serving Mexican immigrants try to assign Spanish-speaking clergy to immigrant communities to better serve their specific needs in making the adjustment to the United States. Due to the historically low number of Mexican or Mexican-American priests, however, it is difficult to staff all parishes with a large number of Mexican immigrant members with priests who share a cultural heritage. In addition to the role it plays in officiating at religious life cycle rituals such as baptisms, weddings, and funerals, the Catholic Church takes an active role in providing help to newly arrived Mexican immigrants. In its attempts to provide this assistance, local Catholic churches make a concerted effort to have a bilingual, Spanish-speaking staff. Throughout Mexican immigrant communities, Catholic churches often provide a variety of human services. Housing assistance represents an important program essential to the successful settlement of Mexican immigrants. Parish staff members maintain lists of referrals to local housing authority agencies, often providing translators to assist Mexican immigrants in making initial contacts and completing the necessary application forms required by most human services agencies. In addition to linking Mexican immigrants with official housing agencies, local Catholic parishes often refer immigrants to housing complexes that have a record of assisting immigrants. Over the last few years, rising housing costs, specifically rental costs, have increased astronomically. Catholic clergymen in many parishes such as those in San Jose, California, and San Antonio, Texas, have worked with local- and state-elected officials and heads of government agencies in their attempts to provide access to low-income housing.

With Pope Paul's papal letter in which he called for both clergy and lay people to be guided by a philosophy that gives a preferential treatment for poor and marginalized people, local parishes with significant numbers of Mexican immigrant congregants have expanded their social services. Guided by a philosophy of social justice activism, parish priests have given their support and leadership to a wide range of causes, including fair wages for immigrant day laborers, farm workers, domestic workers, and other Mexican immigrant workers who are most likely to experience economic difficulties and discrimination.

RELIGIOUS PRACTICES

Although a group's religious beliefs and practices are spiritual in nature, many aspects of religion function to retain a sense of cultural identity, particularly among Mexican immigrants, the majority of whom are Catholic. Mexican immigrants have developed and refined certain aspects of Catholicism in a way that reinforces their Mexican culture and identity.

Specific Catholic religious holidays assume a Mexican style among immigrants. All these holidays and festivals retain their religious function, but, as among other immigrants, Mexican immigrant Catholics have given these events their own particular and recognizable Mexican motifs.

Christmas represents a celebration that has always been marked with specific Mexican cultural traditions. The Feast of the Virgin of Guadalupe on December 12 marks the beginning of the Christmas celebration and ends with the celebration of the Tres Reyes—the three kings who brought gifts to the baby Jesus. Christmas celebrations among Mexican immigrants feature distinctive music and special holiday foods. The tradition of the "posadas" is one that is being replaced with more American forms of Christmas celebrations. Posadas derive from the sixteenth-century Spanish missionary miracle plays called "actos sacramentales." During the days leading up to Christmas, posadas consist of a reenactment of the traditional story of Mary and Joseph leaving their home, traveling to Bethlehem, and looking for lodging for the night during which Christ would be born. A Mexican couple recreates this religious scene by visiting each other's homes, sometimes carrying statues of Mary and Joseph. By a previously agreed-upon plan, the couple is refused shelter until they enter a designated house. Once they arrive, a celebration follows consisting of traditional Mexican foods, including hot chocolate and sweet bread. In some areas of the Southwest, the houses participating in a posada are decorated with "luminarios," bags of sand in which a lighted candle has been placed. The light from the candle provides a beautiful, illuminated decorative piece. Due to the fire hazard involved, this custom is rarely practiced. The major posada takes place on Christmas Eve during which time the parish church is the last stop of the couple playing the roles of Joseph and Mary. This usually takes place around midnight. Once the parishioners are in the church, the priest celebrates midnight mass called "Misa de Gallo." All age groups are encouraged to attend this midnight mass, including young children. After the conclusion of the mass, children taking turns breaking a piñata—a clay pot containing candy and covered with brightly colored paper. Piñatas can take any shape, including a star or globe. It is now customary for most Mexican immigrants to distribute Christmas gifts on December 25 instead of on January 6, the day of the Three Kings, which is still the day on which Mexicans living in Mexico open their presents. Many Mexican families now distribute gifts on Christmas day and on the Feast of the Three Kings.

MUSIC

Music adds cultural continuity to any immigrant group's national, religious, and family celebrations. Like other immigrant groups, Mexican immigrants continued their musical traditions once they moved to the United States. The influence of music traditions from Mexico, particularly regional music, has always played an important role in the lives of Mexican immigrants. Music, according to anthropologists, reflects the cultural worlds of any group. An immigrant group's musical heritage represents an important factor in the group's maintenance of national and cultural identity within the larger American society.

Throughout Mexican immigrant communities in the United States, distinctively Mexican music styles continue to flourish. Although a diversity of musical styles eventually develops within all immigrant groups, traditional music usually continues within a specific sector of the immigrant community. "Música Norteña" (music from north of Mexico) represents one of the major and most recognizable styles of music from Mexico. Música norteña refers to a music genre that originated in the northern states of Mexico such as Nuevo León, Tamualipas, and Chihuahua, and along the U.S.–Mexico border states, particularly Texas. From the earliest phases in their immigrant history, Mexican immigrants brought música norteña with them to their new communities in the United States where the music evolved within their communities, blending new elements with those of the past.

Música norteña can be traced back to the latter part of the nineteenth century and the early part of the twentieth century. Mexican musicians and songwriters built on the influence of German immigrants who brought their distinctive music styles with them from Germany in the nineteenth century to South Texas and Northern Mexico. Within their communities, Germans listened and danced to German polkas and mazurkas. Immigrants from Germany introduced the accordion to their new homeland. As a result música norteña developed as a musical genre that blended elements of two cultures: German and Mexican.

Musicians played música norteña throughout the early years of Mexican immigration. From about 1900 through the 1940s, this traditional music style could be heard at major celebrations within Mexican communities. It was played at public concerts, dance halls, and private parties. Música norteña evolved over the years, changing the more German-sounding rhythms by introducing various innovations. One early development involved the use of the accordion, the traditional instrument of German music. Mexican immigrant musicians changed the way Germans played the accordion by almost completely abandoning the use of their left hands. By playing the accordion with their right hands, Mexican immigrant musicians achieved an almost exaggerated treble sound with a "snappy" quality to it that made it even more ideal for dancing polkas than German music. They relied on a guitar accompanist to carry the bass melody, a practice not found among German immigrant musicians.

Música norteña continues to be played wherever Mexican immigrants settle in the United States. It continues to evolve, changing over time with the influence of modern American music such as rock, pop, and techno. Many música norteña groups, such as the celebrated and award-winning "Los Tigres del Norte" (The Tigers from the North) from San Jose, California, have sold hundreds of albums in both the United States and Mexico. They have appeared in fourteen films geared toward a Mexican and Mexican immigrant audience. Using the "corrido" or story song, Los Tigres del Norte have carried on Mexican traditional cultural forms with thirty-one recordings. The group's most famous corridos have thrilled fans for over thirty years. The group consists of four brothers, a cousin, and a close friend. In 1968, they crossed the border, like so many other Mexican immigrants, looking for a better life in the United States. The band members came from the state of Sinaloa and made one of their earliest appearances at the Mexican Independence Day parade in San Jose, California. Their dreams were to improve their standard of living while keeping their Mexican culture and traditions alive. While singing at various Mexican festivals and community dances, Los Tigres del Norte gained the attention of promoter and record producer Art Walker who started Fama Records, which soon became the most important Spanish-language record company on the West Coast. Los Tigres del Norte are responsible for making música norteña an international genre. Their music, recorded in their San Jose, California, community, spread to all parts of Mexico and even into El Salvador and Nicaragua. The group created a type of música norteña that skillfully and creatively blended boleros, cumbias, and hard rock.

Their songs go directly to the heart of Mexican immigrants. Los Tigres del Norte tell the stories of the immigrants: their problems, hopes, and dreams. Their first recording dealing with the immigrant theme was the 1976 "Vivan Los Mojados" (Long Live the Wetbacks). They sing of the hard work endured by immigrants that strengthens the American economy. Their song poses the question: What would happen to the American economy if all the Mexican immigrants were returned to Mexico? The immigrant community made this song an overnight hit. In the early 1980s, Los Tigres del Norte hired record producor Enrique Franco, a Mexican immigrant who pushed the group to new heights in exploring a wide variety of themes dealing with the struggles and triumphs of Mexican immigrants. Their recording success in the mid-1980s developed at the same time that the United States was discussing the latest immigration reform (IRCA) eventually passed by Congress in 1986.

In 1984, Los Tigres released what would soon become their signature immigrant song and the Mexican immigrant community's most beloved song, "La Juala de Oro" (The Golden Cage). The song tells the all-too-common story of the Mexican immigrant: enjoying some level of economic opportunity in the United States but, at the same time, feeling homesick for Mexico. The group won a Grammy in 1987 for its corrido "Gracias America Sin Fronteras" (Thank You America, without Borders). Los Tigres continue to release a series of recordings, and in 2000 they won a Grammy for Best Norteño Performance for their "Herencia de Familia" at the first annual Latino Grammy Awards.

8

Families and Changing Gender Relations

Mexican immigrant families living in the United States have always attempted to retain many aspects of their traditional Mexican culture. With the passing of time, Mexican immigrants experienced many changes taking place within their own families. Social forces from the larger American society introduce Mexican immigrant families to different values, and as this chapter shows, different gender roles and gender behavior may eventually develop. As a result, although most Mexican immigrants retain a sense of pride and loyalty to Mexico and their traditional cultural values and practices, they adopt new gender roles and behavior patterns that usually lead to changes in their family.

UNDERSTANDING MEXICAN IMMIGRANT FAMILISM

Any study of changing gender roles within Mexican immigrant families must keep in mind that there is no one general type of Mexican immigrant family. Differences exist based on time of immigration to the United States, region of Mexico, number of family members, social class, occupation, education, and other similar social factors. Nevertheless, it is possible to discuss some general characteristics that can be used to study Mexican immigrant families within the context of changing gender roles and behavior patterns.

Familism is perhaps the most well-known characteristic identified with Mexican families. Maxine Baca Zinn (1982b), a Mexican-American studies sociologist, outlines the various types of familism. Familism refers to the belief and value that a person's family represents the most central group to which one gives unconditional loyalty. Familism can be defined in more detail by identifying specific types. Demographic familism refers to the total number of people residing under one roof. Structural familism refers to the multigenerational dimension of families. Mexican immigrant families take many multigenerational forms, including both the nuclear family consisting of parents and children, and the extended family, consisting of such relatives as grandparents, in-laws, aunts, uncles, and cousins. Normative familism involves the degree of value a person places on family loyalty and unity. Behavioral familism is related to all of the other dimensions, but it refers specifically to degree of interaction between both nuclear and extended family members. For the most part, Mexican immigrant families display the following characteristics: their families are larger than families in the larger American society, and they tend to include extended family members, usually grandparents. In addition, Mexican immigrants believe that their families are the most central group in their lives and, as such, demonstrate high levels of interaction with family members. In fact, when Mexican immigrants refer to their "families," they are usually referring both to their immediate nuclear family and their extended family members, who may or may not live under the same roof.

Familism as a multifaceted characteristic provides Mexican immigrants with much-needed assistance during their early years of settlement in the United States. Close family ties, for example, assist immigrants during various stages of the migration process. Throughout the history of Mexican immigration, immigrants already living in the United States serve as a magnet for attracting members of their immediate and extended family to make the trip to the United States. Living in close proximity and maintaining high levels of kinship interaction allows newly arrived Mexican immigrant families to adjust to their new lives. Even after immigrant families have settled in, familism creates a strong support network that assists the immigrant family in time of need. Families lend each other money, provide child care, assist with the elderly and sick, and join together to celebrate important dates.

Research on Mexican immigrant families continues to document the effects of high levels of familism. For example, over 50 percent of Mexican immigrants established their places of residence in the United States with the help of family members (Portes and Bach, 1985). Mexican immigrants living in the United States continue to maintain their ties, both direct and indirect, with family members still living in Mexico, even those who do not intend to come to the United States (Rouse, 1996). Community studies of Mexican immigrants document an extensive and intricate set of kinship interrelationships between Mexicans living in the United States and their compatriots living in Mexico. Studies of communities such as the one in Redwood City, California, conclude that events that take place in a Mexican immigrant's hometown in Mexico have an impact on his or her life in the United States. The same is true for those Mexicans who continue to live in an immigrant's hometown in Mexico as events in the United States, in turn, affect them. This process through which a binational community of Mexican immigrants and their counterparts in Mexico form a type of community is called the transnational migrant circuit (Rouse, 1996). These types of transnational migration patterns involve the in-and-out flow of immigrants as they enter the United States; return to their country of origin, in this case Mexico; and then return to the United States. Mexican communities will continue to flourish as the exchange of goods, services, and communication networks becomes even more sophisticated and as transnational migration continues. Interestingly, a few immigration studies have already documented how this transnational migrant circuit is contributing to dramatic changes in gender relations among Mexican immigrants.

MACHISMO AND GENDER ROLES

A study of changing gender roles and behavior within Mexican immigrant families usually begins with an understanding of one of the most commonly identified characteristics associated with traditional Mexican immigrant families. Perhaps the most widely identified theme involves what is referred to as "machismo." Machismo comes from the Spanish word for male: "macho." Machismo is defined as a form of masculinity involving an exaggerated sense of male bravado; it is also associated with the belief that the Mexican male is the sole, unquestionable authority within the household. Recently social scientists used the term "patriarchy" to describe this type of family form in which men exhibit various degrees of male dominance. Machismo, therefore, is an extreme form of male dominance and is often associated with a double-standard of sexuality for men. Men are expected to demonstrate their sexual prowess whereas Mexican women and their families are expected to guard their virginity until marriage at all costs. Some people believe that machismo is most likely to be found among lower working-class immigrant families, but studies show that it exists in varying degrees within all social classes and educational levels.

Social scientists continue to debate the positive and negative aspects of machismo as a form of exaggerated masculinity and male dominance (Baca Zinn, 1982a). Some suggest that machismo has served as an adaptive mechanism for traditional Mexican men who come to the United States and experience high levels of prejudice and discrimination. In this case, machismo can be seen as a survival strategy for Mexican men, protecting them from the problems associated with living in a society characterized with varying degrees of anti-Mexican immigrant sentiments. On the other hand, machismo is seen as a form of patriarchy in which women are treated as inferior by their male counterparts. As such, machismo is not seen as exclusively a Mexican family characteristic but rather as one level of male dominance, occurring in all families, immigrant or not, Mexican or not. The most current research on Mexican immigrant families suggests that both approaches—the one that views machismo as a survival tool for men and the one that views it as detrimental to women—can help in the understanding of Mexican immigrant families. A more recent and different perspective believes that Mexican families have been stereotyped by those researchers who believe that machismo is an ingrained gender value exclusive to Mexican society and culture. In the last few years, immigration studies of Mexican families have found that machismo is not a universal value or gender behavioral pattern central to Mexican families. In addition, these new studies have found that Mexican immigrant families residing in the United States exhibit a wide range of gender values with machismo being only one, and when it does exist, it can appear with varying degrees of intensity.

IMMIGRATION AND CHANGES IN GENDER ROLES

Current research on the transnational nature of Mexican immigration at the end of the twentieth century suggests that certain patterns of immigration produce changes in gender relations within Mexican families. In general, the nature of immigration works as a transformative agent for existing gender relations. Under certain conditions Mexican immigrant men and women are very likely to experience a shift from a traditional male-dominated family to a more egalitarian form of family structure.

Early studies of Mexican immigrant families examined the process through which Mexicans transplanted their cultural values in American society (Baca Zinn, 1980). Findings point out that the Mexican immigrant women experienced a more difficult adjustment to life in the United States specifically when they did not have members of their extended family living in close proximity. Mexican traditional cultural values stressed the importance of women's support networks, particularly for household work and child rearing. As a result, Mexican immigrant families often decide to live close to their relatives in order to best meet the needs of their families, particularly their children. In this way, Mexican family values and gender relations patterned after those characteristic to Mexican society were easier to re-create in the United States.

Although Mexican immigrants tended to migrate as a family group in the first half of the twentieth century, a new development involves the migration of the father with the rest of the family staying in Mexico. Mexican men who arrive in the United States by themselves usually made the decision to migrate on their own, deciding that this would benefit the entire family. Joint decision making, a characteristic of an egalitarian family structure, is usually not evident in Mexican families whose head of household immigrates to the United States. Oral histories support this perspective. One Mexican woman discussed her relationship with her husband, criticizing him for his long absences from home:

> He would leave and come back, and sometimes he would leave for three years, four years. Every time that he returned home to visit I became pregnant, and I had children, and more children, as they say, "fatherless" children. The check that they [immigrant fathers] send, that's very different than being a father. . . . They are fathers only by check. They are fathers who in reality have not helped raise the children. (Hondagneu-Sotelo, 1992: 403)

Other immigrant women in this study expressed deep-rooted resentment that their husbands did not consult with them when they decided to move to the United States, leaving them and their children in Mexico. Some women agreed that when their husbands worked in the United States, they were able to improve their lives as a result of the money they sent back to Mexico. Nevertheless, Mexican women believed that they should be consulted by their husbands regarding family issues. These women resented that they had to take on all the family responsibilities. Wives of husbands who have been working in the United States without their families believe that their husbands find it more convenient for them to stay in Mexico. Immigration studies of the past ten years, however, suggest that more and more Mexican women and their families are leaving Mexico to be reunited with their husbands, some of whom had been in the United States for many years.

Mexican women who decide to make the journey to the United States to join their husbands usually have to develop some kind of belief in their independence from their husband's wishes and authority. Mexican women often ask their own extended family members living in the United States to assist them in their migration, often against the wishes of their husbands.

After the new immigration laws of 1965, many Mexican men gained legal residency in the United States. Those family members, like their wives, who wanted to enter the United States to join their families had to have the legal resident's permission. This situation produced widespread conflicts between those Mexican men who are now permanent residents in the United States and their Mexican wives who wanted to enter the United States. For those women who successfully persuaded their husbands to sponsor their legal immigration, studies document that they experienced a change in their traditional Mexican values. These women begin to see themselves as active decision makers within their families, more so than they ever did in Mexico. Their immigrant experience leads to a decline in traditional Mexican gender roles. In fact, Mexican women often design innovative strategies in exerting their newly gained sense of independence. Hondagneu-Sotelo (1992: 406) tells the following story to illustrate this.

> In 1974 Tola Bonilla, an illiterate woman, managed with the help of a friend, to write letters to her husband in California, asking that he either return home or bring her and the children to the United States. Luis Bonilla ignored his wife's pleas, so Tola secretly borrowed money from her mother and sister, both women worked in California, and after Luis had unexpectedly arrived home for a brief visit due to an expulsion by the Immigration and Naturalization Service (INS), she used these funds to go north. She accompanied him when he departed, yet separate income funds covered their migration costs.

Other Mexican women share Tola Bonilla's experience, exhibiting new gender roles in relation to their husbands. Oral histories document that this type of immigration experience represents one of most important ways in which Mexican immigrant families undergo gender role transformations. Interestingly, these families, whose structure may show signs of becoming less traditional and more egalitarian, often continue to support the retention of other Mexican traditions. Although machismo dominance and patriarchy still persist in varying degrees within Mexican families, many Mexican women who decide to become immigrants often change themselves, their husbands, and eventually their children into New Americans with more egalitarian gender roles.

OTHER PATTERNS OF EGALITARIANISM WITHIN MEXICAN FAMILIES

In addition to those produced by the immigration process, gender relations changes occur within Mexican families as women become more integrated into American society. Increased levels of education and participation in the paid labor force tend to change gender relations in all families, including Mexican immigrant ones. The more education a woman has and the more hours she works in the paid labor force, the more likely it is that changes in gender roles will develop between husbands and wives, particularly those families with more traditional cultural values from Mexico. Mexican women who work either part or full time in the paid labor forces report that their relationships with their husbands changed the longer they worked outside the home. One Mexican woman tells the following story. She works a full-time swing shift in a furniture factory and also works an eight-hour day on Saturdays and Sundays at a motel. Maria recalls that before she entered the paid labor force, she did all the housework and her husband only did such jobs as taking out the trash or mowing the lawn. She describes the change in her family soon after she became a wage earner: "Before I used to do everything. Now I put my cards on the table and he is doing his chores. In other words, we have made an agreement that he does so much and I do so much. I have worked hard for this, that is why it has changed" (Pesquera 1993: 189).

In many cases, daughters of immigrant parents, particularly immigrant mothers, received encouragement to better themselves, usually through education. For example, in her autobiography *Immigrant Daughter: Coming of Age as a Mexican American Woman* (2000), Frances Esquibel Tywoniak recalls how her mother, who had only had a few years of school, always supported her daughter's goal of obtaining a higher education. Even when her father expressed some resistance in giving her permission to participate in certain afterschool activities, Frances remembers that her mother always succeeded in changing her father's mind. Her immigrant mother recognized the importance of higher education for her second-generation daughter living in the United States. Frances remembers that her mother supported her steadfastly throughout her education: "My mother always gave her unswerving support to any school sanctioned activity. I trusted her and expected her to take care of getting my father's approval. . . . My mother always spoke fondly of her brief school experience. She was an advocate for education" (Tywoniak, 2000: 114).

Oral histories of other Mexican immigrant women also document the development of changes in traditional gender roles. As they gain more experience in American society, American culture, and, most importantly, the labor force, immigrant women see themselves as capable of expressing some level of independence in relation to their husbands. The more they contribute to the family income, the more they see themselves as copartners with their husbands. Research findings point out that these immigrant mothers socialize their American-born daughters to view themselves as equal to men. It should be pointed out, however, that the type of change in gender relations does not develop among all Mexican immigrant families. Frances Tywoniak recalls that other Mexican immigrant parents were not as supportive as hers: "Unlike other Mexican families who, I learned, prohibited their children from participating in certain school activities, my family never did so if they felt they would further my education" (Tywoniak, 2000: 113–14).

It should be remembered that Mexican immigrant families represent a diversity of experiences. Even during the first major wave of immigration, Mexicans who came to the United States, although they shared a common Mexican nationalism, came from divergent backgrounds: rural, urban, working class, middle class, upper class, unskilled, skilled, professional, and other types of social backgrounds. As a result, a diversity of gender relations within Mexican immigrant families existed. During all periods of Mexican immigration, relations between recently arrived immigrants and those having lived in the United States for a longer period of time reflect differences based on gender roles and relationships between the two groups. Similarly, because immigration from Mexico, unlike immigration patterns from other countries, has remained constant, without any definite cut-off points, families with different types of gender relations coexist side by side with those Mexican immigrant families that have experienced changes in gender relations for all the reasons discussed. Recently, Mexicans and Mexican Americans—both women and men—have experienced another social force within American society that has led to changes in gender relations within families: the development of a feminist movement among Mexican women.

FEMINISM AMONG MEXICAN AND MEXICAN-AMERICAN WOMEN

The continuous influx of Mexican immigrants has always affected the nature and composition of Mexican-American communities. In turn, Mexican immigrants experienced the effects of social forces originating within communities of second-generation Mexicans. Social, political, cultural, and economic forces within American society, therefore, will always have an impact on Mexican immigrants living alongside second, third, fourth, and older generations of Mexican Americans. The development of various political movements, such as a feminist movement among Mexican-American women, draws immigrant groups closer to the mainstream of American politics and culture. The impact of a Mexican-American feminist movement reached both the general population of Mexican Americans and Mexican immigrant women.

The contemporary Mexican-American women's movement began in the 1960s and coincided with the other social protest movements of that period: the Black Power Movement, the anti–Vietnam War Movement, and the second wave of the Women's Movement. Mexican-American feminists inherited a historic tradition of political activism dating back to the first wave of Mexican immigrant women who, together with their families, crossed the border into the United States at the turn of the century. Mexican immigrant women and their families fled the upheaval produced by the Mexican Revolution of 1910. As discussed in chapter 2, communities of Mexican immigrant families developed throughout the Southwest, joining preexisting communities of Mexicans created after the U.S.–Mexico War of 1848. El Paso, San Antonio, San Diego, Los Angeles, and Santa Barbara all experienced dramatic societal transformations that would shape future generations of Mexican Americans. Throughout contemporary Mexican-American history, women have played active roles in their communities in a struggle for social and cultural equality. Their political activism shaped the course of major reform movements within communities of Mexicans in the United States. Recent scholarship is recovering this historical legacy by documenting the participation of women at all political levels (Garcia, 1989, 1997).

The political struggles of Mexican and Mexican-American feminists during the late 1960s and through the 1970s reflected a continuation of women's activism that paralleled the experiences of other women in the United States. A Mexican-American feminist movement, like that of African-American women, assessed the gender relations and patterns of gender inequality within their families and communities. In general, one of their main objectives involved improving gender relations by supporting specific changes within Mexican and Mexican-American families that would create equal relations between men and women. Another broad objective focused on changing those practices of gender discrimination in the paid labor forces that led to persistent gender inequalities for Mexican women and, thus, produced problems for entire Mexican communities.

Although it is difficult to determine the extent to which Mexican immigrant women support a feminist movement and participate within it, an examination of the issues addressed during the initial phase of contemporary Mexican-American feminism shows the movement's concern for issues of particular concern for Mexican immigrant women. For example, a recurrent issue addressed by newspaper articles written by Mexican-American feminists during the 1960s and 1970s focused on the growing anti-immigrant climate in the United States. Specifically, Mexican-American feminists expressed their concern for the deportations of all undocumented Mexicans; however, they stressed the often more serious difficulties experienced by undocumented Mexican women who faced deportation, particularly those who were single heads of households with children. Conferences dealing with Mexican-American feminist activities usually included workshops or panel discussions addressing such issues (Garcia, 1997). Other issues included child care, general health care, prenatal services, birth control, under-utilization rates for health care delivery systems, and prescription drugs for the elderly. At one of the early conferences organized by Mexican-American women, panel discussions addressed the language needs within the health care delivery system serving communities of Mexican immigrants with limited English language skills. One conference participant summarized the problem:

[Mexican American] women must contend with . . . the lack of bilingual medical staff. In addition, economics limit . . . choice of medical facilities to state and county health clinics which usually have inadequate health services. Depending on the availability of a bilingual volunteer among the patients [Mexican-American women], most doctors treat monolingual Spanish-speaking patients with less than adequate diagnosis. (Nieto-Gomez, 1974: 40)

The organization Mujeres Activas en Letras y Cambios Sociales (Women Activists in Letters and Social Change [MALCS]) represents one of the major organizations established by Mexican-American women to deal specifically with women's issues within the university and the general community. Consisting primarily of academic women, MALCS works closely with women from a variety of community organizations within Mexican communities. MALCS has built a strong bridge between Mexican-American scholars and Mexican-American and Mexican immigrant women. One of the organization's summer conferences focused on Mexican women immigrants and their adjustment experiences in the United States.

As a result of all the activities spearheaded by Mexican-American feminists, Mexican-American and Mexican immigrant women have addressed a variety of gender relations issues. Although solutions to family and gender inequalities have proceeded at a gradual rate, actual changes in gender relations and roles within families and the larger society will continue to develop. At whatever level of support, Mexican immigrant women were exposed to the larger Mexican-American feminist movement. As one woman concludes: "There has always been feminism in our ranks and there will continue to be as long as [Mexican Americans] live and breathe in the movement" (Cotera, 1977: 12). As they examine the existing gender relations and, more importantly, the changes in these gender relations, Mexican immigrant women will move closer to creating communities of Mexican women transformed into "New American women."

9

Paths toward Citizenship

Mexican immigrants, like all other immigrants to the United States, face the issue of identity transformation: the process through which their identity changes from one of being Mexican to a New American identity. This process involves one in which Mexican immigrants recognize that their lives as immigrants, newcomers to the United States, change them in ways that lead them to redefine themselves, their families, and their relations with their American-born children. The transition from immigrant to American citizen represents a change in orientation for Mexican immigrants as they become full members of American society. The path toward citizenship and the consequent gaining of citizenship changes the identities of immigrants who now begin to see themselves less as immigrants living in the United States and more as persons who are functioning as New Americans.

CITIZENSHIP IN HISTORICAL CONTEXT

Beginning with the first major influx of Mexican immigration to the United States in the early twentieth century, the issue of naturalization confronted both Mexican immigrants and the larger American society. Proponents for naturalization debated its positive aspects for Mexican immigrants with those who opposed their becoming citizens by stressing the negative consequences for American society. As early as 1920, the American labor movement, under the leadership of the American Federation of Labor (AFL), opposed policies that would increase Mexican immigration, basing the opposition on their view that a large supply of cheap Mexican workers would keep wages low for American workers. Furthermore, the AFL argued that an abundance of Mexican laborers increased unemployment by taking jobs away that would otherwise be filled by American workers. Others argued that the AFL's policy of not admitting Mexican nationals into their ranks produced a situation that led employers to prefer Mexican workers willing to work for lower wages. Without the ability to join unions whose contracts established wage standards, Mexican immigrants would continue to provide employers with a cheap and abundant source of labor, cheaper than the unionized American ones. Ultimately, the AFL became one of the strongest supporters for the naturalization of Mexican immigrants in an effort to guarantee a cheap source of labor. The AFL pressured Congress to pass legislation that would facilitate the naturalization of Mexican workers and thus, allow for their admission to the union. Ironically the AFL launched an anti-Mexican campaign intended to pressure both employers and other sectors of American society to curb Mexican immigration. American newspapers document the AFL attacks against all Mexican immigrants, stereotyping Mexican immigrants as having morally reprehensible cultural values and living habits. Such racist attacks, nevertheless, existed side by side with the AFL's support for naturalization. Even though the labor unions wanted to place strict quotas on future Mexican immigration, they also wanted to encourage those Mexicans already living and working in the United States to become citizens, making them eligible for unionization in an attempt to increase their membership and gain more political clout.

As a result, statistics show that this support for naturalization did not result in a dramatic increase in Mexicans becoming American citizens from 1910 to 1930. In 1910, the U.S. Census Bureau reported that 102,009 Mexicans living in the United States became naturalized citizens, representing only 11 percent of all Mexican immigrants. In 1920, only 5 percent of all Mexican immigrants became citizens. Moreover, between 1923 and 1924 this percentage fell below 1 percent. Despite support from American labor unions for the naturalization of Mexican immigrants, other factors during these early years of the twentieth century worked against any significant naturalization patterns.

Ever since Mexicans began to enter the United States in large numbers during the Mexican Revolution of 1910, strong xenophobic sentiments existed that fueled opposition to their naturalization despite efforts by the AFL to increase the numbers of naturalized Mexicans. Xenophobic sentiments among a large section of Americans, including elected officials at the local, state, and national level, existed long before the first wave of Mexican immigrants entered the country. American society exhibited anti-immigrant sentiments against Italians, Irish, and Eastern Europeans, particularly Eastern European Jews. These lingering xenophobic sentiments turned into attacks against Mexicans in the 1920s. In addition, the Great Depression triggered an even deeper animosity against Mexicans living in the United States, culminating in large-scale deportations. As a result of a growing anti-immigrant climate, Mexican immigrants demonstrated a reluctance to become naturalized even though most recognized the benefits they would receive as American citizens. In sum, the combined effects of discrimination and segregation produced strong impediments to the naturalization of large numbers of Mexicans.

An interesting development took place within certain groups in American society that tried to mitigate the negative climate for immigrants. Certain key American institutions and reformers attempted to inculcate what they considered to be "American" values among Mexican immigrants. The American public school system represented a key institution in achieving this end. Throughout the Southwest, Mexican immigrant children attended American schools once their parents achieved some type of stable residency. Among the public school administrators and members of school boards, many reform or progressive-minded individuals made the Americanization of Mexican immigrants a major objective. American public schools with a large student body of Mexican immigrants designed a curriculum intended to smooth the transition to American citizenship. Although many children of immigrants were American born, significant numbers of children were Mexican citizens who had made the trip north with their immigrant parents. The school system, under the leadership of progressive educators, believed that English-language instruction and American civics courses would make Americans out of Mexican children. However liberal minded their motivations, American public school administrators and teachers, particularly in Texas, designed "Americanization" programs that contained implicit and explicit assumptions about Mexican immigrant culture as less "advanced" than American culture. Thus, an Americanization curriculum usually involved courses on hygiene, morality, and health care, as well as traditional civics lessons in American history and government. The majority of Mexican children were tracked into nonacademic studies such as woodworking for boys and domestic services for girls. The actual implementation of Americanization programs designed for Mexican children in the 1920s and 1930s functioned more as training sites for future low-skilled workers than as a basis for naturalization for American citizenship.

Like the public school system, religious organizations designed and implemented Americanization programs for children of Mexican immigrant parents throughout the Southwest. Catholic religious orders such as the Sisters of Loretto established grade schools and high schools for Mexican girls. Along with a more rigorous academic curriculum, these religious schools focused on Americanization classes. They trained young Catholic girls in the manners and values of American society, always emphasizing the specific roles and values related to womanhood. Girls attending schools run by the Sisters of Loretto and other Catholic religious orders received instruction on the "proper" American way to behave as future wives and mothers. All-boys schools played a similar role in the education of Mexican immigrant children. Mexican boys were taught American patriotism, loyalty, and the standard values of American society.

Despite these attempts at Americanization, Mexican immigrants kept a sense of Mexican nationalism that made them suspicious of Americanization programs that they believe viewed the Mexican culture as something to be eliminated as a prerequisite for citizenship. Interviews with Mexican parents whose children experienced these types of Americanization programs recall that they were offended by the programs' inference that American culture and society were better than Mexican. Contemporary attempts to encourage the naturalization of Mexican immigrants are designed to stress the benefits to be gained by naturalization. Social forces in Mexico and the United States account for both Mexican immigration and subsequent naturalization patterns. An immigrant's family represents the key to immigration and naturalization. Family circumstances, as outlined earlier, provide the conditions that lead to specific actions by immigrants regarding their decisions to become American citizens. Mexican immigrants, like immigrants from other countries, realize that citizenship opens the doors to full participation in American society, bringing with it the benefits belonging to all Americans.

NATURALIZATION POLICIES

Immigrants meeting the naturalization requirements receive all the rights and responsibilities of American citizenship. Historically changes in naturalization requirements have reflected periods in American history when immigrants were either welcomed or not welcomed to the United States. In this way, naturalization policies are directly associated with the political climate and public sentiments in the United States regarding immigration. For example, the increased influx of Chinese in the late nineteenth century created an anti-immigrant climate in the United States. Americans believed that the Chinese would take jobs away from Americans and bring cultural qual-

ities that would threaten the moral fabric of American society. Such preju-
diced and xenophobic national feelings led to very strict immigration and
naturalization policies. In fact, anti-Chinese feelings eventually led to the
Chinese Exclusion Act of 1892, barring any future immigration of Chinese
workers and, more importantly, declaring that Chinese were ineligible for
naturalization. The question of whether American-born children of Chinese
immigrants were American citizens led to the 1898 U.S. Supreme Court
decision *United States v. Wong Kim Ark*, which declared that the place of
birth, in this case the United States, constituted the basis for American citizenship—not race as stipulated by the existing naturalization laws.

Despite this Supreme Court decision, attempts to restrict the naturalization of immigrants continued for many years. Discriminatory naturalization
policies developed against specific immigrant groups such as Eastern Europeans. Eventually Congress passed the Naturalization Act of 1906. This act
represented an attempt to codify various naturalization policies and, a few
years later, served as a basis for the establishment of the Bureau of Naturalization. Subsequent naturalization policies stipulated that immigrants who
pledged loyalty to the United States and satisfied the naturalization requirements could gain full American citizenship rights. Nevertheless, restrictions
on immigration continued through the use of quotas. Mexican immigration
history reflects upward and downward trends in restrictive immigration policies.

BECOMING AMERICAN CITIZENS

A comparison of immigrants from Asia, Latin America, and Africa reveals
marked differences in rates of naturalization. An understanding of the process
related to the acquisition of citizenship by Mexican immigrants requires an
overall understanding of naturalization rates for other groups. Several key
factors demonstrate a greater likelihood that immigrants from a particular
country will seek citizenship. These factors include the economic and educational background of immigrants, their geographic mobility to the country
of origin, and, perhaps most importantly, the percentage of undocumented
immigration.

Historic and contemporary records illustrate that Mexican immigrants
have the lowest rate of naturalization among immigrant groups entering the
United States. The demographic profile of Mexican immigrants discussed in
chapter 5 provides evidence that Mexican immigrants have less socioeconomic advantages than other immigrant groups. The history of low naturalization rates among Mexican immigrants can be seen by a comparison with

other groups. Between 1976 and 1993, naturalization rates for Mexican immigrants remained about 5 percent of the total number of all immigrants becoming citizens. This trend takes on a greater significance because Mexican immigrants accounted for the greatest percentage of immigration from all countries. Statistics for citizenship rates between 1970 and 1993 reveal that even with the immigration reforms of the mid-1960s and the subsequent increase in Mexican immigration, the percentage of Mexicans who become citizens was only 17 percent of the total population of Mexican immigrants. Researchers explain this low percentage on their persistently low educational and economic levels when they entered the United States. For example, citizenship rates among Vietnamese was 89 percent; for Filipinos and Chinese, 66 percent; and for Indians, 56 percent. Immigrants from these countries represented significantly higher levels of educational and occupational levels. In addition, unlike Mexico, countries such as Vietnam, Cuba, and the Philippines had historic ties with the United States that led Congress to amend (or in some cases, develop) immigration laws favoring both their immigration to the United States and their naturalization. Cubans fleeing from Castro's regime in the late 1950s received many advantages once they came to the United States as political refugees. The large migration of Vietnamese in the mid-1970s reflected an American foreign policy that favored the immigration of those Vietnamese that supported the United States in Vietnam.

During this same period, Mexico did not benefit from any of these types of agreements with the United States. Immigration patterns from Mexico show a continued preference by American employers, particularly agribusiness in California and Texas, for cheap Mexican labor. Furthermore, the fact that the cheapest and most abundant sources of labor were undocumented Mexicans accounts for their low rates of naturalization. Another reason for low naturalization rates involves the proximity of Mexico to the United States. With their country of origin adjacent to the United States, Mexicans have always been able to move back and forth. This trend is also characteristic of Canadian immigrants, who have the second-lowest rates of naturalization among all immigrants to the United States. On the other hand, the farther an immigrant's country of origin, the greater the propensity to seek American citizenship status. During the twenty years between 1970 and 1990, Mexican immigrants had the lowest rates of naturalization—a pattern that social scientists say will continue due to the high rates of undocumented immigration from Mexico (Ueda, 1994).

CALIFORNIA'S PROPOSITION 187

Increases in naturalization rates among immigrants, including Mexicans, have always been related to an anti-immigration climate. For example, Mexican immigrants living in California in 1994 when Proposition 187 was introduced expressed more interest in becoming American citizens. An understanding of the political development of Proposition 187 contributes to our understanding of how Mexican immigrants moved along the path toward citizenship.

In November 1994, Californian voters approved Proposition 187, a resolution banning undocumented immigrants from receiving such social services as health care and education. Various factors explain the approval of Proposition 187. The proposition appeared on the ballot after a successful signature drive, "Save the State," sponsored by the Pioneer Fund, an ultraconservative organization. California's then-governor Pete Wilson gave his political support for Proposition 187, stating that his state's economic recession was a result of undocumented workers taking jobs from American workers. Wilson soon found himself facing political defeat for re-election as a result of California's economic decline.

Proposition 187 contained the following key provisions: First, Proposition 187 would make undocumented immigrants ineligible for public social services, public health services (except for emergencies as stipulated by federal law), and public education (elementary, secondary, and postsecondary). Second, Proposition 187 would require employees of public agencies to report any person suspected of being undocumented to either of two government agencies—the office of the California attorney general or the INS. Last, proposition 187 would make it a felony to print, sell, and/or use false citizenship documents.

During the statewide campaign, California's Latino population mobilized against Proposition 187. Within Mexican communities, both Mexican immigrants (documented and undocumented) and Mexican-American citizens considered Proposition 187 as a potential threat to their civil rights. A combination of political organizations sponsored community workshops and forums to disseminate information on the proposition and to mobilize an effective opposition force. One of the largest demonstrations against Proposition 187 took place in Los Angeles, where 100,000 protesters marched to show their opposition. Other organizations joined in these efforts, including the League of United Latin American Citizens (LULAC) and university student groups from all over the Southwest. Even with growing opposition developing from various social groups in California, Proposition 187 was approved by 59 percent to 41 percent. Support for the proposition varied by race: 63 percent of whites voted for Proposition 187, whereas 77 percent of Latinos voted against it. A survey conducted of a sample of Californians who supported Proposition 187 concluded that these voters shared similar views. They believed that the state's economy was deteriorating and that undocumented immigrants posed the major economic threat (Alvarez and Butterfield, 1997).

The approval of Proposition 187 led to further complications. Immediately after its approval, groups opposed to it filed various court injunctions in an effort to prevent its implementation. The federal courts placed a temporary halt to its enforcement. Tensions increased in many California communities with Mexican Americans reporting increased incidents of discrimination. A spokesperson for the California Rural Legal Assistance Foundation, Juanita Ontiveros, recalled that Latinos were "being harassed because of looks, language and mannerisms" (*Time Magazine*, November 28, 1994). Hotlines were set up to handle the growing number of complaints of discrimination. At the same time that federal courts were assessing Proposition 187, community organizations reported an increase in Mexican immigrants wanting to apply for American citizenship. Fearing the repercussions if Proposition 187 were upheld by the courts, Mexican immigrants became convinced that this was a good time to begin the naturalization process (*Time Magazine*, November 28, 1994).

In March 1998, Judge Mariana Pfaelzer declared Proposition 187 unconstitutional citing the 1982 Supreme Court decisions in *Plyler v. Doe* that all children under eighteen years of age are entitled to public education, regardless of their immigration status. In addition, Judge Pfaelzer overturned Proposition 187 because immigration law is a federal and not a state-level issue. This decision was appealed by Governor Wilson, but his successor Gray Davis decided to send the issue into mediation. The settlement bars the enforcement of Proposition 187's major provisions. The only provisions that were upheld involved the sanctions placed on making, using, distributing, or selling false citizenship documents. Although Proposition 187 faded into the political background, events surrounding its introduction, passage, and challenges produced another period of anti-immigrant sentiments within which Mexican immigrants, both documented and undocumented, had to live. This climate pushed many immigrants to begin the necessary steps toward American citizenship.

Recent political development may also facilitate an increase in the naturalization rates of Mexican immigrants, both documented and, perhaps more significantly, undocumented, which will facilitate the transition to American citizenship. In December 2000, President Bill Clinton signed a new immigration law that eased the existing residency criteria for naturalization. The existing law disqualified immigrants for naturalization if they left the country, even for a brief time, during their application for naturalization. Clinton attached an amendment to a pending budget bill in order to allow for changes in the immigration law. Clinton's amendment eliminates the requirement stipulated by the 1986 IRCA that stated that undocumented immigrants who wanted to apply for citizenship had to leave the country and apply for readmission to the United States, a process that could last as long as ten years. Furthermore, this new immigration law provides for a shorter time period for immigrants applying for naturalization to obtain a resident visa and thus speed up the process for family reunification.

Despite these improvements, the revised immigration law contains some specific shortcomings. Many Democratic members of Congress who have been lobbying for immigration reforms believe that the number of immigrants provided for under this law should have been increased by at least 100,000. In addition, strong advocates for increased leniency in naturalization requirements had hoped that Clinton's immigration law would provide for residency status for those undocumented immigrants that have lived in the United States continuously since 1986. Another provision not included relates to a reform that would have given residency to those undocumented immigrants from El Salvador, Honduras, Guatemala, and Haiti who fled their countries' political and economic conditions. Supporters of this amendment pointed out that a 1997 measure granted residency to Nicaraguans and Cubans who entered the United States for similar reasons. As a result, Democrats in Congress intend to reintroduce what they are calling the "Central American parity law."

The immigration reforms signed into law by President Clinton represent important developments for Mexicans and other Latinos. During the election year of 2000, both Democratic and Republican candidates targeted Mexicans who were naturalized citizens and Mexican Americans as a growing voting block. Immigration reform was seen as a key to winning their votes. Nevertheless, anti-immigration groups organized to defeat the immigration legislation; they opposed establishing more lenient naturalization requirements, fearing a potential influx of undocumented immigrants becoming citizens. The Coalition for Immigrant Reform led the opposition to this bill's Section 245(I) of the Immigration Reform and Control Act that, as outlined earlier, removed the requirement that undocumented immigrants had to leave the country before applying for citizenship.

With the election of President George W. Bush in 2000, supporters of continued legislation for further leniency in the naturalization process fear that the most conservative wing of the Republican Party will be able to pressure President Bush in vetoing immigration reform laws. While he was governor, Bush maintained a record that demonstrated his political goal of establishing "good neighbor" relations with Mexico by not pressing for strict anti-immigration policies. From the earliest months of his presidency, Bush continued this policy favoring the path of binational cooperation between the United States and Mexico. Bush and his Latin American foreign policy advisors maintained that increasing Mexican economic development would be the best way to curb illegal Mexican immigration. As a result, President Bush moved closer to a centrist position regarding immigration than many conservative Republicans in the House and Senate. During the summer months of 2001, the Bush administration focused more on the status of the millions of undocumented Mexicans living in the United States rather than on those newly arrived undocumented. Bush indicated support for a White House task force on immigration that would give legal status to the more than 3 million Mexicans living in the United States. Mexican President Vicente Fox Quesada has supported what both countries now call a "regularization" of Mexican migrants living in the United States and, in fact, believes that this is a basis for creating new bonds between the two countries. By the end of the summer, it appeared that the immigration debate would not only be the basis for a new era in U.S.–Mexico relations, but it would have the potential to lead to a reexamination of immigration policy for the first time in fifteen years.

The tragic events of September 11, 2001, when terrorists destroyed the twin towers of the World Trade Center in New York, altered the course of immigration policies that had been under consideration throughout the summer months. A tightening of American national security represented one of the immediate consequences of 9/11. The Bush Administration echoed widespread public sentiments by calling for an analysis of current immigration laws. The Administration answered the terrorist threat to American society by delaying initiatives to grant amnesty to Mexicans living in the United States and, more important, by supporting antiterrorist policies designed to expand the government's ability to restrict or deport those immigrants identified as having terrorist links. A Foreign Terrorist Tracking Force was designed to monitor immigrants under suspicion of terrorist association. Many legislators expressed their concern that such antiterrorist policies had the potential of initiating widespread incidents of civil rights violations. Although he was quick to express his outrage at the events of 9/11 and his sympathy for the American public, Fox Quesada was fearful that Mexico would most likely feel the brunt of antiterrorist policies with the establishment of an anti-immigrant climate. President Fox Quesada called for a judicious application of immigration restrictions and urged restraint in the treatment of Mexicans and other immigrants living in the United States, the majority of whom have no ties to terrorist organizations.

DUAL CITIZENSHIP

In addition to legislation dealing with immigration reforms, the issue of dual nationality of immigrants represents another key issue in the contemporary study of immigration to the United States, particularly Mexican immigration. Almost half the world's countries recognize dual citizenship. Mexico passed a law in 1996 that allows Mexicans to hold a dual nationality. This law stipulates that Mexican nationals living in the United States who become naturalized American citizens do not have to relinquish their Mexican citizenship. This has enabled between 4 and 5 million Mexican residents in the United States to have access to rights as citizens of both countries. Up until the passage of this Mexican law, it is estimated that large numbers of Mexicans living in the United States who were eligible for naturalization did not pursue citizenship because they would lose their rights as Mexicans, particularly their right to own property and to vote in Mexico.

The 1996 law allows people born in Mexico, or with one parent born in Mexico, to hold dual citizenship, but they will not be allowed to vote, hold political post, or join the Mexican army. The law, however, does provide for them to maintain property rights, travel to Mexico without a visa, and invest in Mexico without the restrictions placed on foreigners. This law permits those Mexicans born in the United States to apply for dual nationality by registering in any Mexican consulate. Similar laws have been passed in other Latin American countries such as Colombia.

The U.S. government does not encourage dual citizenship but does recognize Mexico's law. The State Department maintains the right to revoke American citizenship for those individuals who run for office in another country, but it has seldom exercised this prerogative. Opponents to dual citizenship fear sentiments of divided loyalty among immigrants with dual nationality and thus believe that their patriotism and support for the United States, particularly in times of crisis, will be compromised. Evidence for such fears remains to be discovered. In fact, the U.S. Supreme Court has declared as unconstitutional the forced denationalization of U.S. citizens who obtain dual nationality. Interestingly the requirement that an immigrant renounce allegiance to another country as a prerequisite for naturalization was hardly ever enforced. The increased tolerance for dual citizenship reflects a changing international context, one that does not consider this to be a threat to a country such as the United States. The collapse of communism in the Soviet Union, signaling an end to the Cold War, represents a major international development contributing to the growing and widespread acceptance of dual citizenship. Nevertheless, because the largest number of permanent residents in the United States are from Mexico, the issue of dual citizenship will be a key one for years to come.

Another dimension to the issue of dual citizenship involves the changing nature of relations between the United States and Mexico. The 2000 Mexican presidential election stands as a turning point in the political and diplomatic history of both countries. For Mexico, the electoral victory of Vicente Fox Quesada, the candidate from the opposition party—PAN—ended the seventy years of political rule of the Revolutionary Institutional Party (PRI). Up until its defeat, the PRI, established at the end of the Mexican Revolution of 1910, remained the party that had been in power for the most years in all of Latin America. Its defeat signaled the potential for a dramatic shift in both national Mexican politics and, more important, for the question of dual citizenship in the relations between Mexico and the United States.

In the first days after his election, Vicente Fox Quesada outlined his political agenda regarding Mexican immigration to the United States. Although he announced a national economic program intended to improve Mexico's long-standing economic problems of unemployment, poverty, low wages, and inadequate social services, the newly elected president recognized that Mexicans would continue to see immigration to the United States as a major, if not only, remedy for their economic difficulties. With this in mind, Fox Quesada called for specific changes in the international relations between the United States and Mexico. First, he called for the development of more effective policies aimed at Mexican immigrants living in the United States, particularly those laws and policies of the INS. In his visit with President Clinton, Fox Quesada criticized the past record of the INS for its violations of the international rights of Mexican citizens. Fox Quesada also urged President Clinton to encourage American law enforcement agencies to be more vigilant in patrolling the U.S.–Mexico border in order to deal with those individuals who transported Mexicans across the border in dangerously overcrowded vehicles.

In addition, Fox Quesada announced other political objectives related to the current binational situation of Mexicans entering the United States to work, live, and, in some cases, become American citizens. He discussed a political plan that he hoped would be in place within ten years. His plan, a

delicate and almost immediately controversial one, would open the U.S.–
Mexico border as a free zone, allowing Mexicans to come and go across the
border without being encumbered by immigration documents. In addition
to helping curb the human rights violations of both the INS and unscrupulous transporters of immigrants across the border, Fox Quesada's call for
an open border reflects his political view that Mexico and the United States
stand to benefit by the creation of a labor force that could move, with very
little legal constraints, between the two countries. Some labor unions and
anti-immigrant lobbies issued their strong opposition to Fox Quesada's announcement. Although the issue of open borders will continue to be hotly
debated, it will affect the more immediate implementation of policies dealing
with dual nationality. The future of citizenship patterns among Mexican
immigrants, therefore, will be shaped by these two mutually related and
intertwined issues; dual citizenship and open borders between Mexico and
the United States.

10

Forging a New American Political Identity

As the process through which Mexican immigrants, like all other immigrant groups, forges a new political identity, becoming "New Americans" represents a critical key to understanding both the nature of the immigrant experience and the constant transformation of the United States as a complex and culturally diverse society in the twenty-first century. Immigrants construct new identities in many ways. Studies of immigrants from different countries reveal that immigrant identity transformation does not follow one general pattern. This chapter analyzes several of the key factors involved in the forging of a new political identity among Mexican immigrants: the increased use of the English language, the development of political associations and organizations, and the development of electoral politics within Mexican communities. Although this chapter examines the experiences of Mexican immigrants, an important framework for the study of their political identity and participation in the United States needs to include an examination of the parallel development of the role of American-born Mexican heritage individuals. This chapter discusses the political interrelationship between these two groups.

PATTERNS OF ENGLISH LANGUAGE ACQUISITION AND USAGE

Studies have challenged the long-standing view of American society as a "melting pot," which results from a process of cultural assimilation that replaces "old country" culture with a modern American culture. Classic studies of immigration have viewed the immigrant experience as one characterized by "uprootedness," a disruptive departure from the "soil" of the immigrant's homeland and their traditional way of life. Immigrants move from one culture to another: from the "traditional" world of Mexico to a "modern" American world. Successful assimilation can be seen as a process through which the immigrant generation leaves behind their Mexican immigrant heritage with their continued exposure to mainstream American culture (Glazer and Moynihan, 1963; Gordon, 1964; Handlin, 1951; Redfield, 1907).

The melting pot model of immigrant adjustment to a new society can be modified by pointing out that immigration does not erase all the traces of an immigrant's traditional culture (Bodnar, 1985; Gans, 1962; Ruiz, 1993; Sanchez, 1993). Recent studies of immigrants document how their lives are shaped by both their past experiences in their countries of origin and those in the United States. Mexican immigrants continue to hold on to their Mexican culture even as they forge an American identity. This process is not always a smooth one; it usually reveals tensions, conflicts, and negotiations between immigrants and American society and culture. Within Mexican immigrant communities in the United States, Mexicans construct new American identities as they attempt to keep the best of both worlds.

The daily lives of Mexican immigrants are characterized by attempts to maintain cultural traditions, such as retention of the Spanish language. They also are introduced to cultural changes such as the acquisition of English. This process is best illustrated by examining the process through which Mexican immigrants make the transition to an increased use of English while maintaining their Spanish. The first wave of Mexican immigrants in the early twentieth century displayed a reluctance to use English in their homes and in public. As Manuel Gamio (1930) pointed out, the majority of Mexicans who established immigrant communities along the U.S.–Mexico border and in other areas of the Southwest and Midwest could function quite well in their jobs without a command of English. For the most part, Mexican immigrants, as discussed in previous chapters, worked in unskilled and semi-skilled occupations, requiring little spoken interaction with their supervisors. Mexican workers spoke Spanish among themselves at their various work sites such as the railroad yards, mines, and agricultural fields. In addition, these early Mexican immigrants preferred to speak Spanish in their homes. Within Mexican immigrant communities, Mexicans conducted their business in Spanish in the various types of establishments, such as restaurants, barber and beauty shops, and retail stores. Mexicans read Spanish-language newspapers and listened to Spanish-language radio stations.

Nevertheless, the more time that Mexicans spent in the United States, the more they began to make some degree of transition to speaking English. For most Mexicans, those who came during the first major wave of immigration in 1910 and those who have just recently arrived, the acquisition of English often originated with the development of code-switching, a process through which a person uses their primary language, in this case, Spanish, with a sprinkling of English words. Mexican immigrants often changed certain English words to "sound like" a Spanish language version. For example, Gamio (1930) listed the following English words and their "translation" into a kind of Spanish by Mexican immigrants:

Dime—"Daime"	Sweater—"Suera"
Nickel—"Nickle"	Bills—"Biles"
Track—"Traque"	Tickets—"Tiquetes"
Lunch—"Lonche"	Chance—"Chansa"
Market—"Marqueta"	Watching—"Guachando"

Mexican immigrants from the middle or upper classes are less likely to use words such as these. In addition, Mexicans living in Mexico, particularly in the interior and Mexico City, would never use these hybrid English–Spanish words and, in fact, usually look down on these linguistic styles—associating them with the lower classes. This poses a considerable problem for those Mexican immigrants who return to Mexico for some length of time. In addition to using an intermingling of Spanish and English and hybrid English–Spanish words, another common practice among Mexican immigrants living in the United States involves the usage of grammatically incorrect Spanish. Gamio (1930) noted that working-class Mexican immigrants who had very little schooling made the mistake of not using the subjunctive. Studies of more contemporary Mexican immigration show that the likelihood that Mexicans will move toward greater English language usage and skills is directly related to their interaction with their American-born children. As Mexican immigrants remained in the United States and raised children born in the United States, they began to make a more definite and complete transition to learn the English language although they usually retained Spanish, often preferring it over English. Although many Mexican immigrants continued to dream about their eventual return to Mexico, most did not; many remained in the United States where they and their American-born children have settled on a permanent basis. Mexicans lived in their immigrant communities with people like themselves, sharing a new, often perplexing, family experience. Although many Mexican immigrants came to the United States with their children, many continued to have children after they arrived in the United States. By the early 1940s, the Mexican population in the United States had more American born than foreign. This trend has never been reversed even though immigration from Mexico will continue well into the twenty-first century.

As immigrant parents of American-born children, Mexican parents who were predominately Spanish-speaking attempted to raise their children in a Spanish-speaking family environment. Many Mexican families included one or both grandparents who themselves were Mexican immigrants. These grandparents preferred overwhelmingly to live their lives in the United States as Spanish speakers, with very little, if any, capacity to speak English. Given the necessity for most immigrant parents to work in the paid labor force, grandparents very frequently assumed the responsibility of child care for the American-born grandchildren. This pattern accounts for their grandchildren, referred to in studies of immigrants as the "second-generation," learning some level of Spanish in order to communicate with their grandparents.

Once the children of Mexican immigrants entered the American educational system, a dramatic change developed within their families. As their children progressed in American schools, they became more and more conversant in the English language. With the reversal of bilingual education, this trend will continue. Prior to the introduction of any widespread bilingual educational programs, second-generation children left their Spanish-speaking families and encountered the English-speaking world of education. For those children who, for reasons already discussed, started school with a limited knowledge of English, this transition represented a difficult challenge. For the most part, schools teaching Spanish-speaking children of immigrants relied on a total English immersion curriculum. In his autobiography, Francisco Jiménez depicts poignantly his experiences when he entered the first grade as a Spanish-only speaker. He recalls how he relied on another Mexican boy who understood English to tell him what the teacher was saying. Most of the time, however, the young "Panchito" did not understand his teacher.

Miss Scalapino started speaking to the class and I did not understand a word she was saying. The more she spoke, the more anxious I became. By the end of the day, I was very tired of hearing Miss Scalapino talk because the sounds made no sense to me. I thought that by paying close attention, I would begin to understand but I did not. I only got a headache, and that night, when I went to bed, I heard her voice in my head. (Jiménez, 1997: 18)

As their children advanced in school, Mexican immigrant parents eventually began to learn more and more English. One historical incident illustrates this transition from Spanish to English. In addition, this example shows how Mexican parents reacted to episodes of discrimination against their children by policies adopted by public school boards and administrators. The "Lemon Grove California Incident," as historians have called it, depicts one of the most dramatic examples of language change among Mexican immigrants. In 1928, the school board in Lemon Grove, California, adopted a school policy to build a separate elementary school for its Mexican students. They based their decision on the grounds that Mexican students spoke more Spanish than English and, therefore, lagged behind their Anglo peers. When the Mexican immigrants learned of this decision, they mobilized themselves into an informal committee to challenge the actions of the school board, calling for it to halt the construction of a separate school for Mexican students, many of whom were American-born children of Mexican immigrant parents. They initiated a school boycott, keeping their children home from school rather than seeing them segregated into what they considered an inferior learning environment. Eventually they hired a lawyer and won their discrimination lawsuit. In a collection of oral histories taken from the Mexican immigrants involved in this case and featured in the film *The Lemon Grove Incident*, parents expressed feelings of frustration due to their lack of English skills. Although they succeeded in both mobilizing themselves and winning their case, these Mexican immigrant parents shared a common view that if they had known more English, they could have been successful earlier in the course of this incident. Immigrants also expressed their feelings that they and their children were now going to be residing permanently in the United States, and, more importantly, their children were entitled to the same full rights as all American citizens.

As the Mexican immigrants attempted to defend the civil rights of their American-born children, they recognized the importance of being able to maneuver successfully within an English-speaking American society and political culture. The historical record shows that this process of cultural change occurred throughout the United States, particularly in Texas where segregated schools were still the norm even after segregation was ruled unconstitutional by the 1954 U.S. Supreme Court Decision of *Brown v. Board of Education*. Immigrants established informal and formal political organizations as they struggled to secure equal treatment for their children, beginning with the American public school system. To the extent that Mexican immigrant parents increased their active participation in school and local politics, they began to see themselves as "citizens" more than immigrants, even if they had not completed the formal naturalization process. Their intentions of returning to Mexico some day also decreased as they mobilized themselves to defend the civil rights of their American-born children. Mexican immigrant men and women began to transform themselves into New Americans. An examination of the development of political associations and organizations among Mexican immigrants continues to tell the story of how Mexican immigrants forged a "New American" political identity.

THE DEVELOPMENT OF POLITICAL ASSOCIATIONS AND ORGANIZATIONS

All immigrant groups that came to the United States faced many common problems as they adjusted to their new lives in American society. One problem encountered by all immigrants at some point in their immigration experience involves their reaction to the development of anti-immigrant legislation and practices. A comparative study of immigrant groups shows that immigrants, such as Mexicans, were exposed to varying degrees of prejudice and discrimination that, in turn, created a societal climate within which immigrants felt unwelcome. Nevertheless, this same comparative study also documents the political response, both formal and informal, developed by immigrants in their attempt to fight specific cases of discrimination. Immigrant groups entering the United States, at whatever point in American history, found it difficult to deal with a hostile social environment. Without a sufficient knowledge of English, American culture, and the American political system, newly arrived immigrants lacked the skills with which to express their concerns. Similarly, immigrants took time to gain the skills and cultural expertise that would eventually lead to the rise of immigrant political associations and organizations to voice their concerns with the troubles they were experiencing. Nathan Glazer (1972), a preeminent scholar of immigrant groups in the United States, has studied this process through which immigrants respond collectively to social discrimination and prejudice. Immigrant group solidarity and political organization increases when group members experience specific instances of discriminatory beliefs and actions. Glazer documents the development of political mobilization among immigrant groups, emphasizing that during instances of anti-immigrant actions by the larger American society, some immigrants react and organize and in so doing, find themselves becoming New Americans as they participate in the political system.

LEAGUE OF UNITED LATIN AMERICAN CITIZENS

The history of immigrant groups in the United States reflects diverse patterns and variations in the development of political associations and organizations. Many factors combine in shaping the types of political groups started by immigrants, allowing for both comparisons and contrasts in studying any one particular immigrant group such as Mexicans. For all immigrants, nevertheless, an immigrant group's ethnicity and immigrant status served as major organizing forces. An overview of Mexican immigration will document the rise of Mexican and Mexican-American political groups beginning approximately in the 1940s.

The establishment of the League of United Latin American Citizens (LULAC) stands as a major transition in the history of Mexican immigrants and Mexican Americans. Although Mexican Americans represented the majority of the founders of LULAC, the organization, its leadership, and its ideology directly affected Mexican immigrant communities. The league mobilized both Mexicans and Mexican Americans in the struggle against prejudice, discrimination, and inequality experienced by generations of Mexicans and Mexican Americans. It directed its attention to the struggle for the civil rights of American-born Mexicans, but, in fact, this struggle would have a direct impact on those Mexicans who either became naturalized American citizens or had children who themselves were American citizens by birthright.

Other civic organizations existed long before the founding of LULAC in 1929. The "Alianza Hispano Americana" (Hispanic American Alliance) dates back to 1894. In 1924, other organizations played an important role in Mexican communities, including "La Sociedad Mutualista Mexicana" (The Mexican Mutualist Society). At this same time, many organizations developed under the auspices of the Catholic Church and functioned to foster close links between Mexican immigrant communities and Mexico. In addition to providing social services, these church-sponsored organizations encouraged the retention of Mexican culture and the renewal of Mexican patriotism and national loyalty.

The history of LULAC reversed this trend by creating an organization that would both unite Mexicans and Mexicans Americans (LULAC used Mexican and Latin American interchangeably) and inculcate an ethos of Americanization among its members. During its formative years, LULAC addressed those issues in the Mexican community that emerged as the most critical in the years between 1930 and the mid-1940s. The league's archives document a tragic list of injustices suffered by Mexicans. Many incidents of brutality, including murder, of Mexicans took place during this same time period. Throughout the Southwest, owners of businesses, especially restaurants, placed "No Mexicans Allowed" and "No Mexicans Served Here" signs. Mexican Americans faced common practices aimed at their disenfrancisment such as voting poll taxes and white primaries. In addition, in many southwestern states, strict prohibitions barred Mexicans from buying homes in certain neighborhoods. Wage discrimination confronted documented and undocumented Mexican immigrants and Mexican Americans. LULAC set out to challenge all these forms of discrimination. Their efforts culminated in political victories that affected all Mexican-origin individuals regardless of their immigrant and citizen status.

Three organizations joined efforts in creating LULAC: the Knights of America, the Council Number 4 of the Order of the Sons of America, and the League of Latin American Citizens. These organizations, all established in Texas, came together to be united under one umbrella association. Although all three groups believed that one united organization would have a greater likelihood to wield more political clout, their leaders and rank-and-file members engaged in long debates concerning its structure and ideology. In 1927, the three groups met in Harlingen, Texas, to establish the organization and set up its bylaws. The most heated debate occurred over the qualifications for membership, with some delegates favoring the restriction of membership to American-born Mexicans. This caused an intense conflict among the majority of the delegates who were also Mexican immigrants without American citizenship. Without reaching a compromise, the 1927 meeting adjourned until a second meeting in 1928. With their overwhelming support for an umbrella organization, delegates organized a constitutional convention in May 1929 in Corpus Christi, Texas. They resolved the membership issue by including a bylaw limiting membership to native-born or naturalized citizens and stating that English would be the official language for conducting organizational business. Although the founders of the League of Latin American Citizens faced criticism for such membership qualifications, the LULAC archives record that the founders wanted to stress the nature of LULAC as a civic organization that would fight for citizenship rights for its members but still understand that its victories would have an impact on Mexican immigrants. By 1932, LULAC chapters existed in Arizona, Colorado, New Mexico, and California; eventually LULAC chapters could be found in all states (R. Garcia, 1991).

Women have always participated in every aspect of LULAC. Although women in LULAC recognize the existence of sexism within the organization, they have persisted in working to strengthen its support for the equal status of women. In 1938, the league established a national office for women. Women have always constituted half of the membership. LULAC, under the direction of the national office for women, holds an annual national conference, "Adelante Mujer Hispana" (Forward Hispanic Women).

During the last seventy years, LULAC has been at the forefront of the struggle for civil rights. Mexican communities have benefited from its concerted efforts to pave the way for social, political, and economic changes to reduce conditions of inequality. LULAC has served as the model for many Mexican-American and Latino organizations, including the Mexican American Legal Defense and Educational Fund (MALDEF). LULAC continues to function as a key lobby in local, state, and national politics. Its legal victories created a more humane community for Mexicans and Mexican Americans and, thus, for the larger American society whose attempts to achieve diversity continue to the present day.

The LULAC archives lists the following milestones in the organization's history and the history of Mexicans and Mexican Americans in the United States. This partial list includes victories in law, politics, housing, employment, health care, and education.

- 1930: Desegregation of public places in Texas
- 1931: Provided organizational and financial support for the first class-action suit against segregated "Mexican schools" in Texas (*Salvatierra v. Del Rio Independent School District*)
- 1940: Assisted in filing discrimination cases for the Federal Employment Practices Commission, the first federal civil rights agency
- 1946: Filed the *Mendez v. Westminister* lawsuit in Santa Ana, California, which ended almost one hundred years of public school segregation in California
- 1948: Filed the *Delgado v. Bastrop Independent School District* lawsuit that ended the segregation of Mexican-American children in Texas
- 1954: Argued the *Hernandez v. State of Texas* lawsuit before the Supreme Court that won the right for Mexican Americans to serve on juries
- 1966: Provided financial support to the United Farm Workers Movement
- 1986: Outlined a position regarding the 1986 Immigration and Reform Act
- 1986: Lobbied the Texas Senate subcommittee hearings on English only and succeeded in stopping the resolution from going outside the committee
- 1995: Established the "Commitment with America" to improve Mexican and Latino communities

This brief overview of the League of Latin American Citizens provides some examples, among many, of the process through which Mexican immigrants and native-born Mexican Americans experienced a change in consciousness and ideology (R. Garcia, 1991). With continued episodes of prejudice and discrimination, these groups began to focus their attention more closely on American society, its embedded inequalities, and, above all, their place within the United States. Mexicans and Mexican Americans joined collectively in such organizations as the League of Latin American Citizens to channel their energies and thus become a more effective political force capable of achieving political victories such as those listed for the League of Latin American Citizens. As a result, these "New Americans" fought for and began to gain a voice in American society.

POLITICS OF SOCIAL PROTEST

Influenced by the black nationalist movement and the Mexican-American community's historical legacy of discrimination and structural inequality in American society, a generation of Mexican Americans channeled their collective energies into a militant civil rights and ethnic nationalist movement in the late 1960s and 1970s. Surrounded by a radical climate of national political protests and insurgency such as the Black Power Movement, the anti–Vietnam War Movement, and the second wave of the Women's Movement, the movement focused on social, political, and economic self-determination and autonomy for Mexican-American communities throughout the United States (Barrera, 1974; Muñoz, 1989; Navarro, 1974; Rosales, 1996). Although most of the social protest activists were American born, many had Mexican immigrant parents. In addition, the various aspects of this civil rights movement, particularly the United Farm Workers Movement, had an immediate impact on Mexican immigrant farm laborers, particularly in California.

The Chicano Movement evolved from various struggles with specific leaders, agendas, and organizational strategies and tactics. The New Mexico Land Grant Movement, for example, headed by Reies López Tijerina, fought for the rights of dispossessed "Hispanos," as those from New Mexico called themselves, whose lands had been lost as a result of the war between the United States and Mexico (1846–1848). In California, Cesar Chavez and Dolores Huerta organized migrant farm workers into the United Farm Workers Union whose strikes, boycotts, and victories against the state's agribusiness would become the soul and inspiration of the Chicano Movement, as well as a national and international symbol of the struggle for social justice and equal rights. The urban-based Colorado Crusade for Justice, spearheaded by Rodolfo "Corky" Gonzales, mobilized Mexican-American communities around the issues of political self-determination. In Texas, José Angel Gutiérrez founded a third political party, the Raza Unida Party, and challenged the state's political system for its systematic exclusion of the Mexican-American community. Gutiérrez and the Raza Unida Party's electoral victory in Crystal City, Texas, in 1970 represented a major political milestone (Shockley, 1974). In high schools and universities throughout the Southwest, Mexican-American students organized their collective efforts into a radical confrontation with an educational system that they criticized for its patterns of discrimination. Generations of Mexican-American parents had identified an inadequate educational system as a major barrier to their children's achievement of the American dream: upward social mobility. After decades of educational neglect, young Chicanos and Chicanas organized school boycotts, known as blowouts, as a sign of militant protest (San Miguel, 1987). Drafted in large numbers into the military and out of proportion to their population in the country, Chicanos organized their own significant anti-war movement. This protest reached its zenith when over 20,000 demonstrators, mostly Chicano, protested the war in the National Chicano Anti-War Moratorium in East Los Angeles on August 29, 1970.

Culturally, the movement released a new energy of artistic and literary expression in what constituted a "Mexican American Renaissance." Poets, writers, playwrights, and artists mobilized art as a political weapon for "La Causa" (The Cause). The movement was not the first time that Mexican Americans had protested their second-class status. Indeed, a strong historical legacy of protest existed, but the movement was the largest and most widespread expression of Mexican-American discontent (M. García, 1981, 1994; R. García, 1991). Sharing ideological roots with black cultural nationalism, Chicano cultural nationalism—"Chicanismo"—advocated an ideology and spirit of active resistance within Mexican-American communities throughout the United States.

Cultural nationalism emphasized cultural pride as a source of political unity and strength capable of mobilizing Chicanos and Chicanas into an oppositional political group within the dominant political landscape in the United States. The ideology of Chicanismo contributed to the development of a collective ethnic consciousness directed at bringing about social change for Mexican and Mexican-American communities. In the 1960s, Mexican Americans and Mexican immigrants still faced fundamental social inequalities in comparison to many other ethnic groups, especially Euro-Americans. More than one-third of all Mexican Americans lived in poverty, and the average educational attainment for Mexican Americans was less than eighth grade, the lowest in the country. Jobs and wage discrimination added to poor housing opportunities only compounded the Mexican-American position in the United States.

Cultural nationalism served as a dynamically effective tool capable of mobilizing divergent struggles within the Chicano Movement. By the late 1960s, cultural nationalism served a dual political purpose. Chicanismo provided a unifying world view for El Movimiento while, at the same time, it provided the ideological link that cut across such groups as the Raza Unida Party, the United Farm Workers, the Crusade for Justice, and the student movement.

Many women, active within every sector of the movement, began to raise their voices collectively to protest the specific inequalities that they faced. Developing first as cultural nationalists, these Chicanas began to see and experience some of the contradictions they encountered in their everyday lives. Many were daughters of Mexican immigrants who held the hope of attaining the American dream. Their children—second-generation Americans—believed that American society was characterized by many forms of discrimination and inequality that prevented them from realizing their parents' dreams.

Chicana feminists inherited a historic tradition of political activism dating back to the immigrant generation of Mexican women who, together with their families, crossed the border into the United States at the turn of the century. Mexican immigrant women and their families fled the upheaval produced by the Mexican Revolution of 1910, as well as from economic displacement and poverty. Communities of Mexican immigrant families developed throughout the Southwest, joining preexisting communities created after the U.S.–Mexico War of 1848. El Paso, San Antonio, San Diego, Los Angeles, and Santa Barbara all experienced dramatic societal transformations that would shape future generations of Mexican Americans. Throughout contemporary Mexican-American history, women played active roles in their communities in a struggle against persistent patterns of societal inequality. Their political activism shaped the course of major reform movements within communities of Mexicans in the United States.

The political struggles of Chicana feminists during the late 1960s and late 1970s reflected a continuation of women's activism that paralleled the experiences of other women of color in the United States. A Chicana feminist movement, like that of African-American women, originated within the context of a national social protest movement. Dolores Huerta is the most prominent Mexican-American political activist and labor leader in the United States. Huerta is the co-founder with the late Cesar Chavez of the United Farm Workers Union. Huerta has served as a staunch advocate for farm workers, particularly Mexican immigrant farm workers, for thirty years. She was born in 1930 in northern New Mexico. Her father entered the United States in the late 1920s. Her mother, a single parent, raised Dolores and her siblings during the Great Depression. In her early twenties, Dolores Huerta began what would be a lifelong crusade for social justice for Mexican and Mexican-American communities. She worked in various grassroots community organizations, the most important of which was the Community Service Organization (CSO). In 1972, she joined with Cesar Chavez to found the United Farm Workers Union. A forceful leader and speaker, Dolores Huerta worked closely with the various groups that had emerged during this social protest period. Reminiscing about the civil rights movement among Mexicans in the United States and her own life as a political activist, Dolores Huerta said, "I think we showed the world that non-violence can work to make social change" (www.gale.com/freresrc/chh/huerta.htm).

ELECTORAL POLITICS

Racial and ethnic groups, including immigrant groups, develop a strong sense of cohesion as they participate in the political process. Although Mexican immigrants cannot vote until they become naturalized American citizens, the next generation of American-born Mexicans can participate actively in electoral politics by voting, campaigning, mobilizing voter registration drives, and other forms of political behavior within their Mexican-American communities. Through such political activities, native-born Mexican Americans have the potential to change conditions. Mexican immigrants who are exposed to ethnic politics, as the history of other immigrant groups documents, are more likely to begin the process of forging a new political identity. Historian Ronald Takaki's study (1993) of racial/ethnic groups in the United States shows how Irish, Italians, and Jewish immigrants evolved into a vital political force once they became American citizens, acquired a new sense of American identity different from an immigrant mentality, and served as role models for their fellow immigrants who had not yet become American citizens. Other immigration scholars point out that the election of ethnic candidates represents an even stronger force in forging a New American identity among specific immigrants such as Mexicans.

Mexicans have won electoral victories in American politics since the nineteenth century. Between 1879 and 1883, Romualdo Pacheco served as California's congressman. José Manuel Gallegos served as New Mexico's representative to Congress from 1853 to 1855. Between 1855 and 1912, when New Mexico ended its status as a U.S. territory and became a state, eight other Mexicans were elected to Congress. In 1914, Benigno Hernández

Mexican-American women at a Los Angeles rally during the
early 1990s. "Chicano" was the term used by militant Mexican
Americans and referred to men and women. The inclusive form
is "Chicana/o." Courtesy of Raul Ruiz.

won New Mexico's single congressional seat. In 1929, Octaviano A. Larra-
zolo, the former governor of New Mexico, ran a successful senate campaign
for New Mexico. Dionisio "Dennis" Chavez represents another important
political figure. Chavez served in the House of Representatives as well as the
Senate, where he served from 1935 to 1962. Chavez's political career serves
as an excellent example of the relationship between American-born Mexicans
and Mexican immigrants. During his tenure as the senator from New Mexico, Chavez sponsored legislation designed to improve conditions for New

Protest march in Los Angeles, California, early 1970s. Courtesy of Raul Ruiz.

Mexico's communities, including Mexican. In 1944 and 1948, Chavez sponsored a bill to establish a federal Fair Employment Practices Commission which was ultimately defeated by the vote of a bloc of conservatives. Chavez became a major supporter for both the Civil Rights Acts of 1957 and 1964.

After Chavez's death in 1962, a New Mexican congressman, Joseph M. Montoya, won his seat in the Senate in 1964. Like Chavez, Senator Montoya's political career demonstrated his importance in sponsoring and supporting legislation that would be of dramatic importance for Mexican communities, including Mexican immigrants. Montoya introduced the Bilingual Education Act of 1968 and its amendments in 1974. In addition, he introduced three other bills of direct importance to Mexicans: (1) a bill to create the Cabinet Committee on Opportunities for the Spanish Speaking, (2) a bill to establish a commission on immigrant labor, and (3) a bill to train bilingual workers in the health care system. In the 1970s, Senator Montoya supported the Voting Rights Act and other amendments to the civil rights acts of the 1960s. Montoya lost his Senate seat in 1976 and died a few years later, leaving an impressive record of political reforms, most of

Congressman Edward Roybal, 25th District, Los
Angeles, California. Congressman Roybal served
his district from 1962 to 1992. Courtesy of Edward R. Roybal Institute for Applied Gerontol-
ogy, California State University, Los Angeles.

which contributed directly to improvements in both Mexican and other ethnic communities (Vigil, 1994).

Two other Mexican-American elected officials highlight this process
through which Mexicans forged a "New American" political identity. The
achievements of Edward Roybal of California and Henry B. González of
Texas show how the political lives of native-born Mexican Americans serve
as role models for Mexican immigrants. Such politicians can sponsor legislation capable of having a significant impact on Mexican immigrants, particularly when these immigrants become naturalized American citizens
capable of participating directly in electoral politics.

Edward Roybal's political career spanned over thirty-nine years, beginning in 1949 when he became the first Mexican American since 1882 to win

a seat on the Los Angeles City Council. In 1962, Roybal was elected to the U.S. House of Representatives from California's 25th District (Los Angeles). The political career of Congressman Roybal stands as testimony to a lifelong commitment to reforming American society through the political system at the local, state, and national level.

The first of eight children of Eloisa and Baudilio Roybal, Edward Roybal was born in 1916 in Albuquerque, New Mexico. His father, like many Mexican immigrants and Mexican Americans living in the Southwest in the early twentieth century, worked for the railroads. An unsuccessful railroad strike cost many workers their jobs in 1920, and Edward Roybal's family moved to the Boyle Heights community of Los Angeles which was home to a large working-class Mexican community. Although his family stressed the importance of education, the Great Depression made it difficult for Roybal to continue his studies after his graduation from high school. Roybal joined the Civilian Conservation Corps (CCC) created by Franklin D. Roosevelt as an answer to the chronic unemployment produced by the Great Depression. With the general economic recovery, Roybal left the CCC and was able to continue his education. He enrolled as an accounting major in the School of Business Administration at the University of California at Los Angeles. After graduation, Roybal went to work for 20th-Century Fox Studios.

Roybal became interested in health care as he participated in community affairs and became aware of the high incidence of tuberculosis within the Mexican-American and Mexican immigrant communities. He volunteered to work with the Tuberculosis Association and eventually was hired to operate its mobile X-ray unit used to test for the disease. Roybal was appointed as the public health educator for the Los Angeles County Health Association but left this position to volunteer with the U.S. army during World War II. At the end of the war, Roybal returned to his position and became a well-known and respected figure in the Mexican immigrant and Mexican-American community.

In 1947, Roybal entered the election for the Los Angeles City Council and lost by only a small percentage. He continued his community activism and joined long-time community organizer Fred Ross and his Community Service Organization (CSO). With the CSO's support and a large community following, Roybal won the 1947 race for the Los Angeles City Council; he became the first Mexican American to sit on the council since 1882. Roybal lost his next two election campaigns: the 1954 election for California's lieutenant governor, and the 1959 election for a seat on the Los Angeles Board of Supervisors. Nevertheless, Roybal continued to serve on the city council until 1962, winning twice without opposition. In 1962, Roybal embarked on what was to be his national political career. He ran for the U.S.

House of Representatives in California's 25th District, and his victory represented a major breakthrough for Mexicans. Roybal's distinguished work as a congressman spans from 1962 until his retirement in 1992.

Roybal's political concerns always centered on issues critical to all his constituencies, but he specifically addressed issues confronting the Mexican-American community. He introduced legislation reforms dealing with health care, housing, and the elderly. He also distinguished himself by serving on the Foreign Affairs Committee, the Subcommittee on Inter-American Affairs, the Appropriations Committee, the Select Committee on Aging, the Committee on Veterans Affairs, and the Subcommittee on Education and Training. In 1967, Roybal introduced a bill that would have long-lasting implications. He wrote the federal bilingual education act that was successfully passed. Roybal fought sustained opposition to this bill for years, particularly during the Reagan administration.

Roybal served as one of a handful of Mexican-American political figures with a national reputation. He championed the need for increased citizen participation in the political civic arena. He founded the National Association of Latino Elected and Appointed Officials (NALEO)in 1975, and in 1977 he played a prominent role in the creation of the Congressional Hispanic Caucus. This caucus included all congresspersons of Latino background. As caucus chair, Roybal led the struggle against the Simpson-Rodino IRCA of 1986. Roybal was active in many other organizations, including the Democratic National Committee, the American Legion, the Knights of Columbus, and the Boy Scouts. His unwavering commitment to public life earned him numerous prestigious awards, including the Excellence in Public Service Award from the American Academy of Pediatrics and the Joshua Award for his advocacy of Jewish-Latino Relations. His daughter, Lucille Roybal-Allard, now holds his congressional seat.

Like his contemporary Edward Roybal, Henry B. González dedicated his life to reforming the American political system by addressing specifically those issues that most affected his Mexican-American constituency and those Mexican immigrants who would become American citizens. González was elected to the Texas Senate in 1956; he was the first Mexican American to do so in one hundred years. In 1961, González was elected to the U.S. House of Representatives—the first Mexican American from Texas ever elected to national office.

González was born in San Antonio, Texas, on May 3, 1916, when his upper–middle-class parents fled the turmoil of the Mexican Revolution. His father had been the mayor of a small town in Durango, Mexico, and after his immigration to Texas continued his public career when he became an

Congresswoman Lucille Roybal-Allard, California District. Courtesy of the Office of U.S. Representative Lucille Roybal-Allard, Los Angeles, CA.

editor of *La Prensa,* a major Mexican immigrant newspaper. Despite his father's professional status, González's parents experienced economic hardship, making it difficult to provide adequate financial support for their six children. As a result, they instilled in their children the value of education as a key to upward mobility. In 1936, González accomplished the first of many lifelong successes as a second-generation Mexican American: he earned admission to the University of Texas at Austin as an engineering major. The Great Depression made it impossible for González to continue working to pay for his college expenses. Returning to San Antonio, he eventually was able to attend St. Mary's University from which he was awarded an honorary Doctor of Jurisprudence degree, twenty years later.

After World War II, González left his position as a nonenlisted employee in the offices of both army and navy intelligence to begin his long and illustrious political in the early 1950s when he served as a member of San Antonio's city council. By the end of the 1950s, González had gained a respected reputation as a national political figure. Throughout his political life, he devoted his legislative energies to the struggles for social justice. He was at the forefront of efforts to end segregation, improve housing conditions, and increase educational opportunities and civil rights for his constituency in the 20th Congressional District of Texas, a predominantly Mexican-American district. One of his major victories was his role in ending the Bracero Program, which was responsible for keeping a ceiling on agricultural wages. More important, González's political campaign to end the Bracero Program was a result of his criticism regarding its sustained violation of the civil rights of the hundreds of Mexican immigrant workers who had been brought to the United States to deal with the high rates of unemployment in the agricultural fields throughout the Southwest.

As a result of his political successes and seniority in Congress, González was appointed chair of the House Banking and Currency Committee. His long-standing political philosophy focused on the need to pass specific legislative reforms and monitor the policies of the Federal Reserve System Board in order to expand economic opportunities available to minority populations. He became an ardent supporter for political reforms on issues such as the poll tax, restrictive covenants in housing, and mortgage restrictions aimed at economically marginal groups. González was a prominent member of the House Banking Committee, its chair for three terms, and the force behind key housing legislation to repair the Federal Deposit Insurance Corporation. He was also a major force in dealing with the savings and loans scandal of the early 1990s. González, affectionately known as "Henry B," was famous for his avid criticism of Republicans, particularly President Reagan, calling for his impeachment after the 1982 Grenada invasion and the 1987 Iran-Contra scandal. He also called for the impeachment of President George Bush after the Persian Gulf War in 1991.

In 1976, together with Congressman Edward Roybal and the three other Hispanics in Congress at that time, González founded the Hispanic Congressional Caucus in order to advocate for all Hispanics. Congressman Gonzalez retired in 1998 and resided in Texas until his death in 2000. His son, Charles A. González, now serves as the congressman from the same Texas district as his father.

For the last twenty years, the number of Mexican Americans holding elected office has increased continuously but not dramatically, given the growing population of Mexican Americans. By the 1980s, the Hispanic Cau-

Congressman Henry B. González, 20th District, San Antonio, Texas. Congressman González served his district from 1961 to 1998. Courtesy of the Office of U.S. Representative Charles A. González, San Antonio, Texas.

cus, not limited to Mexican Americans but including other groups such as Cuban Americans and Puerto Ricans, doubled in size. The 1980 census revealed significant population increases in the sunbelt states, where a large percentage of the total Mexican-American population resides. The 2000 census shows that California's population has increased and will add another congressional representative. In the 2000 presidential and state elections, the Mexican-American vote was sought by candidates from all political parties. In the last three presidential elections, Mexican Americans have voted overwhelmingly for Democrats. Many more significant factors in electoral politics all point to the continued importance of both Mexican-American office-holders and the Mexican-American voting bloc—both of whose political participation affects the growing population of Mexican immigrants. Once

Charles A. González. Courtesy of the Office of U.S. Representative
Charles A. González, San Antonio, Texas.

they become naturalized citizens, Mexican immigrants will be able to become
participants themselves in American electoral politics—the result of their
ever-unfolding "New American" political identity.

PUBLIC POLICIES AND THE CONGRESSIONAL
HISPANIC CAUCUS

Since its development, the Congressional Hispanic Caucus has played a
key role in supporting major legislation related directly to Mexican and other
Latino communities. Although members of the Congressional Hispanic Caucus did not always reach consensus on all issues due to different political
ideologies and backgrounds, the caucus gained a reputation for its position
on two issues: immigration reform and the English-only movement. During

the congressional debates of both issues, the Congressional Hispanic Caucus distinguished itself as an advocate for the civil rights of Latino communities.

As discussed in chapter 4, the 1980s witnessed the emergence of immigration reform legislation as a major issue on the national political agenda. In 1983, members of the Congressional Hispanic Caucus led an organized battle against the Simpson-Mazzoli Immigration Bill. Their actions led to the bill being suspended during that congressional session. Spokesmen for the Caucus gained widespread national recognition through their extensive media appearances. Their position on the Simpson-Mazzoli Immigration Bill did, however, lead to disagreements with other Hispanic political organizations, some of whom believed that this bill would lead to some long-needed immigration reforms, although the bill did lack an acceptable position on family reunification. During all of the 1980s, the congressional debate on immigration reform would continue with the Congressional Hispanic Caucus remaining a key player, if not always united, in the call for immigration reform.

The Congressional Hispanic Caucus failed to agree on a united position during the debates over the IRCA in 1986. For various reasons, key members of the Caucus did not support the bill's provision outlining penalties for employers who hired undocumented workers. Opponents argued that such sanctions would lead to an increase in discrimination of those Hispanic citizens whom employers would be reluctant to hire out of fear of being held in violation of the proposed immigration law.

Discrimination in hiring practices of Hispanics who were American citizens represented one of the unforeseen consequences of such immigration reform legislation as IRCA. According to a study conducted in 1990 by the U.S. General Accounting Office, close to 1.5 million of the 4.1 million employers polled admitted that they had given their tacit approval to informal, often formal, hiring policies that discriminated against job applicants whom they believed, based on their "foreign" appearance, were undocumented (Vigil, 1994). Despite the efforts of Congressman Edward Roybal to eliminate the employer penalties clause in the IRCA, the bill remained intact. The IRCA passed, but further congressional debates over immigration reform continued throughout the 1990s with the Congressional Hispanic Caucus playing a national role.

At the same time that the Congressional Hispanic Caucus took an active role in reforming existing immigration laws by challenging those provisions with the potential to violate the civil rights of Hispanic citizens, it also turned its attention to the national "English-only" movement. Fueled by anti-immigrant sentiments and a growing concern with the economy, communities throughout the United States, particularly California, initiated organized efforts to pass resolutions that would declare the English language the official language within the United States. Although the use of English has long been the official language for public transactions, the Congressional Hispanic Caucus and other political groups considered the "English-Only Movement" as a rallying theme for a thinly veiled ethnocentric, usually discriminatory, anti-immigrant belief system. The Caucus argued that English-only resolutions had the potential to prohibit any practices that would bar the use of other languages in official government documents such as voting and social services publications. Despite their efforts, seventeen states passed English-only resolutions. Congress deliberated on several English-only bills in the early 1990s. More significantly, Congress debated a proposal to amend the U.S. Constitution to make English the official language in the United States. All this legislation was defeated with the political climate fostering anti-immigrant sentiments submerging for a while only to reappear in alternating cycles up to the present. These debates will continue for decades to come.

Mexicans and Mexican Americans continue to be one of the fastest-growing groups in the United States. Their political influence, however, has not increased as fast as their population. Since 1980, Mexican-American community and political organizations have initiated national projects to strengthen their voice in the political world. A variety of strategies have developed within Mexican-American communities. The success of many of these programs has had an immediate and a long-range impact on Mexican immigrants, particularly among those Mexican immigrants who have become naturalized citizens. Successful voter registration drives, for example, increased the importance of Mexican Americans as a voting bloc with the potential to be courted as a swing vote by politicians from both the Democratic and Republican Parties. Political organizations in Texas and California initiated legal challenges to gerrymandering political districts. The practice of gerrymandering refers to the practice of drawing voting district boundary-lines with the intent to scatter them as a block of voters, such as Mexican Americans, over several districts. As a result, Mexican-American communities with histories of political gerrymandering did not have a majority in these districts. In only a few instances, Mexican Americans achieved political victories. Federal courts agreed with Mexican-American activists that the practice of establishing voting districts with the purpose of splintering Mexican-American communities should be stopped, and, more important, voting district lines should be redrawn to keep long-established communities intact. Mexican-American activists advocated these reforms, hoping that with such new boundaries, more Mexican Americans would be elected to office. Although the redistricting of communities took place in both California and Texas, Mexican Americans did not always win elections in these voting districts. Nevertheless, the political struggle to reform electoral politics remains a symbol for Mexican immigrants and Mexican Americans that they can change the American political system, making it more sensitive to redressing past discrimination.

ELECTORAL POLITICS AND MEXICAN-AMERICAN VOTERS

Political interest in the Mexican-American vote dates back to the 1960 presidential election between John F. Kennedy and Richard Nixon. As a Catholic, Kennedy established a direct connection with Mexican Americans throughout the Southwest. The Democratic Party helped mobilize "Viva Kennedy" clubs that sponsored events targeting Mexican Americans, particularly those living in Texas. The large voter turnout by Mexican Americans, particularly in Texas, helped to secure Kennedy's narrow victory over Nixon. President Kennedy appointed El Paso Mayor Raymond L. Tellez as ambassador to Costa Rica; he became a major voice for the Mexican-American and Mexican immigrant community through his rise to national prominence. Later, in 1968, the Mexican-American vote in Texas gave Hubert Humphrey an electoral victory in Texas over Nixon, who, nevertheless, won the presidency. In the 1994 California Senate race, Mexican Americans helped Democratic candidate Dianne Feinstein beat her Republican opponent, Michael Huffington.

During the presidential elections of 1996 and 2000 and other general elections, politicians viewed the Mexican-American vote and the Hispanic vote in general as a potential swing vote, particularly in hotly contested races. As with other aspects involved in the forging of a New American political identity, Mexican immigrants, although not able to vote, became exposed at different levels to the American political arena. For those recently naturalized Mexicans, voter registration efforts, such as the Southwest Voter Registration Project in Texas, canvased Mexican immigrant communities in order to bring these New American citizens into politics. Voter registration efforts have proven successful, but project coordinators believe that the numbers could increase. Voter turnout remains another citizenship issue because Mexicans have a record of low turnout rates. The study of presidential politics and electoral politics in general demonstrates the interrelationship among Mexican immigrants, naturalized American citizens, and American-born Mexican Americans.

The national debate over Mexican immigration represents a contemporary issue that has emerged at the center of major political contests, including presidential elections. Prior to the 1996 presidential election, various reports by such research centers as the Tomás Rivera Center in California concluded that Mexican immigration would continue to represent an important political issue for Mexican-American voters. Although Mexican Americans have not always voted as a bloc, researchers predict that Mexican immigration policies will prove an important factor in determining which politician and political party captures the majority of the Mexican-American vote. In a 1996 study, Mexican Americans supported public policies that made immigrants eligible for the same social services as U.S. citizens. Polls also show that they are in favor of undocumented immigrants receiving social services if they pay taxes. In addition, Mexican Americans support continued accessibility to public schools by children of undocumented immigrants. California represents the state in which the impact of the Mexican-American vote remains key to understanding electoral politics. Political campaigns focus on the strength of the current population of Mexican-American voters and potential voters to be found among Mexican immigrants once they become American citizens.

The presidential election of 2000 witnessed increased attention by both the Democrats and the Republicans to mobilize the Mexican-American vote into their respective camps. Each political party knew that the Mexican-American vote has been historically democratic. As a result, Democrats wanted to maintain this democratic allegiance and Republicans hoped to bring in significant numbers of Mexican-American voters. In general, the Mexican-American vote remained democratic. Poll results consistently showed Mexican Americans supporting the Democratic Party on the basis of concrete political issues. Mexican Americans and Hispanics in general believed that the Clinton Administration had improved their economic situation—they believed they were even better off in 2000 than in 1996. Results also show that Mexican Americans believed that the Democratic Party had always supported more favorable immigration policies than Republicans. Mexican Americans also supported national and local Democratic leaders whom they believed called for a more humane position on undocumented immigrants. Furthermore, and more directly related to communities of non-voting Mexican immigrants, Democratic candidates supported stronger social services and, perhaps most important, educational programs for undocumented immigrants.

The Mexican-American vote will continue to play an important role in shaping the nature of American politics. Their views on issues directly related to immigration will continue to shape the gradual path toward a New American political identity among Mexican immigrants. For those Mexican immigrants who are not voters, seeing Mexican Americans participate in American electoral politics will continue to be a valuable civic lesson that ultimately will assist in the transition from immigrant to New American.

11

Children of Immigrants: The Second Generation

Immigrant groups arrive in the United States with dreams of beginning a new and better life. They leave their homeland with specific reasons that vary across groups. Some immigrants, such as Russian Jews in the nineteenth century, fled their country as persecution against them increased. Others, such as the Irish, left their homeland to escape the severe economic hardships brought on by the potato famine of the 1800s. All immigrants, including Mexicans, share a common dream: to assure a better life for themselves and for their children, particularly their American-born children. The process through which Mexican immigrants transform themselves into "New Americans" is shaped both by their own adjustment to their new country and by the experiences of their second-generation children.

ETHNIC IDENTITIES

As shown in previous chapters, immigrant culture was kept alive within immigrant communities long after the initial phase of immigration. This process was not a smooth one and was characterized by many identity conflicts and identity readjustments. Community studies of Italian immigrants, for example, illustrate that they created little "urban villages" within the larger Boston community. These Italian immigrants saw themselves as both Italian and American (Gans, 1962). More recently, Asian immigrants show a similar pattern of ethnic identity viewing themselves as both Asian and American (Cerulo, 1997; Espiritu, 1992; Posadas, 1999).

Mexican immigrants undergo this same process of identity formation (Garcia, 1999; Hondagneu-Sotelo, 1994). Mexican immigrants experience a transformation of identity as they increase their participation in American society and institutions. Their "memorias" or memories of their lives in Mexico become a source of cultural retention and, as the years go by, a source of cultural change. Mexican immigrants keep many of their Mexican cultural practices and values while blending American ones with their more traditional ones. Mexican immigrants transform themselves into New Americans with multiple sources of ethnic identity. A sense of being Mexican does not disappear as a new American identity emerges. Their American-born children experience a similar process of ethnic identity formation. Their identity develops both from the influence of their immigrant parents and their own experiences as American citizens. These Mexican-American children see themselves as bearers of two sources of ethnic identity that shape their own lives and that of their immigrant parents. This blending of ethnic identity is also influenced by their different experiences of social class, gender, and other important social experiences such as religion and region of the country.

Second-generation Mexican Americans express a sense of ethnic identity that cuts across two cultures. Many of their experiences within the larger American society are quite different than those of the immigrant parents. Many oral histories and essays by these children of Mexican immigrants capture the difficult position within which they find themselves in American society. The Latina writer Gloria Anzaldua captures this experience in one of her biographical essays: "I am a border woman, I grew up between two cultures, the Mexican (with a heavy Indian heritage) and the Anglo. . . . I have been straddling the tejas-Mexican border, and others, all my life. It's not a comfortable territory to live in, this place of contradictions" (Anzaldua, 1987: preface).

One way of understanding how second-generation Mexican Americans define their ethnic identities is to examine the different ethnic labels they confront while living in the United States with Mexican immigrant parents and extended family members. As one Mexican-American woman recalls:

> I used to work every summer in a large wholesale store that employed high school students from my neighborhood. I would hear a lot of different names used. I remember that one guy said his friends used Chicano but his parents said they didn't like it. I sometimes use Mexican American but sometimes I say Chicana. It is sort of a judgement call by me and even depends where I am. At home we use "Mexican" especially around my grandmother but it's mostly to avoid arguments

with her. She's from Mexico but has lived with us a long time. When I am with my friends from the softball team, I usually don't see myself like "ethnic" but I do say I have a Mexican heritage but I guess, now that I talk to you, that I still see myself as different, you know my skin is darker. But, it sounds confusing. (Interview with Emma Sanchez [ficitious name at interviewee's request] by Alma M. Garcia, 1997)

In her autobiography *Hoyt Street*, Mary Helen Ponce, herself an American-born daughter of Mexican parents (1993, 143), captures similar patterns of identity ambiguities when she describes her coming of age in a small town in southern California:

Our church did not have a statue of the Virgin of Guadalupe. This really bothered me. After all, *were we not Mejicanos?* Father Mueller constantly assured me that the Virgin Mary and Guadalupe were one and the same, but I never believed him. How could they be? One was from *Mexico* and had appeared to an Indian named Juan Diego. And the other? *She was American*, with blue eyes and blonde hair. Although I accepted them both as holy women, I *actually preferred the Virgin Mary*, she at least *understood English* (emphasis added).

Like Ponce, second-generation Mexican Americans maintain multilayered aspects of ethnic identities. They recognize that their identities are complex and always blending aspects of two or more cultures that they confront in American society like all other immigrants. On the one hand, like Ponce, their narratives document the early development of an ethnic Mexican way of life within their "Mejicano" families. Yet, on the other hand, second-generation Mexican Americans see themselves as different from their immigrant parents. Ponce says that she does not identify with an "American" version of the Virgin Mary with Anglo features. Yet in her autobiography, the young Mary Helen identifies ultimately with the English-speaking image of the Virgin Mary. Nevertheless, Ponce prefers English yet says she is "Mejicana." Many Mexican immigrant parents thought that they could best protect their children from discrimination if they made sure that they spoke English as a primary language.

Other autobiographical stories told by Mexican Americans reveal a basic understanding that their immigrant parents want a better life for them. Their stories are full of expressions of sincere gratitude that their parents left Mexico to improve their economic circumstances in order to secure a better future for their children. One Mexican-American woman related numerous family stories in which her parents recalled their immigration to the United States and the difficulties they encountered:

> My mom and dad were always telling me and my brothers that they dreamed of a better future for us. You know, they started out as farm workers and now my mom works in a box factory and my dad in construction. They don't want us to work at these kinds of jobs. Once my mom told me that she wanted me to be some kind of professional. (Interview with Dianna Gomez [fictitious name at interviewee's request] by Alma M. Garcia, 1997)

The formation of ethnic identity among Mexican Americans suggests that the transition from Mexican to American is not simple. Historian Vicki L. Ruiz's study (1993) of second-generation Mexican women who came of age during the 1930s and 1940s illustrates the generational conflicts between Mexican immigrant parents and their daughters as these young women experience the complex worlds of a traditional Mexican culture and the rise of an American "flapper" culture of the "Roaring Twenties." Using oral histories of Mexican women, Ruiz records the personal stories of these second-generation Mexican-American women. Ruiz concludes that Mexican-American women were not caught between two worlds: "[the] young Mexican woman may have looked like a flapper as she boarded a streetcar on her way to work at a cannery: yet she went to work (at least in part) to help support their family, as part of her obligation as a daughter. . . . Their experiences reveal the blending of the old and the new, fashioning new expectations, making choices, and learning to live with those choices" (Ruiz, 1993: 23).

An understanding of the lives of Mexican immigrant families requires an understanding of the lives and identity of second-generation American-born children of immigrant parents. This process is beautifully captured in Pat Mora's poem (1987) "Legal Alien":

> Bi-lingual, bi-cultural,
> able to slip from "How's life?"
> to "Me'stan volviendo loca" [They are driving me crazy],
> able to sit in a paneled office
> drafting memos in smooth English,
> able to order in fluent Spanish
> at a Mexican restaurant,
> American but hyphenated,
> viewed by Anglos as perhaps exotic,

perhaps inferior, definitely different,
viewed by Mexicans as alien,
(their eyes say, "You may speak
Spanish but you're not like me")
an American to Mexicans,
A Mexican to Americans,
a handy token
sliding back and forth
between the fringes-of-both-worlds
by smiling
by masking the discomfort
of being pre-judged—
Bi-laterally.

EDUCATIONAL ATTAINMENT LEVELS OF SECOND-GENERATION MEXICAN AMERICANS

Demographic information on Mexican Americans shows persistently low levels of education for this group. Although population differences relate to such factors as parents' immigrant status and geographic concentrations produce marked diversities within their communities, Mexican Americans have historically lacked access to high school and college. Major gaps exist between the Mexican-American population and whites. In 1990, 79 percent of the white population completed four years of high school or more in comparison to 44 percent for Mexican Americans. Data for 1998 show little improvement with 83 percent of the white population completing four years of high school or more in comparison to 48 percent for Mexican Americans. Over the last eight years, the gap between these two populations has not decreased significantly (U.S. Census Bureau, 1999).

Similar patterns are found when the two populations are compared using data from the census category of "persons who have completed four years of college or more." Over the last thirty years, the Mexican-American population has lagged significantly behind the white population. The increase from 1970 (2.5 percent) to 1998 (7.5 percent) is only 5 percent. For whites, the increase from 1970 to 1998 in college completion rates is 13.7 percent (1970: 11.39 percent; 1998: 25 percent). Although one-fourth of the white population has completed college or higher, less than 10 percent of the Mexican-American population has graduated from college.

The statistical data for Mexican-American women are difficult to obtain. When the U.S. Census Bureau provides data separated by race and ethnicity, it does not always control for gender. When it does, the umbrella category

"Hispanic" is typically used; this category includes Cuban Americans, Puerto Ricans, and Mexican Americans. The problem of using this umbrella category is that the data for Cuban Americans inflate the percentages due to this population's higher socioeconomic level. Specific data on the educational attainment levels of Mexican-American men and women are not available. The gender gap within the white population is larger than that for the Hispanic population from 1960 to 1998. White females have lower rates than their male counterparts than Hispanic females with Hispanic males. The average difference between white females and white males for the years 1960 to 1998 is 6.4 percent, whereas that in the Hispanic population is 1.71 percent. In 1998, the gap between white females and white males was 4.5 percent, whereas the comparable rate between Hispanic females and males is .2 percent. Thus, for Hispanics, ethnicity, not gender, is a more salient characteristic.

Although research findings suggest that Mexican-American women will continue to have limited access to higher education, research on those women who, against all odds, do attend and complete colleges and universities will contribute to the further understanding of the changing dynamics within second-generation Mexican-American communities.

Research studies on Mexican-American students and the educational system have pointed out several major factors in explaining their low levels of educational attainment in comparison to the total population. Some explanations have pointed to the following barriers to educational success among Mexican Americans: distinct cultural values and behavior patterns, low levels of achievement motivation, high levels of delayed gratification and other cultural factors. (Lareau, 1984; McClelland, 1965; Ringawa, 1980; Romo, 1984). The most recent studies stress the importance of the historic and contemporary barriers to higher education such as segregation, tracking, cultural biases in administrative and curricular organizational structures and institutional discrimination within the educational system, and the stresses and strains of high levels of poverty (Romo, 1984; Romo and Falbo, 1996; Segura, 1986; Solórzano, 1986). Research has also focused on the gender-specific effects of education on Mexican-American women in high schools and colleges. An early study concluded that structural barriers, not Mexican cultural values, worked against Mexican-American women achieving success within the educational system (Gándara, 1982). Other studies identified inadequate university support services and faculty mentoring as major factors in high dropout rates among Mexican-American women (Chacón et al., 1982). Although demographic profiles from the early 1980s are now quite dated, these pioneering studies found a direct relationship between persistent structural inequalities and the low levels of educational attainment among Mexican-American women:

> The structural inequities which seriously compromise the educational experience of Hispanic women at all levels of education, unfortunately are numerous. Beginning with tracking/ability grouping, we can progress to those inequities posed by racial segregation, improper teacher behavior, inappropriate instructional practices, lack of appropriate same sex/ethnic group role models, [and] inadequate counseling encounters. (McKenna and Ortiz, 1988: 11)

Various structural barriers are responsible for the underrepresentation of Mexican-American women and men in higher education. Education levels produce direct influences on the types of occupations and incomes of second-generation Mexican Americans. As indicated earlier, the Mexican-American population has not shown comparable educational levels with the total U.S. population although their educational attainment levels are higher than Mexican immigrants. One of the most striking differences between the Mexican-American population and the larger U.S. population is found in the rates of high school dropouts. The high school dropout rate for the total white population is 13 percent, whereas that for Hispanics, including Mexican Americans, is 45 percent. Education reflects a person's occupation and income, and higher education usually leads to better occupations and higher incomes.

A NATION IN TRANSITION

The latest report from the U.S. Census Bureau points out the dramatically changing nature of the country. The United States continues to emerge as a highly diverse society, and Hispanics have now reached parity with African Americans as the nation's largest minority group. According to the Census Bureau, the population increases witnessed during the last ten years have resulted from the massive increases in both the Asian and the Latino population. Latinos represent 12.5 percent of the 281.4 million people in the United States. The Latino population increased 58 percent since the 1990 census and now stands at 35.8 million. Immigration is seen as the major factor for this increase. The Asian population has followed similar trends. The Census Bureau estimates the increase in the Asian population as between 52 percent and 74 percent. In addition to the overall population increases, the Census reports that Latinos and Asians are moving into geographic areas of the country which historically have been home to only a small percentage of their population.

With the publication of these preliminary population figures obtained in the 2000 Census, many social issues will undoubtedly confront American society, for example, the diversity in population with the dramatic growth of such groups as Latinos. Many foresee the rise of social conflict among this diversity of racial and ethnic groups, particularly among recently arrived immigrants. Such issues as bilingual education, welfare, subsidized health care, and housing will be at the forefront. Another major issue will be the growing political potential of Latinos.

Latinos now hold 5,138 elected political offices in the United States. This number includes nineteen members of the House of Representatives. It is always important to draw comparisons between the Latinos and African Americans. African Americans hold 8,936 elected offices, including fifty-nine members of the House of Representatives. Although increases in population do not automatically produce an increase in political power, Latinos will continue to be targeted by both Democrats and Republicans in an effort to harness their voting power. Historically, African Americans developed various types of political and community organizations in their attempts to form a significant voting bloc. In the past, Latinos, particularly Mexican Americans due to continued Mexican immigration, have had more difficulties than African Americans in securing their political base of power. Approximately 39 percent of all Mexicans over the age of eighteen are not American citizens. The Mexican-American population continues to be a much younger population than all other racial/ethnic groups in the United States. For these reasons, it is understandable that Mexican Americans face vastly different obstacles related to political mobilization than African Americans. Nevertheless, Mexican-American community organizations are (1) increasing their efforts to help Mexican immigrants become American citizens, and (2) organizing voter registration campaigns for those already citizens and American-born Mexicans. Political scientists expect that the twenty-first century will see the rise of key political organizations within Latino communities. According to Harry Pachón, president of the Tómas Rivera Policy Institute, located in Claremont, California, "Latinos are penetrating every institution of American society. America is being Latinized, and Latinos are being Americanized" (*San Jose Mercury News*, March 13, 2001, p. 20A).

THE LATINO WAVE IN AMERICAN CULTURE

Over the last decade, Latinos, including second-generation Mexican Americans, have created a cultural wave that has contributed to the growing diversity of American society and culture. Magazines such as *Time*, *Newsweek*, and *Business Week* have all carried articles on the growing impact of Latino culture in the United States. The children, grandchildren, and even great grandchildren of Mexican and other Latino immigrants are contributing a Latino cultural flavor to American society, particularly in popular culture such as music, television, and films. Many factors contribute to this ever-rising Latino wave. The American-born Mexican population has increased dramatically due to high birthrates and immigration. The Latino population has increased by 38 percent since 1990, whereas the overall population has grown only 9 percent. In addition, the Latino population is very young, with more than one-third younger than eighteen. By 2005, Latinos will be the largest minority in the country, surpassing the African-American population. As a result of such trends in population growth, particularly growth in American-born and legal immigrants eligible for citizenship, an important Latino influence in politics is already developing. Although Latinos represent a small portion (6 percent) of all voters, they are concentrated in eleven states holding 217 of the 270 electoral votes needed to elect the president. All over the country, in national, state, and local elections, candidates from different political parties recognize the importance of developing specific campaign strategies to win Latino votes. These campaigns have produced television, radio, and printed media political campaigns aimed at Latino communities.

The emerging Latino wave is most visible in popular culture. The Latino population represents a diversity of backgrounds, and each particular group of Latinos, such as Mexican Americans, leaves its own distinct mark on American society. *Newsweek* calls this Latino wave the "Generation ñ" (Spanish letter of the alphabet pronounced "en-yay"). Others, including many Latinos themselves, refer to the "Generacíon Latino." A feature story in *Newsweek* (July 12, 1999) on Latino culture examines this diversity of cultural experiences: "Latinos can't be neatly pigeonholed. They come from 22 different countries of origin, including every hybrid possible. Many are white, some are black, but most are somewhere in between. Some Latino families have been in the United States for centuries, since the days when much of the Southwest was still a part of Mexico."

This Latino cultural influence can be seen in the growing Latinization of dance and music on the American youth scene. Salsa music is heard throughout Latino communities. Nightclubs with a predominately Anglo clientele have regular "Salsa Nights" but also integrate the Latin Beat on a regular basis. Tejana music singer Selena Quintanilla Perez remains one of the most widely known Mexican-American vocal artists, particularly after her untimely murder in 1995 at the age of twenty-three. Originating from South Texas of Mexican-American parents, Selena started her singing career at an early age with her own band that included her brother and sister. Their band, Los Dinos, drew large audiences throughout the Southwest and eventually in Mexico, where she charmed music critics and journalists alike with her mixture of English and Spanish, a common practice among many Mexican Americans. Selena confronted the world of Tex-Mex music, a traditionally male-dominated music genre. She won the Female Vocalist of the Year from the Tejano Music Awards in 1987, and then in 1994 she received a Grammy award for her recording "Amor Prohibido" (Forbidden Love). She eventually began singing and recording in Spanish, which she learned phonetically since, like many Mexican Americans, she had a very limited command of the Spanish language. Her single "Como la Flor" (Like the Flower) reached number one on the charts in a matter of weeks. Selena made a cameo singing appearance in the film, *Don Juan De Marco*, and her image in a long white floral gown became one of her signature fashion pieces. In 1995, Selena drew the largest audience in the history of Houston's Astrodome, an attendance record that still stands. When she was killed by her fan club president, the *New York Times* carried the article on its front page. For hundreds of young Mexican-American adolescent girls, Selena became and remains a pop icon. Her dark features and curvaceous body resonated with a large cross-section of young Latinas whose features often differed from the tall and slender image popularized in most media images. Soon after her death, a Selena Barbie-like doll sold out in a few days at toy stores across the Southwest. The movie *Selena*, starring Latina Jennifer Lopez, brought this singer's short life to the attention of national American audiences. In addition, this starring role helped the acting career of the then-aspiring actress Jennifer Lopez, who soon starred in many hit films. Lopez has now branched out into the recording industry.

Other musical forms, the more traditional Mexican ballads, continue to be played by radio stations throughout the United States, which feature such rising stars as Enrique Iglesias, Alejandro Fernández, and other Latino artists, including those with Latin American cultural heritages other than Mexican. Even the Mexican-American boxing sensation Oscar de la Hoya has burst onto the music scene and received a Grammy nomination in 2000. Recently pop diva Christina Aguilera produced a cross-over Spanish-language CD with her recording of "Mi Reflejo." Ricky Martin's appearance on the Grammy

Awards in 1999 heralded him into the American culture. Martin was even featured on the cover of *Time* a few months later. Other Latino artists are continuing to ride on the Latino wave. Rapper Big Pun is the first Latino hip hop artist to have a recording go platinum. The group Co-Note is one of the new "boy-group" artists. Enrique and Julio Iglesias Jr., sons of romantic singer Julio Iglesias, continue to expand their singing careers in both the United States and Latin America. Other artists such as Marc Anthony, Shakira, and Chayanne are popular among Latinos and Anglos. In general the diversity within Latino communities produces an equally diverse spectrum of musical styles, including Mexican banda, TexMex, Salsa, mariachi, and a growing trend in American-style pop, rap, and hip hop music. Given the population projections for the early years of the twenty-first century, the Latino wave will surge to even greater heights.

The television industry has been quick to recognize the growing Latino market by adopting strategies targeted to this population. Demographic changes have speeded the development of Latino television programming. In the past, the television industry separated their corporate planning categories into general audiences and Latino audiences. But with the ever-growing Latino market, television networks are integrating their Latino viewers' interests into their mainstream offerings. They base these new strategies on such population trends as the fact that there are some 31 million Latinos in the United States, the majority of whom are television viewers representing a significantly large consumer market. A growing percentage of revenues from paid commercial advertising is coming from advertisers who target this expanding Latino market. A recent estimate by the National Hispanic Merchants' Coalition puts the Latin purchasing power at $370 billion. Several American soap operas have featured Latinos, the most famous being megastar Ricky Martin who appeared on *General Hospital* before his explosion on the American music scene with his recording of "La Vida Loca." Syndicated news programs include regular feature stories of interest to Latino audiences with some directly related to Mexican-American communities. Television programming, particularly situation comedies and dramas, have lagged behind with only a limited number of shows featuring a Latino actor. Mexican-American Hector Elizondo is one example with his starring role in the popular drama *Chicago Hope.* In the past, such actors as Desi Arnaz (*I Love Lucy*) and Ricardo Montalbán (*Fantasy Island*) became trailblazers for the small number of Latinos presently appearing in television programs.

Programming for Latino-American audiences is not limited to the American television industry. Spanish-language television networks such as Univision and Telemundo target Mexican-American and Latino viewers in general. Some programming is geared to older audiences with a strong command of the Spanish language, but the newest trend is to aim at younger Latinos who may have only limited or no Spanish language skills. The SITV production company develops Latino-based programs that are mostly in English for such networks as the cable station Galavision. Although these production companies and networks understand that the growing numbers of young Latinos prefer the English language, many older viewers continue to live in bilingual worlds, preferring mainly Spanish-language programming. According to one network spokesperson: "Language should be used situationally, to reflect how real Hispanics live. At work, a character would speak to his boss in English, at home, speak to his family in Spanish, and later think about his boss in Spanish" (*American Demographics*, March 1999).

Mexican immigrants come to the United States and, as the years go by, undergo the complex process of becoming New Americans. Their American-born children—the second generation—represent a major force that shapes the new lives of Mexican immigrants. The experiences of the second generation affect the daily lives of their immigrant parents. Together the experiences of the first and second generations contribute to the diversity of cultures in American society.

12

The Future of U.S.–Mexico Relations

With the election of President Vicente Fox Quesada, the first opposition party candidate in the history of modern Mexican politics who broke the monopoly of the ruling political party (PRI), Mexico set itself on the road to economic reform. Mexicans viewed President George W. Bush's visit to Mexico, his first foreign trip after his election, as an important sign that Mexico had turned the corner in terms of its position in the world political and economic scene. With all the reforms realized through the implementation of the North Atlantic Free Trade Agreement (NAFTA), Mexico, under the leadership of President Fox, hopes to put its cycle of economic crises in its past by revamping its national economic programs. During his presidential campaign, Fox pledged to bring Mexico full circle from its former financial setbacks and economic and political scandals to a place alongside countries such as the United States, but many obstacles are confronting Mexico in its attempt to modernize its economy.

MEXICO'S BORDER PROBLEMS

Mexico's northern border region experienced the impact of a bilateral industrialization policy between Mexico and the United States, called the Maquiladora Program, which involved the introduction of assemblyline computer and electronic work. Although the Mexican government hoped that this type of industrialization would bring the country out of its economic stagnation, the immediate and long-range consequences of maquiladora industrialization has fallen short of what Mexican leaders and economic advisors had anticipated. The Mexican border region has always helped to shape the nature and extent of Mexican immigration to the United States, and developments in this region further emphasize the relationship between Mexico's economic and social difficulties and increased Mexican immigration to both Mexico's northern region and to the United States.

Another problem directly related to economic conditions along the border involves the changing nature of working conditions within the maquiladoras. Since their origin in the late 1960s, border assembly plants have represented new opportunities for obtaining an improved standard of living for many Mexicans, particularly young women. Attracted by their modern, urban setting, the plants have drawn a constant stream of workers. According to recent investigations, the Mexican border is experiencing many new social problems that researchers estimate will lead to the growth of Mexican immigration, which will in turn contribute to changing demographic patterns in the United States. When the largest maquiladoras were established in the 1960s, Mexico's unemployment had reached an all-time high, suggesting the possibility of widespread social unrest and political instability. The maquiladoras relied almost exclusively on a supply of steady workers, mostly women who had never been in the paid labor force. The maquiladora industrialization program never fully succeeded in significantly lowering Mexico's spiraling unemployment. NAFTA produced an increase of employment opportunities in the border region. Although the maquiladora program had previously resulted in a large-scale migration of workers from other parts of Mexico, NAFTA sparked an even larger increase in migration rates within the country and a renewed influx of international companies setting up plants all along the Mexican border. Companies such as Alcoa, Delphi Automotive Systems, and General Electric have all been attracted to Mexico as a result of a growing source of cheap labor and the introduction of new tax breaks resulting from NAFTA.

Since the mid-1990s, most assembly plants have increased their production, bringing even larger numbers of workers from all regions of Mexico to the border. An example of this population explosion can be seen in Ciudad Acuña, a town opposite Del Rio, Texas. Alcoa moved its automotive wiring system plants from Mississippi to Ciudad Acuña, attracting large numbers of workers. The city grew faster than any other city in northern Mexico. The 2000 Census recorded 110,390 residents, representing an increase of about 80,000 from the late 1970s. A total of sixty maquiladoras have been established in this city. Ciudad Acuña, like other border towns with new maquiladora plants, was not prepared for this population increase; available housing for workers was very limited. In order to survive, Mexican workers began a practice that workers in urban centers throughout Latin America have adopted for decades. Workers built makeshift housing units, creating what are referred to as "squatter settlements": slumlike housing settlements whose residents face poverty on a daily basis. Adjacent to almost every maquiladora plant, squatter settlements now dot the border's urban landscape as assembly plant workers often find themselves worse off than they were in their hometown, before they moved to Mexico's border region (*New York Times*, February 11, 2001, pp. 1, 6).

The social costs of these economic developments are becoming more evident. Although Mexican workers are attracted to these new employment opportunities in an effort to improve their lives, Mexican border cities experienced the negative impact of such a rapidly growing population. All along the U.S. and Mexican border, Mexican cities find themselves overburdened by this sudden surge in population density. It is estimated that between 1996 and 2001, 5 million Mexicans have left their homes in other areas of the country to settle in such cities as Ciudad Juarez, Mexicali, and Reynosa.

Both Mexican and American economists see the border as the site for new trends in business and employment policies best fitted for the twenty-first century, but, at the same time, they also recognize that this area is experiencing and will continue to experience major social problems. Border cities find themselves without the social and economic resources to deal with the tremendous strain placed on them by such a dramatically increasing population. Given their financial resources, cities are finding it difficult to handle the basic social service needs of their residents. Meeting the basic needs of health care, education, housing, and water and energy represents some of the major problems associated with the new industrialization patterns in this border region of Mexico. Estimates indicate that border cities can treat less than 35 percent of their sewage needs. Almost one-third of their citizens lack adequate housing, and 12 percent lack any reliable source of potable water. Workers living along Mexico's border express their deteriorating living conditions. The wife of a bus driver whose bus line takes maquiladora workers to and from the plants expressed her concern with the lack of sufficient water for her family, particularly her children. She limits herself to one glass of water a day in order to meet the needs of her children. She told a journalist that during the winter her rationing of the water supply keeps her children from being thirsty, "but in the summer, they need a lot of water. And there is not always enough" (Thompson, *New York Times*, February 11, 2001, p. 6).

Many maquiladoras have initiated policies to help alleviate some of the harsh conditions experienced by their workers both in the assembly plants and in their neighborhoods. Wage increases have been taking effect, but on the whole these increases have been minimal. More success can be seen in the actual working conditions, including better lighting, improved ventilation, on-site medical services, and renovated workers' cafeterias. Alcoa is one of the maquiladoras that has made large, direct contributions to local governments, such as Ciudad Acuña. The company donated a $50,000 ambulance in 1998, and in 1999, it joined Ford Motor Company in starting the Ford–Alcoa elementary school. Alcoa has set the standard for other assembly plants by donating about $170,000 for several community projects in Ciudad Acuña, including a recreational facility. Despite these efforts, the general standard of living in this region of Mexico has left many Mexicans with few options. One option that is the most common today, as in the past, is immigration to the United States.

Continued increases in Mexican immigration to the cities along the American side of the border has led to deteriorating conditions in these areas. All along the border, particularly in Texas, Mexican immigrants face similarly harsh living conditions. During their first visit with each other, President George W. Bush and President Vicente Fox identified the increased economic difficulties experienced by local communities along the U.S.–Mexico border as a top priority for their respective administrations. Many experts estimate the cost of a border assistance program would be about $20 billion. Both governments have pledged major contributions in an effort to improve living conditions along the border. President Fox called for an increase in the taxes paid by owners of maquiladoras to the Mexican government. Many plant owners are delaying their plans for greater expansion into Mexico until Fox's tax plan is fully revealed. President Fox has increased his commitment to focus on the social ills plaguing the country's northern border region. Mexicans on both sides of the border will continue to be affected by social and economic difficulties along the border. Future changes in the nature of the maquiladora assembly plants, the taxation policies of the Mexican government, the role of the United States in assisting Mexico deal with its economic problems, and the economic situation in the United States will all continue to affect the rates of Mexican immigration to the United States.

A growing problem associated with increases in Mexican immigration, specifically undocumented immigration, involves the often tragic consequences associated with the journey to the United States. Historically, the 2,000 mile border, "la Frontera," has been characterized as an open door, with law enforcement agencies facing the monumental task of keeping undocumented immigrants from entering the country. Over the last few years, the Border Patrol has adopted new and improved technology aimed at making their jobs more successful by apprehending and deporting those Mexican immigrants who circumvented the legal process of immigration by taking their chances of crossing the border undetected. Although the Border Patrol has increased its numbers of apprehensions and deportations, most undocumented Mexicans who experience deportation usually reenter the United States by crossing at more remote and less patrolled areas. Mexican immigrants attempting to enter in this way face numerous obstacles. Many cross into the United States by way of the Arizona desert and are ill-equipped to handle the extremely high day temperatures, the lack of water, and the low night temperatures.

Robbery and murder of undocumented immigrants are also on the rise— often at the hands of unscrupulous agents who are contracted by the undocumented to assist them in the border crossing. During the brief period from February 8, 2001, to September 21, 2001, a total of twenty-eight persons died or were killed along the border. The INS reported 261 immigrant deaths in 1998, and 369 in 2000. More deaths were most likely not reported. The Border Patrol divides the border region into various sectors, and its Tucson, Arizona, and El Centro, California, sectors had the highest number of reported deaths because these regions are characterized by exceptionally treacherous deserts and rugged mountains. About 40 percent of these deaths were due to exposure. The Border Patrol has increased its rescue capabilities in an effort to reduce death rates among immigrants. In 1999, 1,041 persons were rescued, and in 2000, this number doubled to 2,054 (Zeller, *New York Times*, March 18, 2001, p. 14).

A study conducted by the Center for Immigration Research at the University of Houston found that the number of immigrant deaths near their border crossings has increased as the surveillance and apprehension practices of the Border Patrol have increased. The study points out that illegal border crossings have always posed a serious threat to the safety of Mexican immigrants with drowning accounting for large numbers of deaths. Homicides and pedestrian accidents have also been common along the U.S.–Mexico border. The growing practice among Mexican immigrants of stowing away in boxcars and secret compartments in trucks has led to an increase in deaths by suffocation and heat stroke. Current research by the Center for Immigration Research has focused on the recent years during which the Border Patrol has significantly increased its actions in controlling the flow of undocumented persons. The study concludes that although these efforts do contain the entrance of large number of undocumented Mexican immigrants in those areas of increased Border Patrol activity, the general flow of immigrants shifts to another point along the border, usually to those isolated and more treacherous locations such as the Tucson and El Centro sectors. One Mexican immigrant attempted to enter the United States in one of these more remote areas after a smuggler suggested that he try to cross the border near Nogales, Arizona. The Mexican immigrant paid the smuggler $1,000 for a ride in a poorly ventilated van, overcrowded with other immigrants. When the Border Patrol stopped the van and ordered him and the other immigrants to get out, he escaped by running deep into the desert. This undocumented worker was eventually rescued by the Border Patrol. Although this Mexican came close to death from exposure to the desert, he admitted that he would keep trying to enter the United States in search of work and a better life (www.uh.edu/cir/death.htm).

RETURN MIGRATION FROM THE UNITED STATES TO MEXICO

The process of return migration to Mexico represents one of the newest developments in the study of Mexican immigrants living in communities throughout the United States. At the same time that a constant flow of Mexican immigrants is increasing, particularly in California, a growing number of immigrants return to Mexico for extended periods of time before returning to the United States. Throughout the twentieth century, during each major wave of Mexican immigration, a certain percentage of Mexicans did not remain in the United States, preferring to return to their Mexican towns and villages usually after they had saved enough money to help them improve their lives upon their return to Mexico. Information gathered from both the U.S. Census and recent studies of Mexican immigrant communities suggest an increase in return migration. An overview of the process of return migration, the return of immigrants to their homeland after staying a few years in their host country, will contribute to a deeper understanding of Mexican immigrant communities.

A summary of the major conclusions outlined in several studies of return migration begins with the finding that some undocumented immigrants are more likely to return to Mexico after a few years. Interviews with immigrants suggest that the longer their experiences with unemployment, the more likely they will be to leave the United States and return to Mexico. The high levels of unemployment of undocumented workers is due largely to their lower educational levels in comparison with documented Mexican immigrants. For example, about one-half of documented Mexicans with less than a grade school education return to Mexico within two years. Nevertheless, undocumented immigrants still have higher rates of return migration than the documented immigrants: 50 percent of undocumented workers leave the United States within the first year of immigration. Undocumented women have a slightly lower rate of return migration than their male counterparts. Both men and women who are undocumented and undergo return migration have resided in only one location during their stay in contrast to those who decide to make their homes in the United States.

The financial cost of social services used by immigrants has always been one of the major public policy issues that has shaped America's view of immigration. Studies of return migration suggest that those Mexican immigrants who are largely undocumented and who eventually return to Mexico represent a very small percentage of those immigrants who use such services as public assistance and other social welfare services. Return migrants do, however, use emergency medical services and regular health care that the Medicaid program covers. In addition, undocumented workers, whether they return to Mexico, do not qualify for the Special Supplemental Food Program for Women, Infants, and Children, food stamps, and other similar programs unless their children are American citizens. Documented immigrants, however, are eligible for services but only after a stipulated waiting period. They can receive food stamps and Supplemental Security Income after they have worked for a given period of time. Interestingly, those documented Mexican workers who stay the longest—more than ten years—usually have the highest levels of education, best job skills, and lowest unemployment rates and as a result have the lowest utilization rates for social service programs. One final conclusion regarding the rates of Mexican immigration must always be kept in mind: regardless of the levels of return migration, future rates of Mexican immigration will continue to increase as long as Mexico's economy continues to hold only limited avenues for improved living conditions for those Mexicans near the bottom of the country's economic ladder (Reyes, 1997).

An additional way of understanding the issue of return migration is to understand the transnational feature of contemporary movements of Mexican immigrants back and forth between Mexico and the United States. A developing trend among Mexicans is to return to Mexico for a given period of time, from a few months to a few years, and then return to the United States. For many, this process is repeated throughout their lives. This transnational immigration is usually referred to as migration patterns in order to highlight the repeated process of movement between one country and another. Such a migration pattern is not found among all immigrants due to a variety of reasons, including the proximity to Mexico, social and political conditions, transportation costs, and other factors. In addition, the host country's legal provisions for reentry by immigrants may also work as an obstacle to transnational migration. Given the nature of the U.S.–Mexican border, Mexicans find it relatively easy to include return trips to Mexico. Some Mexicans attempt to circumvent the residency requirements for citizenship that call for uninterrupted residence in the United States by reentering the United States without going through the border checkpoints. Immigrants who experience transnational migration contribute to the cultural and social experiences of the communities within which they live in the United States and Mexico. In turn, these experiences affect all Americans.

MEXICAN PRESIDENTIAL POLITICS AND MEXICAN IMMIGRANTS

Vicente Fox Quesada was inaugurated as Mexico's president on December 2, 2000, and beginning with his inaugural speech, Fox pledged to move Mexico on the path of popular democracy and national and regional economic development by initiating a series of reforms aimed at breaking Mexico's political and economic stalemates. Although his National Action Party (PAN) failed to win a majority in the Mexican Congress, Fox and his cabinet ministers outlined a political program that promised to usher in a new era of Mexican politics, particularly foreign relations with the United States. The Mexican president identified Mexican immigration as one of the major issues he will address, pointing out that the struggle for a better Mexico is tied to Mexican immigration to the United States.

A steady increase in Mexico's level of economic growth, according to Fox, will enable the country's most at-risk social groups, such as low-skilled or unskilled urban workers, to find suitable employment that will provide them with a decent standard of living for themselves and for their families. The success of such an economic plan will check the constantly increasing flow of Mexican immigrants across the border. Fox hopes to provide the financial support necessary for national industries to be able to increase their production and be in a better position to provide stable employment for the large numbers of Mexicans who find themselves chronically unemployed. The Mexican president also included the introduction and passage of legislation that will facilitate specific types of foreign investment, particularly from the United States, which, in turn, will further bolster a more diversified and dynamic economy in the country, decreasing the need for immigration, particularly undocumented immigration.

Fox stressed the theme of mutual political and economic cooperation between Mexico and the United States when President George W. Bush visited Mexico, the site of his first foreign trip as president. The two leaders met on February 16, 2001, and outlined a bilateral plan for improved relations that will be implemented over the next few years with the approval of both. The focal point of this plan involves short- and long-term economic strategies designed to sustain growth and stability. Both leaders agreed that the most effective remedy for the influx of undocumented Mexicans into the United States is to provide the foundations for a more prosperous Mexican economy. Secretary of State General Colin Powell summarized this strategy during his visit to Mexico: "The thing that really has to be done to solve this problem is to continue to help the Mexican economy grow, so that jobs are in the south [Mexico], so that the great magnet is no longer just in the north [United States], but it is also within Mexico" (*New York Times*, January 31, 2001, p. 31). According to preliminary data gathered by the U.S. Census Bureau and the INS, the number of undocumented Mexican immigrants has already decreased since the election of Vicente Fox.

President Fox's commitment to this bilateral policy is directly related to his concern for the millions of Mexican immigrants currently living in the United States. Fox made it clear during his first months in office, during his visit with President Bush, and during his own trip to California in March 2001, that his administration wants to find a remedy for the plight of Mexican immigrants, specifically undocumented immigrants who confront a precarious existence as workers in the United States. Prior to his meeting with President Bush, Fox traveled to the border during Christmas, a time when many Mexicans living in the United States make the trip back to their homes in Mexico. All along his stops on the border, Fox repeated his pledge to investigate the conditions of Mexican immigrants. At one such stop in Nogales, Mexico, a border town on the Arizona border, the Mexican president went so far as to call Mexico's population of immigrants modern-day "heroes" for their courage in making their annual Christmas trip back to Mexico, although they are usually confronted by long delays and even harassment by American immigration border officials when they try to reenter the United States. Undocumented Mexicans face even greater risks and dangers as they attempt to enter the United States after their stay in Mexico.

Although still in the planning stage, President Fox has proposed a plan for dealing with the immigration issue. During his tour of the border, Fox included talks with ordinary Mexicans, departing from his predecessor's practice of interacting primarily with Mexican political elites and American diplomats. Fox listened to the descriptions of immigrant living conditions in the United States provided by those who had spent some time there. Fox repeatedly voiced his dismay that the working and living conditions of Mexican immigrants have shown little signs of progress. Although other Mexican presidents have toured the United States and other American presidents have included trips to Mexico on a regular basis, President Fox has expressed his concern, calling for concerted bilateral efforts to alleviate the problems facing Mexican immigrants in the United States. His policy suggestions include facilitating border crossings of documented Mexicans and increasing the total number of visas available for documented Mexican immigrants. Fox is critical of his country's economic policies under the PRI which led to millions of Mexicans making the trip north to the United States in hopes of a better life for their families. Fox stressed that workers leave Mexico out of an economic desperation that will only be alleviated by the implementation of economic measures that introduce sustained growth for the country. Until such a plan can produce this desired goal, Fox remains concerned with the plight of those Mexicans seeking relief as immigrants. He has expressed alarm at the spiraling death rates of undocumented Mexicans as they entered the United States, usually exposing themselves to the harsh desert conditions and threats from robbers. Fox has created a new cabinet-level office that will monitor the conditions along the border and those in Mexican immigrant communities in the United States.

Fox also expressed his support for the legalization of undocumented Mexican workers living in the United States, a long-standing controversial issue for both the United States and Mexico. His position is that the legalization of Mexican workers will prove beneficial for both countries. The United States will be able to reduce the operating budget of both the Border Patrol and the INS and, in addition, will be able to expand its tax base with this increase in citizens who are eligible to pay income tax. According to Fox, Mexico would benefit as a result of the projected increases in the remittances already being sent to Mexico by undocumented immigrants who would be able to make bank transfers without the fear of apprehension and deportation. Remittances by Mexican immigrants represent an important source of revenue for the country. The money that immigrants send home boosts the economy of many towns and villages with which immigrants retain family ties. According to both American and Mexican sources, Mexicans remit anywhere from $6 billion and $8 billion annually, making them the third largest legitimate sector of the country's economy after oil and tourism. Income for drug trafficking also numbers in the billions. Despite President Fox's position on the importance of remittances, he is steadfast in supporting a policy that will provide American citizenship for Mexican undocumented workers. Fox's plan gained support from a broad spectrum of American politics, including some labor leaders; Federal Reserve chairman Alan Greenspan; and senior Republican Senator Phil Gramm. They all support the legalization of Mexican workers in order for them to improve themselves economically, contribute to the overall U.S. economic prosperity, and eventually return to Mexico. In addition, supporters in the United States view this policy of legalization as an important means for strengthening ties between the two countries. Mexico's oil and electricity is seen by many as a potential source of energy to support the ever-increasing needs of states such as California. Such a hemispheric energy policy would meet the needs of the United States and Mexico's economic problems—both of which will continue to challenge each country during this first decade of the twenty-first century. Mexican immigrants represent key players in such bilateral foreign policy decisions. The future will show how effective these developments in Mexican presidential politics have been in dealing with the lives of these New Americans, whether they live as immigrants in the United States, Mexico, or in a transnational world, living in each country for extended periods of time.

13

Toward a Twenty-first Century of Diversity: The New American Society

With the ushering in of the twenty-first century, Americans have started to reflect on the challenges facing them as a society. The framers of our Constitution could never have anticipated the radical social transformations that the United States would experience, particularly in terms of demographic changes brought on, to a large extent, by increasing rates of immigration, specifically from Mexico. The population data from the 2000 Census reveals that American society is moving closer to a nation where no one racial/ethnic group is in the majority in terms of population percentages. The new millennium in American history will be one in which diversity and multiculturalism will take center stage in our country's public life and our own private lives as Americans.

THE TWENTY-FIRST CENTURY AND THE U.S. POPULATION

In general the newly released Census figures document a significant increase in two major groups: Asians and Latinos—specifically Mexicans. Both groups are contributing to the increased diversity in the United States in figures that surpass any ever recorded by the U.S. Census Bureau. The growth rate of the Asian population represents a continuation of a trend seen throughout the 1980s and 1990s. The Asian population increased by at least 52 percent to as much as 74 percent. This increase reflects two patterns among Asians. First, the number of Asians immigrating to the United States has not declined since the 1990 census. Second, this increase reflects the introduction of a new category of "multiracial," which enables individuals to mark more than one racial identification. The Census Bureau estimates that this new category explains the large number of Asians counted in the 2000 Census, with Asians now the third largest minority group. Demographers see Asian immigration as the primary reason for such a population growth and point out that it has been driven by the Immigration Act of 1965 that eliminated the existing quotas for Asian immigration. According to Diane Chin, executive director of the Chinese for Affirmative Action, a civil rights group in San Francisco, California, these population changes will have to be met with more public policy initiatives aimed at integrating these New Americans (*San Jose Mercury News*, March 13, 2001, p. 20A).

Mexican immigration is also contributing to a changing, more diverse American society. Like Asian immigrants, Mexican immigration is considered the primary factor accounting for the dramatic increase of the Mexican population documented in the latest Census figures. Records illustrate that about 50 percent of the population growth in the United States can be attributed to the growth rates of Asians and Latinos, Mexicans, and other Hispanics such as Puerto Ricans and Central Americans. The number of Hispanics grew by 58 percent or 35 million. Latinos are now 12 percent of the total population of the United States, which numbers 282 million according to the most recent Census reports. Latinos will soon be the largest minority group, numbering more than African Americans. They will continue to be characterized by an age structure that distinguishes them from all other groups; the average age of Mexicans is much lower than all other groups.

California is the state that will have to deal with the largest number of Mexicans in comparison to all other states. The year 2000 marks the first year that whites are no longer their largest population. Latinos make up one-third of California's total population of 34 million residents and represent four out of every five of the newest residents. High rates of Mexican immigration and high birthrates that surpass all other immigrant groups account for such population changes in the state. Los Angeles County has more Latinos (4 million) than the total population of Oregon. The largest influx of Latinos is, as in the past, seen in the state's major urban centers such as Los Angeles and the San Francisco Bay area. In the Bay area, the Latino population grew at a similar rate as the entire state (42 percent). The age structure of this urban center reflects statewide trends in which Latinos are characterized as a younger population. California's adult population remains predominately white (52 percent), whereas the population under eighteen years of age is only 35 percent white. The growth in the Latino and Asian populations represents a dramatic demographic shift. The African-American population represented both the largest minority group and the fastest growing group in California. For example, the national population increase for the African-American population was 14 percent during the 1990s, but they were responsible for only 14 percent of the new residents in California during this same time period.

The Census Bureau statistics do not differentiate between immigrant and U.S.-born children of immigrants, but some figures on direct immigration are available from reports from the INS. Between 1900 and 1998, an estimated 3 million legal immigrants, the majority from Asia and Latin America, entered California. The legal immigration of 170,000 to California in 1998 accounted for 26 percent of the country's total legal immigration. A major explanation for the increases in Latino immigration is the cultural similarities between, for example, Mexico and California. Mexican immigrants come to the United States, specifically California, and find an entire array of cultural practices, activities, and networks that make the state appear to be a continuation of their Mexican lives and cultural traditions that they thought were being left behind. Mexican immigrants feel "at home" even if they are now in a new home where they become New Americans.

FUTURE SOCIAL POLICY IMPLICATIONS

The most current Census Bureau information points toward a continuous influx of Mexican immigrants, particularly to California. Such projections have a direct impact in the development and future implementation of social policies to deal with the ever increasing numbers of Mexicans that will shape the course of American society throughout the twenty-first century. Many issues will remain in the spotlight. First, demographic studies predict that the greatest population growth rates of Mexican immigrants will be from the influx of undocumented individuals. Studies of contemporary undocumented Mexicans show that the group's overall educational levels are lower than those in the last twenty years. This education characteristic affects the occupational experiences of Mexican immigrants once they enter the United States. An overall pattern of economic marginality can already be seen among recently arrived Mexican immigrants, specifically undocumented workers, and immigrants will continue to face the reality of limited occupational opportunities. It is expected that Mexican immigrants will continue to have high fertility rates, creating a younger generation of American-born children whose immigrant parents make up an "at risk" population.

A variety of public policies are being proposed in anticipation of these problems. Debates over public welfare and housing have played a key role in local and state elections. Proposals to curb immigration continue to appear at the same time that some policies are being adopted to make citizenship available to undocumented Mexican immigrants. An example of one of the most recent legislative acts addressing citizenship for undocumented immigrants is the Legal Immigration Family Equity Act (The Life Act). This act made provisions for undocumented immigrants to apply for their visas without first returning to their home countries, a stipulation of existing requirements for citizenship. To take advantage of this act, undocumented immigrants are required to have a sponsor and have a close relative who is a U.S. citizen or a permanent resident. At the same time that undocumented immigrants were waiting in long lines to file their citizenship applications under the Life Act, President George W. Bush carried out his 2000 campaign promise to overhaul the Immigration and Naturalization Service by announcing his nomination for chief of the INS. As in the past, both Mexican immigrants and Mexican Americans demonstrate caution whenever a Republican administration issues a call to reorganize the INS. The relationship between the INS and Mexican immigrants, documented and undocumented, will most certainly continue to be an issue into the twenty-first century.

Other public policy issues underline the need to improve the socioeconomic status of Mexican immigrants currently residing in the United States and those who will make the trip from Mexico in the future. Many policymakers and experts on Mexican immigration agree that the starting point is education. Raising the level and quality of education for Mexican immigrants and their children is identified as a cornerstone of public policy that will prove the most effective in improving the everyday living conditions of Mexican immigrants, which in turn will benefit American society in general. An alarming rise in teenage pregnancies is also seen as a major health issue, and many local agencies are attempting to increase their funds in order to maintain strong family planning services. Although family planning centers have been making a difference in lowering the rates of teenage pregnancies, the rates continue to show a marked upswing. As a result, prenatal health care is becoming a serious issue in need of more attention. A slow but rising increase in the elderly population of Mexican immigrants will undoubtedly become a critical issue in the next few years.

IMMIGRANT IDENTITY: OLD TIES AND NEW ALLEGIANCES

The question of identity among immigrants, particularly Mexicans, promises to be a recurring one in this century. From the earliest wave of their immigration to the United States, Mexicans, like other immigrants such as the Eastern European Jews who settled in New York's Lower East Side in the late nineteenth century, were confronted with the individual and collective question: Who are we? Their answers evolved through a complex interrelationship between themselves and the larger American society within which they found themselves. For example, during the Great Depression large numbers of both Mexican immigrants and American-born Mexicans experienced the consequences of the Repatriation Program which was responsible for forcibly returning Mexicans back to Mexico. This repatriation developed as a response to the widely held view that Mexicans were responsible for the high unemployment rates of "native" American citizens. One of the results of this national policy involved the perpetuation of the stereotype of Mexicans, both foreign and native born, as interlopers. The extent to which Mexican immigrants saw themselves as potential American citizens was shaped by their experiences with xenophobic sentiments that prevailed among some Americans as a result of the Great Depression and the national use of all immigrants as scapegoats. As a result, many Mexican immigrants continued to cling to a traditional Mexican identity. The same dynamic continues to exist. As pointed out in chapters 4 and 9, anti-immigrant sentiments develop cyclically with periods of intense anti-immigration, such as that surrounding California's Proposition 187. For the most part, such experiences lead to the immigrants' attempts to maintain a Mexican identity.

Mexican immigrants have gradually negotiated through American society by developing a second level of identity. At the same time that they see themselves as culturally distinct from the larger American society, Mexican immigrants develop an ethnic identity and consciousness that integrates a sense of "American-ness." Mexican immigrants, like all immigrants, become eventually aware of their rights as residents living in the United States, either legally or as undocumented individuals. Mexican immigrants maintain multiple sources of identity that combine old ties and new allegiances. Unlike the earliest research on immigrant identity that focused on the unfolding "Americanization" of immigrants as they shed their traditional culture in order to embrace a new one, current studies have found that immigrants and their American-born children develop multiple identities. They are both immigrants and New Americans. Their interaction with other groups in American society shows how this multiplicity of ethnic identities develops. Contemporary Mexican immigrants do not leave behind a traditional world to enter a new American one; they bring to the new American world aspects of the old. Studies of other immigrant groups reveal this process through which immigrants attempt to keep "the best of both worlds" (Espiritu, 1992). In his study of Italian immigrants, Gans describes the process through which immigrants experience the formation of multiple identities. Immigrants live in a world in which they retain "a nostalgic allegiance to [their] generation, or that of the old country; a love for and pride in a tradition that can be felt without having to be incorporated in everyday behavior" (Gans, 1979: 9). Similarly, Mexican immigrants living in the United States in the twenty-first century promise to combine their sense of Mexicanness with their New Americanness both at the same time.

FROM MELTING POT TO MOSAIC

From its earliest beginnings, the United States has faced the challenge of forging its own national identity. Its first challenge came as the country broke its colonial ties with England and set itself on a course of nation-building based on a diversity of immigrant groups, each bringing with it its own distinctive culture and traditions. Many came willingly; others, through an egregious process of enslavement (African Americans) and conquest and re-settlement (Native Americans and Mexicans). Whatever their path to American shores, waves of immigrants shape and change the collective American identity. In both times of cooperation and conflict, the diversity of racial and ethnic groups have established their immigrant communities in enclaves throughout the United States, forever changing the American landscape. The "melting pot" became the central metaphor for their experiences and collective choices as New Americans.

Mexican immigrants have demonstrated a capacity to retain the old with the new, replacing the melting pot image with that of a mosaic. Traveling through the United States in places with significant numbers of Mexican immigrants, particularly in the Southwest, one experiences many cultural characteristics: Spanish and English or often a creative mixture of the two; mariachi, Salsa, meringue, and hip hop music; traditional Mexican cuisine and California Nouveau Mexican cuisine; bilingual newspapers; and Spanish and English television programming. American society contains a mosaic of Mexican and American cultures. A Spanish-language radio station in San Jose, California, carried a commercial for a popular type of Mexican cheese with the slogan: "It has been too many years since we left our village in Mexico and the foods we love." After a few Mexican songs, another commercial announced an English class at a local community center so that "you can understand current events in the United States." The radio announcer then gave the schedule for the Cinco de Mayo activities. Mexican immigrants will continue to follow the path of Americanization but will experience the balancing of two cultures. Unfortunately, gang violence, drug trafficking, racial profiling, and other overt and covert manifestations of prejudice and discrimination will also confront Mexican immigrants arriving in the United States in the twenty-first century. History will tell how successful the United States will be in welcoming each new wave of Mexican immigrants, the future New Americans.

Appendix: Notable Mexicans and Mexican Americans

CESAR E. CHAVEZ (1927–1993)

Cesar Chavez was born in Yuma, Arizona, on March 31, 1927. The severe economic conditions brought on by the Great Depression of 1929 forced his family to move to California in search of work and a better life. He was the son of migrant farm workers, and, as a result of his family's frequent moves in search of work in the agricultural fields of the Southwest, Chavez attended more than thirty elementary schools. By the late 1930s, the Chavez family had settled in San Jose, California, in a predominately Mexican immigrant and Mexican-American barrio called "Sal Si Puedes" (Get Out If You Can). As a young child, Chavez worked in the fields surrounding San Jose and at this early age came face to face with the problems of farm laborers. His father participated in some of the early labor activities organized to improve the working conditions experienced by farm workers. These efforts failed but served to initiate the young Chavez in the trials of working-class activism.

Chavez entered the public world of community politics in his early twenties. From 1952 until 1962, he worked with a grassroots community organization, the Community Service Organization (CSO), founded by community activist Saul Alinsky. The CSO, under the leadership of Fred Ross Sr., aimed to improve living conditions by emphasizing the need for community members to learn how to organize themselves. During these years, Chavez dedicated himself to registering voters. In addition, he assumed the duties of general director for community relations for the CSO.

After several years of working in the CSO, Chavez left to devote his full attention to organizing farm workers, particularly in California, founding the United Farm Workers Union in 1962. In 1962, he moved to Delano, California, which continues to serve as the headquarters of the United Farm Workers Union. He began his efforts to work for the improvement of farm workers in 1965 when he joined about 1,000 Filipino grape workers in their strike for better working conditions, particularly better wages. An expert strategist in labor organizing, Chavez succeeded in winning the support of many diverse groups. He brought in student groups, urban workers, church groups, and the most liberal Democratic Party members, specifically the Kennedy family. Robert F. Kennedy became one of his closest friends and supporters. Chavez expanded the grape strike into a national and international strike that succeeded in elevating the struggling United Farm Workers Union into a growing and influential group in the labor movement. Chavez went even further by transforming the union's labor struggles to the higher, more universal level of a major civil rights movement, thereby attracting even more members.

A 1966 statewide march from Delano to Sacramento became of the most significant activities organized by Cesar Chavez. Despite several setbacks, Chavez and the United Farm Workers emerged victorious in their dramatic challenge to the powerful groups of growers. In 1970, the United Farm Workers, assisted by the Catholic Bishops Committee on Farm Labor, signed three-year contracts with twenty-six California growers. Unfortunately, various organizational problems led to more setbacks for the union, with the growers eventually signing contracts with the Teamsters Union in an attempt to break Chavez and his union. Over the 1970s, the union declined, losing many supporters. Nevertheless, Chavez turned his attention to the lettuce growers and initiated a national and international strike. The strike was eventually settled with the United Farm Workers winning major concessions; however, serious internal problems continued to plague the United Farm Workers. By the 1980s, the union's membership had dropped to its lowest levels since its creation. Chavez then turned his attention to the use of pesticides in fields, adopting newer strategies such as mass mailings. A new grape boycott was organized in 1984, but it never gained the level of success of the previous one. Chavez went on several fasts to bring attention to the cause of the farm workers. Robert F. Kennedy came to his side when Chavez ended one of these fasts in 1968. The strain of all these fasts compromised his health.

Chavez emerged as one of the central figures in Mexican immigrant and Mexican-American history. His strategy of nonviolence and his lifelong commitment to social justice remains a legacy for Latino communities and all Americans. In 1990, then Mexican president Carlos Salinas Gotari presented Cesar Chavez with Mexico's highest award given to a foreigner: the Aguila Azteca Award (the Aztec Eagle Award). Cesar Chavez died in his sleep on April 23, 1993, during a trip to Arizona where he was testifying in a United Farm Workers court case. His funeral in Delano, California, was covered by national and international media. The San Jose California City Council voted unanimously to establish his home in San Jose as a national landmark. In 1994, President Clinton honored Chavez with the highest civilian award: the Presidential Medal of Freedom. In 1996, Chavez was remembered by a commemorative march through San Jose, California. California now celebrates the struggles and triumphs of Cesar Chavez with a statewide holiday.

HENRY G. CISNEROS (1947–   )

Henry Cisneros became the first Latino and Mexican American to be appointed as U.S secretary of housing and urban development, serving under President Clinton from 1993 to 1997. Cisneros is also one of the two Mexican Americans to be elected mayor of a major city in the United States. He was mayor of San Antonio, which was then the tenth largest American city in 1981, and he was reelected three times, ending his last term in 1989.

Cisneros was born in 1947 in San Antonio, Texas. His parents were migrant farm workers with little education. Both his parents believed strongly in the value of education and supported their son's desire for an education. During his early childhood, his parents experienced an improvement in their economic situation, and Cisneros was able to attend private Catholic schools through high school. He graduated from Texas A & M College with a degree in city planning and eventually earned a master's degree in urban and regional planning. Cisneros continued his education and in 1973 earned a master's degree in public administration from the John F. Kennedy School of Harvard University. He accepted teaching positions at the University of Texas and Trinity University. In 1974, Cisneros received his doctorate in public administration and joined the faculty at the University of Texas at San Antonio in its division of environmental studies.

Cisneros was elected to San Antonio's city council in 1975 and was reelected twice. As a council member, he emphasized economic development, particularly in those areas affecting Mexicans and Mexican Americans who were the largest ethnic group in the city. In 1985, Cisneros was elected president of the National League of Cities. Cisneros left public office in 1989 and became chairman of his own company, Cisneros Asset Management Company. He also hosted a television program and a national daily Spanish-language radio commentary. Later Cisneros became the deputy chairman of the Federal Reserve Bank of Dallas, served as a board member of the Rockefeller Foundation, was appointed chairman of the National Civic League, and was chairman of the Advisory Committee on the Construction of San Antonio's Astrodome.

During President Clinton's first term in office, Cisneros, as secretary of housing and urban development, was responsible for restructuring this agency and making it more efficient. His most important accomplishment was his successful program for redesigning public housing. During Clinton's reelection campaign, Cisneros became embroiled in political scandal over his testimony to the FBI during his confirmation hearing. Cisneros resigned before Clinton began his second presidential term. Upon leaving the Cabinet, Cisneros accepted an appointment as president of Univision Communications Inc., the major Spanish-language television network.

ERNESTO GALARZA (1905–1984)

Ernesto Galarza immigrated to the United States with his family in 1913 as a result of the Mexican Revolution of 1910. He was the first Mexican to be accepted at Stanford University for graduate studies and became the first Mexican to receive a doctorate.

He was born in 1905 in Jalcocotán, Nayarit. His family first moved to Tepic, Mazatlan, and then continued their journey to the United States, arriving first in Tucson, Arizona, and settling in Sacramento, California. Galarza attended public school in Sacramento and eventually became fluent in English. He graduated from high school and, after winning a scholarship, attended Occidental College in southern California. Galarza specialized in Latin America. He won a graduate scholarship to return to Stanford University where he earned his master's degree in political science and history. Galarza then traveled to New York to attend Columbia University, where he was awarded a Ph.D. in 1944. His dissertation on the Mexican electric industry was published in Mexico.

Galarza and his wife, Mae Taylor, worked as teachers and later codirectors at a private school in New York. He also served as a research associate for the Foreign Policy Association in New York and later held a similar position at the Pan American Union (PAU) in Washington, D.C. His success at the PAU led to his appointment as director of its Division of Labor and Social Information, which required him to make extensive trips throughout Latin America. His work for the PAU sparked what would be Galarza's lifelong passion: the conditions and treatment of Mexican immigrant workers in the United States. In 1947, Galarza became a researcher for the Southern Tenant Farmers Union, which changed its name to the National Farm Labor Union. He moved back to San Jose, California, where he would work for over thirty years helping Mexican farm laborers, particularly undocumented workers, to organize for better working conditions.

Beginning in 1959, after he left the National Farm Labor Union, Galarza focused his work on urban workers. He served as a consultant for various government agencies. During the Chicano social protest movement of the 1960s, Galarza worked for various causes but always focused on farm laborers or urban workers. Galarza became a sought-after speaker at rallies and university conferences. He taught at Harvard University and Notre Dame and universities and colleges in California.

Galarza published two important monographs of farm labor that remain the classic books on farm workers and labor organizing: *Strangers in Our Fields* (1956) and *Merchants of Labor* (1964). Over the next decades, Galarza proved himself to be a prolific scholar, publishing over a dozen books and other reports. In 1970, Galarza published one of his most famous works, *Spiders in the House and Workers in the Fields*. In 1971, Galarza wrote his acclaimed autobiography, *Barrio Boy*, in which he recounts his immigration to the United States with his mother and uncles and his adaptation to American society. *Barrio Boy* is considered one of the literary classics in Mexican-American studies and continues to be used in colleges and universities throughout the United States. Galarza is considered to be the dean of Mexican-American studies.

HENRY B. GONZÁLEZ (1916–2000)

Henry González was elected to the Texas State Senate in 1956, becoming the first Mexican-American state senator in one hundred years. In 1961, González was elected to the U.S. House of Representatives, becoming the first Mexican American from Texas ever elected to national office. González was born in San Antonio, Texas, on May 3, 1916, when his upper–middle-class parents fled the turmoil of the Mexican Revolution. His father had been the mayor of a small town in the state of Durango, Mexico, and after his immigration to Texas, he continued his public career when he became an editor of *La Prensa*, a major Mexican immigrant newspaper in the United States. Despite his father's professional status, González's parents experienced economic hardship and difficulties and providing financial support for their six children instilled in them the value of education as a key to upward mobility. In 1936, Henry González accomplished the first of many lifelong successes as a second-generation Mexican American: he earned admission to the University of Texas at Austin as an engineering major. The Great Depression made it impossible for González to continue working to pay for his college expenses. Returning to San Antonio, he eventually was able to attend St. Mary's University from which he was later awarded an honorary Doctor of Jurisprudence degree.

After World War II, González left his position as a nonenlisted employee in the offices of both army and navy intelligence. He began his long and illustrious political in the early 1950s when he served as a member of San Antonio's city council. By the end of the 1950s, González had gained a respected reputation as a national political figure. Throughout his political life, he devoted his legislative energies to the struggles for social justice. He was at the forefront of efforts to end segregation, improve housing conditions, increase educational opportunities, and civil rights for his constituency in the 20th Congressional District of Texas, a predominantly Mexican-American district. One of his major victories was his role in ending the Mexican Bracero Program, which was responsible for keeping a ceiling on agricultural wages. More important, González's political campaign to end the Bracero Program was a result of the program's sustained violation of the civil rights of the hundreds of Mexican immigrant workers brought to the United States to deal with the high rates of unemployment in the agricultural fields throughout the Southwest.

As a result of his political successes and seniority in the Congress, González was appointed chair of the House Banking and Currency Committee. His long-standing political philosophy focused on the need to pass specific legislative reforms and monitor the policies of the Federal Reserve System Board in order to expand economic opportunities available to minority populations. He became a voice for reform for such issues as the poll tax, restrictive covenants in housing, and mortgage constraints aimed at economically marginal groups. Together with Edward Roybal, congressman from California, González founded the Hispanic Congressional Caucus.

Congressman González retired in 1996 and passed away at the age of eighty-four. His son, Henry González Jr., was elected to Congress from the same Texas district as his father.

DOLORES HUERTA (1930–   )

Dolores Huerta is the most prominent Mexican-American woman labor leader in the United States. She was cofounder and first vice president of the United Farm Workers Union, and together with Cesar Chavez, she shaped the course of farm labor history. Over the last thirty years, Huerta has dedicated her life to the cause of the farm workers and to the attainment of social justice. Huerta was born in 1930 in the mining town of Dawson in northern New Mexico. Her maternal grandparents were born in New Mexico, and her paternal grandparents were Mexican immigrants. When she was a small child, her parents divorced, and she moved to Stockton, California, with her mother and two brothers.

Growing up during the Great Depression, Dolores Huerta witnessed both the harsh conditions and the personal struggles of her own mother as a single woman heading a household. As her family's economic condition improved, Huerta was able to attend the local public schools through high school. After graduating from high school, Huerta helped her mother run a small grocery store and later became a secretary. Huerta then set out to become a teacher. She received her Associate in Arts degree from Stockton Junior College in the early 1950s. Soon after, Huerta turned to what would become her lifelong passion: community and labor activism.

In 1955, Huerta became a founding member of the Stockton chapter of the Community Service Organization (CSO). The CSO was a grassroots organization that focused on local community issues such as housing, access to medical care, and police brutality. Huerta established the Agricultural Workers Association within the CSO in 1960. She became one of the organization's most successful lobbyists in Sacramento. Her lobbying efforts contributed to the passage of legislation allowing voters the right to vote in Spanish and the right of individuals to take the driver's license examination in their native language.

Huerta met Cesar Chavez through her work in the CSO. She agreed with his decision to leave the CSO to form an organization for farm workers: the United Farm Workers Union. Together with Chavez, Dolores Huerta became the symbol of the farm workers' struggle. In addition to her work as a picket captain during the famous Delano grape strike in the 1960s, Huerta assumed the role of major negotiator with the various growers organizations with which the United Farm Workers Union entered into contract negotiations. Throughout the years of the Delano grape strike, Dolores Huerta played a key role along with Chavez. She coordinated major activities of the

United Farm Workers in California and throughout the United States. She spoke at local, state, and national conferences and universities. Huerta testified before several congressional committees dealing with farm workers and Mexican immigration. She became a well-known figure in Mexico and other Latin American countries. With Chavez, Dolores Huerta founded the Robert F. Kennedy Medical Plan, the Juan De La Cruz Farm Worker Pension Fund, the Farm Workers Credit Union, the first medical and pension plan, and a credit union for farm workers. They also formed the National Farm Workers Service Center, a community-based housing organization. Huerta is also active in the Fund for the Feminist Majority, an advocacy group for the equal rights of women, and in the Women's Majority Organization whose goal is to encourage women to run for public office.

Huerta has received many awards for her untiring efforts to improve the living conditions of farm workers. In 1984, she was awarded the Outstanding Labor Leader Award by the California State Senate. In 1993, she was inducted into the National Women's Hall of Fame. Huerta also received the American Civil Liberties Union Roger Baldwin Medal of Liberty Awards. In 1998, Huerta was also honored by *Ms.* magazine as one of the three "Women of the Year." She is included in *Ladies Home Journal*'s "100 Most Important Women of the 20th Century."

FRANCISCO JIMÉNEZ (1943–)

Francisco Jiménez immigrated with his family to California from Tlaquepaque, Mexico, and as a child he worked in the fields of California. He is currently a professor of modern languages and literatures and holds the Fay Boyle University Academic Endowed Professorship at Santa Clara University, Santa Clara, California. Having received his B.A. from Santa Clara University and an M.A. and Ph.D. in Latin American literature from Columbia University under a Woodrow Wilson Fellowship, he has served on various professional boards and commissions, including the California Council for the Humanities, Accreditation Commission for Senior Colleges and Universities, the California Commission on Teacher Credentialing, and the Far West Lab for Educational Research and Development.

Jiménez has published and edited several books on Mexican and Mexican-American literature, and his stories have been published in over fifty textbooks and anthologies of literature. His collection of autobiographical short stories, *The Circuit: Stories from the Life of a Migrant Child* (1997, 1999, 2000), was selected as a Booklist Editors' Choice in 1997 and has received several literary awards: the Boston Globe Horn Book Award for Fiction; the Americas Award; the California Library Association John and Patricia Beatty Award; a Jane Addams Honor Book Award; New York Public Library 1999 Book for the Teen-Age; and an American Library Association Best Book for Young Adults. His children's book *La Mariposa*, published in English, Spanish, and Chinese, won a Parent's Choice Recommended Award, made the Americas Commended List, and was a Smithsonian Notable Book for Children. The Pacific Conservatory for the Performing Arts adapted portions of the book for a one-act play performed in various schools and colleges in California, and Audio Bookshelf has published a recording in both English and Spanish (January 2001). His book *The Christmas Gift/El Regalo de Navidad* (2000), an illustrated bilingual book for children, received a starred review in *Publisher's Weekly*. He recently completed *Breaking Through*, the sequel to *The Circuit*, published in 2001.

GLORIA MOLINA (1948–   )

Gloria Molina broke traditional political barriers in 1982 when she won a seat in the lower house of the California legislature. Molina was born to Mexican immigrant parents in Los Angeles, California. She attended the local grade school and high school. After graduating from high school, Molina attended Los Angeles City College where she became active in the Mexican-American student movements during the 1960s. She joined various student organizations that worked to improve the status of Mexican and Mexican-American students in higher education. After graduating from California State University at Los Angeles, Molina took a position as an employment counselor. In 1973, Molina founded the Comision Femenil de Los Angeles (Women's Commission of Los Angeles). The commission developed various social services programs for Mexican and Mexican-American women. During her term as president of the commission (1974–1976), Molina gained a statewide reputation and became an important role model for Latinas and all women.

Molina entered politics in 1982 when she ran a successful campaign for the California State Assembly, where she became a vocal advocate for Mexican Americans. In 1987, Molina ran for the Los Angeles City Council and gained 57 percent of the vote. With this electoral victory, Molina became the first Mexican-American woman to sit on the City Council. Molina has received many awards for her outstanding work as a public official and community advocate. She was selected Hispanic of the Year by *Caminos* magazine in 1982 and received the Woman of the Year Award presented by the Mexican American Opportunity Foundation. She has also been honored by the Los Angeles County Democratic Central Committee. In 1984, Molina was voted Woman of the Year by *Ms.* magazine. The Mexican American Legal Defense and Education Fund gave her its Woman of Achievement Award.

Molina broke new political ground in 1991 when she was elected to the Board of Supervisors. This political victory represented a milestone. She became the first Mexican-American woman to be elected to this key political office. In 1992, Mexican president Carlos Salinas de Gotari presented her with the prestigious Aztec Eagle award, the highest award given to a foreigner by the Mexican government.

EDWARD JAMES OLMOS (1947–   )

Edward James Olmos is one of the most recognized Mexican-American movie and television personalities. He was born in East Los Angeles, California, where he attended high school and college. He started his career as a rock singer but quickly moved to acting. His first major acting experience came when he won the lead role in the musical play *Zoot Suit* (1978), for which he won the Los Angeles Drama Critics Circle Award. Olmos later starred in the 1981 film version. He gained national recognition when he joined the television cast of *Miami Vice* (1984–1989), where he played Lt. Castillo. He won the Emmy as Best Supporting Actor in a Continuing Drama Series for that role. Olmos played the lead character in the film *The Ballad of Gregorio Cortez* (1982). He continued to gain a national reputation starring in the widely acclaimed film *Stand and Deliver* (1988), the true story of a Latino math teacher with a deep commitment to East Los Angeles Latino students. The film brought national attention to the needs of Latino students in the American educational system. Olmos expanded his role as a television and movie personality by traveling throughout the country lecturing on the need for educational reforms, particularly for Mexican students. These efforts led to Olmos appearing on the cover of *Time*. In 1992, Olmos turned to directing with the film *American Me* (1992), a depiction of gang and prison life among Mexicans in East Los Angeles. Olmos played the narrator in the film *Mi Familia/My Family* (1995), and the role of the father of Tex/Mex singer Selena in the film *Selena* (1997).

ANTHONY QUINN (1915–2001)

Anthony Quinn was one of the most widely acclaimed actors who came to the United States as a Mexican immigrant in 1915 from Chihuahua, Mexico, where he was born. His grandfather came to Mexico to escape the severe economic difficulties in Ireland and married a Mexican woman. The entire family fled the Mexican Revolution, moving to the border town of Juaréz. They eventually crossed the border to live in El Paso, Texas. In 1911 the entire family moved to Los Angeles where his father died when Quinn was only eleven years old. His mother faced many economic hardships as a single parent. Quinn dropped out of high school during the Great Depression and worked at a series of odd jobs. Eventually Quinn began to work in theater, obtaining small parts in local productions. He gained his first experience in the motion picture industry when he was hired to play a small role in a Mae West film. This proved to be an important start in his career when he came to the attention of the famous director Cecil B. DeMille. The young Quinn was subsequently cast as a Cheyenne leader in the movie *The Plainsmen* (1936). Quinn later married DeMille's adopted daughter with whom he had five children.

Between 1937 and 1947, Quinn appeared as a supporting actor in a series of films including *The Last Train from Madrid* (1937), *Blood and Sand* (1941), *The Oxbow Incident* (1943), *Guadalcanal Diary* (1943), *Irish Eyes Are Smiling* (1944), and *Back to Battan* (1945). Quinn, who became a U.S. citizen in 1947, turned to Broadway but returned to Hollywood three years later. One of his most memorable roles was in the 1952 film *Viva Zapata* with his portrayal of Eufemio Zapata, the older brother of Mexican revolutionary leader Emiliano Zapata, played by Marlon Brando. This performance earned him the Academy Award, which he won again for his performance as Paul Gauguin in *Lust for Life*. Quinn appeared in many other movies, including *Guns of Navarrone* (1961), *Requiem for a Heavyweight* (1962), and *Lawrence of Arabia* (1963). During the late 1960s and 1970s, Quinn was cast as a Latin American and other ethnic characters in such films as *The Greek Tycoon* (1978), *The Children of Sanchez* (1978), *Lion in the Desert* (1981), and *Onassis: The Richest Man in the World* (1988). The role for which he will always be best remembered is his portrayal of Zorba in *Zorba the Greek* (1964).

LINDA RONSTADT (1946–   )

Linda Ronstadt is a singer, 1970s superstar, one of the 1980s top female vocalists and winner of a dozen platinum and seventeen gold albums. Ronstadt was born on July 15, 1946, in Tucson, Arizona. Her father was a descendant of a German immigrant who came to Mexico and married a Mexican woman. Linda's father, Gilbert Ronstadt, married Ruthmary Copeman, a native of Michigan. Linda's paternal grandfather and her father were both musicians whose Mexican songs influenced the young Ronstadt during her childhood growing up along the U.S.–Mexico border. Although Mexican music predominated within her home, Ronstadt's music reflects the influence of Elvis Presley, the Beatles, Joan Baez, and the Mexican balladeer Lola Beltrán. At age fourteen, Ronstadt began to sing in public in a trio that included her brother and sister.

When Ronstadt turned eighteen, she left Tucson for Los Angeles in search of her dream: a professional musical career. She joined a group called the Stone Poneys, but after a few years of competing with the burgeoning rock and roll scene in California, the group disbanded. The 1960s and 1970s found Ronstadt struggling to break into the national musical world. She struggled with difficult managers and her own self-doubts and insecurities as a solo female vocalist working in a male-dominated musical world.

Her hard work and talent, managed by Peter Asher, led to a major breakthrough when she signed a contract with Asylum Records. Ronstadt's style combines rock and roll, country and western, and pop music. Her 1974 album, *Heart Like a Wheel,* sold more than a million copies, and her next eight albums went platinum. By 1976, Ronstadt earned over $3 million in the music industry she had struggled against as a young Mexican-American singer.

During the 1970s, Ronstadt's singing success was paralleled with her success in gaining tabloid preeminence. She was linked romantically to various public figures including Jerry Brown, the former governor of California; Steve Martin; and Mick Jagger. Beginning in the 1980s, Ronstadt explored a variety of musical venues. She starred in the broadway production of *Pirates of Penzance* in New York City and won favorable reviews. In 1983, Linda appeared in the pop opera production of *La Bohème.* During the 1980s, Ronstadt recorded duets with Dolly Parton, Emmylou Harris, and Ruben Blades. Her 1987 album, *Canciones de Mi Padre,* was popular and widely received in which Linda, singing in Spanish, performed the music of her father and grandfather. She conducted a national tour based on this album, accompanied by some of the most famous mariachi groups from Mexico. In 1995, Linda Ronstadt came out with *Home*, which included duets with Emmylou Harris. Ronstadt remains a valuable role model for Mexican-American women whose lives have confronted male-dominated professions. Ronstadt broke into the music world and eventually gained her rightful and well-deserved place in rock and roll history.

EDWARD R. ROYBAL (1916–)

Edward Roybal's political career spans over thirty-nine years, beginning in 1949 when he became the first Mexican American since 1881 to win a seat on the Los Angeles City Council. In 1962, he was elected to the U.S. House of Representatives from California's 25th District (Los Angeles). The political career of Congressman Roybal stands as a testament to a lifelong commitment to reforming American society through the political system at the local, state, and national levels.

The first of eight children of Eloisa and Baudilio Roybal, Edward Roybal was born in 1916 in Albuquerque, New Mexico. His father, like many Mexican Americans living in the Southwest in the early twentieth century, worked for the railroads. An unsuccessful railroad strike cost many workers their jobs. In 1920, Roybal's family moved to the Boyle Heights community of Los Angeles. Boyle Heights was home to a large working-class Mexican community. Although his family stressed the importance of education, the Great Depression made it difficult for Roybal to continue his studies after his graduation from high school. Roybal joined the Civilian Conservation Corps (CCC), created by Franklin D. Roosevelt, as an answer to the chronic unemployment produced by the Great Depression. After leaving the CCC and with the general economic recovery, Roybal was able to continue his education when he enrolled as an accounting major in the School of Business Administration at the University of California at Los Angeles. After graduation, Roybal went to work for 20th-Century Fox Studios.

Roybal became interested in health care as he participated in community affairs and became aware of the high incidence of tuberculosis within the Mexican-American community. He volunteered to work with the Tuberculosis Association and eventually was hired to operate its mobile X-ray unit used to test for the disease. Roybal was appointed as the public health educator for the Los Angeles County Health Association. He left this position to volunteer with the U.S. Army during World War II. At the end of the war, Roybal returned to his position and became a well-known and respected figure in the Mexican-American community.

In 1947, Roybal entered the election for the Los Angeles City Council and lost by only a small percentage. He continued his community activism and joined with long-time community organizer Fred Ross and his Community Service Organization (CSO). With the CSO's support and a large community following, Roybal won the 1947 race for the Los Angeles City Council, becoming the first Mexican American to sit on the council since 1882. Roybal lost his next two election campaign: the 1954 election for California's lieutenant governor and the 1959 election for a seat on the Los Angeles Board of Supervisors. He continued to serve on the city council until 1962, winning twice without opposition.

In 1962, Roybal embarked on what was to be his national political career. He ran for the U.S. Home of Representatives in California's 25th District. His victory represented a major breakthrough for Mexican Americans. Roybal's distinguished work as a congressman spans from 1962 until his retirement in 1992.

Roybal's political concerns always centered on issues critical to all his constituencies, but he specifically addressed issues confronting the Mexican-American community. He introduced legislation reforms of health care and aging. He also distinguished himself by serving on such committees as the Foreign Affairs Committee, the Subcommittee on Inter-American Affairs, the Appropriations Committee, the Select Committee on Aging, the Committee on Veterans Affairs, and the Subcommittee on Education and Training.

In 1967, Roybal introduced a bill that would have long-lasting implications. He wrote the federal bilingual education act which was successfully passed. Roybal fought sustained opposition to this bill for years to come but particularly during the Reagan Administration. He served as one of a handful of Mexican-American political figures with a national reputation. He championed the need for increased citizen participation in the political civic arena. He founded the National Association of Latino Elected and Appointed Officials in 1975, and in 1977 he played a prominent role in the creation of the Congressional Hispanic Caucus. As caucus chair, Roybal led the struggle against the Simpson-Rodino Immigration Reform and Control Act of 1986.

Roybal was active in many other organizations, including the Democratic National Committee, the American Legion, the Knights of Columbus, and the Boy Scouts. His unwavering commitment to public life earned him numerous prestigious awards, including the Excellence in Public Service Award from the American Academy of Pediatrics and the Joshua Award for his advocacy of Jewish-Latino Relations.

EMMA TENAYUCA (1917–1999)

Emma Tenayuca is an important figure in the labor history of Mexican immigrants and Mexican Americans. She was born in 1917 in San Antonio, Texas. Her Mexican family on her mother's side goes back to the 1700s, while her father was Native American. The Tenayuca family experienced long years of economic hardship. Young Emma worked at various jobs throughout her high school years. Her labor force experience in Texas exposed her to many unfair working conditions. In 1931, while she was still attending high school, Tenayuca helped organize and participated in a march to Austin by unemployed workers calling for improved public assistance benefits. Her participation in this rally led to the beginning of Tenayuca's life as a labor activist and champion of unionization struggles. Tenayuca was jailed at the age of seventeen for marching with striking workers from one of Texas's largest cigar-making companies. After high school, she devoted her energies to building up support for the Worker's Alliance, a communist-supported union. Tenayuca also began her efforts to start a San Antonio chapter of the International Ladies Garment Workers Union. For the next few years, Emma Tenayuca became a symbol of worker militancy for which she was put in jail many times.

By 1937, after she married one of the key members and leaders of the Communist Party, Tenayuca pledged to devote her life to improving the lives of workers, particularly Mexican immigrants and Mexican-Americans. She and her husband, Homer Brooks, published "The Mexican Question in the Southwest," which analyzed the working conditions of Mexicans using a Communist Party framework.

In 1938, over 2,000 pecan-shellers, mostly Mexican women, went on strike, and because of her fame as a labor union activist, Tenayuca was asked by the strikers to serve as their representative. Her unlimited energy, courage, and passionate commitment to the strike earned her the name "La Pasionaria" (The Passionate One) in memory of Dolores Ibarrut, the leader of the anti-Franco forces during the Spanish Civil War (1936–1939).

Throughout her days of labor activism, Tenayuca was viewed as a symbol of worker solidarity. As a communist, she experienced police surveillance, harassment, and threats of violence. Tenayuca moved to California in the late 1940s, eventually settling in San Francisco to attend San Francisco State University, where she received a B.A. in liberal arts. She moved back to Texas to work as a teacher until her retirement in 1982.

Tenayuca remains a role model for Mexican immigrants and Mexican Americans, especially women who see her as a strong advocate for workers' rights and women's rights.

Glossary

alambrista   From the Spanish word for wire, "alambre" refers to a person; an "alambrista" refers to one who crosses the wire fence used along some parts of the U.S.–Mexico border.

basílica   Cathedral, usually refers to the Basilica of Our Lady of Guadalupe, the national shrine of Mexico located in Mexico City.

corridos   Mexican folk ballads.

El Norte   "The North"—used by Mexicans to refer to the United States.

La Llorona   "The Weeping Woman"—a myth concerning a woman who kills her children and is doomed to wander the earth weeping for them.

los mojados   "The Wet Ones"—used to refer to undocumented Mexican immigrants who cross the Rio Grande River to enter the United States; considered a pejorative term.

madrina   Godmother—female sponsor at baptism or other religious ritual.

madrino   Godfather—male sponsor at baptism or other religious ritual.

mariachi   Traditional form of Mexican music.

musica norteña   Mexican music typical of Mexico's northern states and bordering state of Texas; influenced originally by nineteenth-century German polka music brought by German immigrants to Texas.

quinceañera   From the Spanish word for fifteen—"quince"—means one who is fifteen and refers to the coming-out party similar to a sweet sixteen party.

References

Alvarez, Michael R., and Tara L. Butterfield. "The Resurgence of Nativism in California? The Case of Proposition 187 and Illegal Immigration." http://wizard.ucr.edu.polmeth/working_papers97/alvar97d.html. 1997.

———. "Latino TV in Development." *American Demographics* (March 1999).

Anzaldua, Gloria. *Borderlands/La Frontera: The New Mestiza.* San Francisco: Spinsters/Aunt Lute, 1987.

Azuela, Mariano. *The Underdogs.* New York: New American Library, 1915. Reprinted in 1962.

Baca Zinn, Maxine. "Employment and Education of Mexican American Women: The Interplay of Modernity and Ethnicity in Eight Families." *Harvard Education Review* 50 (February 1980): 47–62.

———. "Familism among Chicanos: A Theoretical Review." *Humbolt Journal of Social Relations* 10 (1982a): 224–38.

———. "Chicano Men and Masculinity." *Journal of Ethnic Studies* 10 (1982b): 29–44.

Barrera, Mario. "The Study of Politics and the Chicano." *Aztlan* 5 (1974): 9–26.

Bodnar, John. *The Transplanted.* Bloomington: University of Indiana Press, 1985.

Cerulo, Karen A. "Identity Construction: New Issues, New Directions." *Annual Review of Sociology* 23 (1997): 385–409.

Chacón, Maria, et al. *Chicanas in Postsecondary Education.* Stanford, CA: Center for Research on Women, Stanford University, 1982.

Cotera, Martha P. *The Chicana Feminist.* Austin, TX: Information Systems Development, 1977.

Díaz Del Castillo, Bernal. *The True History of the Conquest of New Spain.* Translated by J.M. Cohen. Baltimore, MD: Penguin Press, 1963.

Espiritu, Yen L. *Asian American Pan-Ethnicity: Bridging Institutions and Identities.* Philadelphia: Temple University, 1992.

Fox, Geoffrey. *Hispanic Nation: Culture, Politics, and the Construction of Identity.* Tucson. University of Arizona Press, 1996.

Galarza, Ernesto. *Barrio Boy.* South Bend, IN: University of Notre Dame, 1971.

Gamio, Manuel. *Mexican Immigration to the United States: A Study of Human Migration and Adjustment.* New York: Dover, 1930. Reprinted in 1971.

Gándara, Patricia. "Passing through the Eye of the Needle: High Achieving Chicanas." *Hispanic Journal of Behavioral Sciences* 4 (1982): 167–79.

Gans, Herbert J. *The Urban Villagers.* Glencoe. IL: Free Press, 1962.

———. "Symbolic Ethnicity: The Future of Ethnic Groups in America." *Ethnic and Racial Studies* 26 (January 1979): 1–20.

———. "Second-Generation Decline: Scenarios for the Economic and Ethnic Futures of the Post-1965 American Immigrants." *Ethnic and Racial Studies* 15 (1992): 173–92.

García, Alma M. "The Development of Chicana Feminist Discourse, 1970–1980." *Gender & Society* (June 1989): 217–38.

———. " 'I Work for My Daughter's Future': Entrepreneurship and Mexican American Women." *California History* 76 (fall 1995): 262–79.

———. *Chicana Feminist Thought: The Basic Historical Writings.* New York: Routledge, 1997.

———. "Identity (Re)Formation among Mexican American Women in a University Setting: A Study of Personal Narratives." Paper presented at the 34th Congress of the International Institute of Sociology, Tel Aviv, Israel, 1999.

García, Mario. *Desert Immigrants: The Mexicans of El Paso, 1880–1920.* New Haven, CT: Yale University Press, 1981.

———. *Memories of Chicano History: The Life and Narrative of Bert Corona.* Berkeley: University of California Press, 1994.

García, Richard A. *The Making of the Mexican American Mind: San Antonio, Texas 1929–1941: A Social and Intellectual History of an Ethnic Community.* College Station: Texas A & M University Press, 1991.

Glazar, Nathan. *American Judaism.* Chicago: University of Chicago Press, 1971.

Glazer, Nathan, and Daniel P. Moynihan. *Beyond the Melting Pot: The Negroes, Puerto Ricans, Jews, Italians and Irish of New York City.* Cambridge, MA: MIT Press, 1963.

Global Assembly Line, The Videorecording. Educational TV and Film Center. PBS Video, 1986.

Gonzales, Manuel. *Mexicanos: A History of Mexicans in the United States.* Bloomington: Indiana University Press, 1999.

Gordon, Milton. *Assimilation in American Life: The Role of Race, Religion, and National Origin.* New York: Oxford University Press, 1964.

Handlin, Oscar. *The Uprooted: The Epic Story of the Great Migrations That Made the American People.* Boston: Little Brown, 1951.

Hernández, José. "Hispanics Blend Diversity." In *Handbook of Hispanic Cultures in the United States: Sociology.* Edited by Felix Padilla, pp. 17–34. Houston, TX: Arte Publico Press, 1994.

Hondagneu-Sotelo, Pierrette. "Overcoming Patriarchal Constraints: Reconstituting Gender Relations among Mexican Immigrant Women and Men." *Gender & Society* 6 (1992): 393–415.

———. *Gendered Transitions: Mexican Experiences of Immigration.* Berkeley: University of California Press, 1994.

Hufford, Charles H. *The Social and Economic Effects of the Mexican Migration into Texas.* San Francisco: R & E Research Associates, 1971.

Jiménez, Alfredo. "Spanish Colonial Culture." In *Handbook of Hispanic Cultures in the United States.* Edited by Alfredo Jiménez, pp. 208–27. Houston, TX: Arte Publico Press, 1994.

Jiménez, Francisco. *The Circuit: Stories of a Migrant Child.* Albuquerque: University of New Mexico Press, 1997.

Lareau, Annette P. "Social Behavior and the Family-School Relationship in Two Communities." Ph.D. dissertation, University of California, Berkeley, 1984.

Light, Ivan. *Ethnic Enterprise in America: Business and Welfare among Chinese Japanese, and Blacks.* Berkeley: University of California, 1972.

———. "Immigrant and Ethnic Enterprise in North Americ." *Ethnic and Racial Studies* 7 (1984): 195–216.

Light, Ivan, and Edna Bonacich. *Immigrant Entrepreneurs: Koreans in Los Angeles, 1965–1982.* Berkeley: University of California Press, 1988.

Matiella, A. *La Quinceañera.* Santa Cruz, CA: Network Publications, 1989.

McClelland, David. "Toward a Theory of Motive Acquisition." *American Psychologist* 20 (1965): 321–33.

McHenry, J. Patrick. *A Short History of Mexico.* Garden City, NY: Dolphin Books, 1962.

McKenna, Teresa, and Flora Ida Ortiz, eds. *The Broken Web: The Educational Experience of the Hispanic American Woman.* Claremont, CA: Tomas Rivera Center, 1988.

McWilliams, Carey. *North from Mexico: The Spanish-Speaking People of the United States.* New York: Greenwood Press, 1948. Reprinted in 1990.

Morrison, Joan, and Charlotte Fox Zabusky. *American Mosaic: The Immigrant Experience in the Words of Those Who Lived It.* New York: New American Library, 1980.

Muñoz Jr., Carlos. *Youth, Identity, Power: The Chicano Movement.* New York: Verso, 1989.

Namias, June. *First Generation: In the Words of Twentieth-Century American Immigrants.* Boston: Beacon Press, 1978.

Navarro, Armando. "The Evolution of Chicano Politics." *Aztlan* 5 (1974): 57–84.

Nieto-Gomez, Anna. "La Feminista." *Encuentro Femenil* 1 (1974): 34–37.

Nuñez Cabeza de Vaca, Alvar. *Naufragios y Comentarios (Shipwrecked).* 1542. Buenos Aires: Espasea-Calpe, 1944.

Pesquera, Beatriz M. " 'In the Beginning He Wouldn't Even Lift a Spoon' ": The Division of Household Labor." In *Building with Our Hands: New Directions in Chicana Studies.* Edited by Adela de la Torre and Beatriz Pesquera, pp. 181–95. Berkeley: University of California, 1993.

Ponce, Mary Helen. *Hoyt Street.* Albuquerque: University of New Mexico Press, 1993.

Portes, Alejandro, and Robert L. Bach. *Latin Journey: Cuban and Mexican Immigrants in the United States.* Berkeley: University of California Press, 1985.

Portes, Alejandro, and Ruben G. Rumbaut. *Immigrant America: A Portrait.* Berkeley: University of California Press, 1996.

Posadas, Barbara M. *The Filipino Americans.* Westport, CT: Greenwood Press, 1999.

Redfield, Robert. *The Little Community: Peasant Society and Culture.* Chicago: University of Chicago, 1967.

Reyes, Belinda I. "Dynamics of Immigration: Return Migration to Western Mexico." http://www.ppic.org.publications/ppic102/indez.html. 1997.

Ringawa, Marcel. "Cultural Pedagogy: The Effects of Teacher Attitudes and Needs in Selected Bilingual Bicultural Education Environments." In *Ethno-Perspectives in Bilingual Education Research: Theory in Bilingual Education.* Edited by Raymond V. Padilla. Ypislanti: Bilingual Bicultural Education Programs, Eastern Michigan University, 1980.

Romo, Harriet D. "The Mexican Origin Populations's Differing Perceptions of Their Children's Schooling." *Social Science Quarterly* 65 (1984): 35–50.

Romo, Harriet D., and Toni Falbo. *Latino High School Graduation: Defying the Odds.* Austin: University of Texas Press, 1996.

Rosales, F. Arturo. *Chicano: The History of the Mexican-American Civil Rights Movement.* Houston, TX: Arte Publico Press, 1996.

Rouse, Roger. "Mexican Migration and the Social Space of Postmodernism." In *Between Two Worlds: Mexican Immigrants in the United States.* Edited by David G. Gutíerrez, pp. 247–63. Wilmington, DE: Scholarly Resources, 1996.

Ruiz, Vicki L. " 'Star Struck': Acculturation, Adolescence and the Mexican American Women, 1920–1950." In *Building with Our Hands: New Directions in Chicana Studies.* Edited by Adela de la Torre and Beatriz Pesquera, pp. 109–29. Berkeley: University of California Press, 1993.

———. *From Out of the Shadows: Mexican American Women in Twentieth Century America.* New York: Oxford University Press, 1998.

Samora, Julian. *Los Mojados: The Wetback Story.* Notre Dame, IN: University of Notre Dame, 1971.

San Miguel, Guadalupe. *Let Them All Take Heed: Mexican-Americans and the Campaign for Educational Equality in Texas, 1910–1981.* Austin: University of Texas Press, 1987.

Sanchez, George J. *Becoming Mexican American: Ethnicity, Culture and Identity in Chicano Los Angeles, 1900–1945.* New York: Oxford University Press 1993.

Segura, Denise. "Chicanas and Triple Oppression in the Labor Force." In *Chicana Voices: Intersections of Class, Race, and Gender*. Edited by Teresa Cordova et al. Austin: Center for Mexican American Studies Publications, 1986.

———. "Slipping through the Cracks: Dilemmas in Chicana Education." In *Building with Our Hands: New Directions in Chicana Studies*. Edited by Adela de la Torre and Beatriz Pesquera, pp. 199–216. Berkeley: University of California Press, 1993.

Shockley, John. *Chicano Revolt in a Texas Town*. South Bend. IN: University of Notre Dame Press, 1974.

Solórzano, Daniel Gilbert. "A Study of Social Mobility Values: The Determinants of Chicano Parents' Occupational Expectations for Their Children." Ph.D. dissertation, Claremont Graduate School, Claremont, CA, 1986.

Stern, Gwen Louise. "Ethnic Identity and Community Action in El Barrio." Ph.D. dissertation, Northwestern University, Evanston, IL, 1976.

Subervi-Vélez, Federico A. "Mass Communication and Hispanics." In *Handbook of Hispanic Cultures in the United States: Sociology*. Edited by Félix Padilla, pp. 304–57. Houston, TX: Arte Publico Press, 1994.

Takaki, Ronald. *A Different Mirror: A History of Multicultural America*. Boston: Little, Brown and Company, 1993.

Thompson, Ginger. "Chasing Mexico's Dream into Squalor." *New York Times*, February 11, 2001, pp. 1, 6.

Tywoniak, Frances, and Mario García. *Migrant Daughter: Coming of Age as a Mexican American Woman*. Berkeley: University of California Press, 2000.

Ueda, Reed. *Postwar Immigrant America: A Social History*. Boston: Bedford Books of St. Martin's Press, 1994.

U.S. Census Bureau. *Statistical Abstract of the United States*, 1999.

———. *Statistical Abstract of the United States*, 2000.

Vásquez, Melba J.T. "Confronting Barriers to the Participation of Mexican American Women in Higher Education." *Hispanic Journal of Behavioral Sciences* 42 (1982): 167–79.

Vigil, Maurilio. "Latinos in American Politics." In *Handbook of Hispanic Cultures in the United States: Sociology*. Edited by Félix Padilla, pp. 80–108. Houston, TX: Arte Publico Press, 1994.

Williams, Norma. *The Mexican American Family: Tradition and Change*. Dix Hills, NY: General Hall, 1990.

Zeller, Tom. "Migrants Take Their Chances on a Harsh Path of Hope." *New York Times*, March 18, 2001, p. 14.

Index

About the Author

ALMA M. GARCIA is a Professor of Sociology at Santa Clara University, California. She specializes in Mexican American Studies, Gender Studies, and the political economy of Latin America. Garcia grew up in El Paso, Texas, the daughter of a Mexican immigrant father and a second-generation Mexican American mother.